DISCOVERING
YOUR
Riches
IN
Christ

CWR, Waverley Abbey House, Waverley Lane, Farnham, Surrey GU9 8EP

Scripture quotations are taken from NIV, unless otherwise indicated. Other versions include:
NKJ, New King James Version, © 1979, 1980, 1982, Thomas Nelson, Inc., Publishers.
RSV, Revised Standard Version, © 1972, Thomas Nelson, Inc., Publishers.
AMPLIFIED, The Amplified Bible, © 1965, Zondervan Publishing House.
TLB, The Living Bible, © 1971, Tyndale House Publishers.
J.B. PHILLIPS, The New Testament in Modern English, revised edition, © 1958, 1960, J.B. Phillips.
KJV, King James Version, © 1984, 1977, Thomas Nelson, Inc.
MOFFATT, The Bible. A New Translation, © 1950, 1952, 1953, 1954, James A.R. Moffatt.
THE MESSAGE, © 2002, Christian Art Publishers.

DISCOVERING YOUR RICHES IN CHRIST
A compilation of excerpts from *Every Day with Jesus* by Selwyn Hughes 1982, 1984, 1986, 1989, 1993, 1988, 1993, 1994, 1995 edited by Erina Botha
© CWR 2003

Concept development, editing, design and production by
Struik Christian Books Ltd.
A division of New Holland Publishing (South Africa) (Pty.) Ltd.
(New Holland Publishing is a member of the Johnnic Publishing Group)
Cornelis Struik House
80 McKenzie Street
Cape Town 8001

Reg. No. 1971/00972/07

DTP by Natalie Moult
Cover design by Joleen Coetzee
Cover photograph by Photo Access
Cover reproduction by Hirt & Carter Cape (Pty) Ltd
Reproduced, printed and bound by Kyodo Printing Co. Pte. Ltd.,
112 Neythal Road, Jurong Town, Singapore, 628599

ISBN 1 85345 280 7

SELWYN HUGHES

DISCOVERING
YOUR
Riches
IN
Christ

Quiet time

Jesus, forgive me
for the selfishness of
hurt feelings and
insensitivity
to the needs
of those around me.
Give me your
keen sight and hearing
to know just where to spread
the healing ointment
of your love.
Please provide a supply
just right for today.
And Lord, tie a string
around my heart
reminding me that
this is your day, not mine.

January / February

Practising the presence of God

March / April

The high-priestly prayer

May / June

The divine Counsellor

July / August

The search for meaning

September / October

The mind of the Christian

November / December

Discovering our riches in Christ

Start the year right

FOR READING AND MEDITATION – REVELATION 3:14–22

'Behold, I stand at the door and knock.
If anyone hears my voice and opens the door, I will come in ...' (v. 20: NKJ)

We begin this new year by focusing on some of the ways by which we can increase and enhance the awareness of God's presence in our lives. Christians have the assurance that they are constantly surrounded by the presence of God, and that the Almighty's presence abides with them through thick and thin. For he has said: 'I will never leave you nor forsake you' (Heb. 13:5, NKJ). And again: 'He keeps his eye upon you as you come and go, and always guards you' (Ps. 121:8, TLB). Although Scripture assures us that we are constantly surrounded by the presence of God, we do not always feel it. There could be many reasons why we do not experience God's presence in our lives, but the fault is always in us – never in him. We ask ourselves therefore: what can we do to increase and enhance the sense of God's presence in our lives?

Before we look at some of the ways, we must make the point that no one can practice the presence of God until first they know God. God can never be known through the practice of religious techniques alone, although they can be helpful to those who know him. We begin to know God when we stop struggling to save ourselves. If you have never surrendered your life to Christ, do it right now. Start the year right by getting right with God.

My Father and my God, I cannot know your presence until first I know you. I surrender my life into your hands – this very moment. You have me, Lord – and now I have you. I am so thankful. Amen.

All the way from eternity

FOR READING AND MEDITATION – LUKE 15:1–7

'... Does he not leave the ninety-nine in the open country and
go after the lost sheep until he finds it?' (v. 4: NIV)

Yesterday we made the point that we must first come to know God.
Some readers will know about God but have never had a personal
encounter with him. If you wonder: 'How do I find God?' know that
you simply have to let him find you. If the Bible teaches us anything, it teaches us that God searches for man. Look again at the
parable before us today and the other two parables – of the lost silver and the lost son. He is saying that the God of the universe is
involved in a persistent and redemptive search for us. How amazing! 'In finding God,' said Gandhi to a missionary, 'you must have
as much patience as a man who sits by the seaside and undertakes
to empty the ocean, lifting up one drop of water with a straw.'

The great man was wrong. These parables let us see the God of
the shepherd-heart who seeks and seeks for the lost sheep until he
finds it; the God who sweeps the universe with the broom of his
redemptive grace until he finds the coin on which his image is
stamped; the God whose love is so powerful that it lays siege to the
hearts of those who have run from their Father's house. The thrilling
truth is that you simply have to accept God's gift of himself.

✎ *O God, I am so glad that I do not have to search for you. You have come
to stand at the door of my heart. I dare not refuse you. My heart is open,
Lord Jesus. Come in. Amen.*

Consent – the key

FOR READING AND MEDITATION – JAMES 4:1–10
'Come near to God and he will come near to you ...' (v. 8: NIV)

We are coming to grips with the fact that God is on a persistent redemptive search for us. It is not so much a matter of trying to find him as of letting him find us. This must not be understood to mean that our individual salvation is now an automatic thing. God has gone to the utmost lengths to save us, but in order to be saved, we must turn to him in an act of contrition and repentance and invite him to take up residence within us.

I have met people who think that because they have felt God's presence in their lives at one time or another, this is sufficient to believe that they are favoured by the Almighty and have no need to invite him into their hearts. They say things like this: 'I know God is with me because he protected me from a serious accident.' I have no doubt that many people sense God's presence around them, but they can never sense God's presence within them unless they invite him to come in. He loves every one of his creation, but he loves them too much to gatecrash the personality. He comes in only as we give our consent. 'No one is constitutionally incapable of finding God,' says Billy Graham. If we do not find him, the problem is in our consent. When, by an act of the will, you decide to let God in ... nothing on earth or in heaven can keep him out.'

✎ *Loving Father, I realise that my eternal destiny is in my own hands. You have done all you need to do – now I must do what I need to do. Loving Father, save me now. In Jesus' Name. Amen.*

Oh, Lord, another day!

FOR READING AND MEDITATION – PSALM 139:1–18

'… When I awake, I am still with you.' (v. 18: NIV)

Now that we are clear about the fact that we cannot practice the presence of God until he resides within us, we are ready to begin looking at some of the things we can do to help us become more conscious and more aware of his indwelling presence. The first suggestion is this – as you awake each morning, turn to God in an attitude of spiritual expectancy. Our first thought upon waking ought to be of him. A friend of mine says that this suggestion, given to him in the early days of his Christian experience, has been the means of sharpening the sense of God's presence in his life more than almost any other single thing. Listen to how an unknown poet put it: 'Every morning lean thine arm awhile, upon the window-sill of heaven, and gaze upon thy God; then with the vision in thy heart, turn strong to meet the day.'

'Turn strong to meet the day.' What an optimistic thought! Anyone who looks into the face of God during the waking moments is fortified to look into the face of anything the day may bring. Someone has said there are two kinds of Christians: those who wake up in the morning, look around the room and say rather gloomily, 'Oh, Lord, another day' – and those who wake up, look into their heavenly Father's face and say brightly, 'Oh, Lord, another day!' Which kind, I wonder, are you?

✎ *O Father, help me to begin every day by looking into your face before I look into anyone else's. Then, with the vision of you in my heart, I, too, will be able to 'turn strong to meet the day'. Amen.*

Good morning, Lord!

FOR READING AND MEDITATION – PSALM 5:1–12

'Each morning I will look to you in heaven and
lay my requests before you …' (v. 3: TLB)

We are looking at the importance of turning to the Lord in the first few moments after we awake in an attitude of spiritual expectancy. Those who study the effect of thought upon the personality tell us that our last thought at night and our first thought in the morning are greatly influential in determining the quality of our sleep and our attitudes toward life. Consider the importance of focusing your waking thoughts on God. How will this help? It gives a divine perspective to the day. If your day begins with God, it is more likely to continue and end with him. How we start determines to a great degree the way we go on and the way we finish. Some Christians say that turning to him as soon as they are awake and saying, 'Good morning, Lord' helps to sharpen their awareness of the fact that God is with them. Sentimental? Some might think so.

Whatever method you use to focus your thoughts on God in the first few moments after you awake is not important; what is important is the fact that your thoughts turn from being self-conscious to being God-conscious. A friend of mine says, 'Every morning, as I awake, I lie in bed for a while and say to myself, "When I open my eyes, the light comes in; when I open my mouth, the air comes in; when I open my heart, Christ comes in."'

O God, help me to begin every day by opening every pore, every cell, every tissue, every artery, every part of my being to you. In Christ's Name I pray. Amen.

Naturalised in defeat

FOR READING AND MEDITATION – PSALM 62:1–12

'My soul, wait only upon God … for my hope and
expectation are from him.' (v. 5: AMPLIFIED)

We continue looking at the first of our suggestions on how to practise the presence of God. One of the things that deeply saddens me is that spirit of non-expectancy that seems to be so prevalent among so many Christians today. Many do not expect anything spiritually exciting in their day – they just expect to muddle through. When one looks at certain countries in the East one sees what the awful power of non-expectancy can do when it falls upon a civilisation. I cannot help but notice how these otherwise lovely people respond so fatalistically to situations by turning over their hands in an attitude of helpless resignation.

The same danger lies at the door of the contemporary Christian church. In some cases it has actually crossed the threshold and laid its paralysing hand upon the hearts of God's people, causing them to become resigned to spiritual defeat and failure. Dr Worcester, a medical practitioner says, 'Most Christians do not expect their religion to do them any great or immediate good. When one tells them that their condition needs not last more than a single hour, they look at you as one who announces strange doctrine. They have become naturalised in defeat.' The first step to a spiritually profitable day is expectancy.

O God, help me to become an expectant person. Teach me how to go into every day as relaxed and receptive as a little child. Then life will become play and my hardest tasks pure joy. In Jesus' Name I ask it. Amen.

Faith – largely expectancy

FOR READING AND MEDITATION – ISAIAH 30:15–26

'And therefore the Lord waits – expecting, looking and longing –
to be gracious to you …' (v. 18: AMPLIFIED)

Many Christians begin their day in a spirit of non-expectancy.
They expect nothing spiritually exciting or profitable to happen to
them. They think it utterly inconceivable that God should want to
speak to them, guide them, or reveal himself to them in some new
and fresh way – they think of such experiences as being strange
and abnormal. How sad. In *Reason and Emotion*, John MacMurray
tells a story of a little girl who was permanently lopsided and was
brought to him for treatment. After working with her for some
time, he managed to get her to stand quite straight. Then he asked
her to walk across the room. She walked perfectly straight for the
first time in her life and then, bursting into tears, threw herself into
her mother's arms, crying, 'Oh, Mummy, I'm walking all crooked!'

Christians who lack a spirit of expectancy are like that – they
think of walking through the day with their heads held high and a
song in their hearts as being something strange. 'Faith,' said Dr
Cyndyllan Jones, a famous Welsh preacher, 'is largely expectancy –
expectancy set on fire by the Holy Spirit.' Begin your day by looking into your heavenly Father's face in a spirit of expectancy and
you will not be disappointed. Push expectantly on the gates of
abundant living and surely those gates will open wide.

✒ *O God, if faith is 'expectancy set on fire by the Holy Spirit', then breathe
upon the embers of my heart today so that my whole being shall be set
aflame with expectancy. Amen.*

Closeness must be cultivated

FOR READING AND MEDITATION – LAMENTATIONS 3:22–36

'… his compassions fail not. They are new every morning;
great is your faithfulness.' (vv. 22–23: NKJ)

Another method to increase and sharpen our awareness of our Lord's presence in our daily lives is to establish a time to spend with him in prayer and contemplation. Nothing sharpens the awareness of God's presence in a believer's life more effectively than the regular practice of a morning Quiet Time. Some people's circumstances prevent them from finding either the time or the place during the first part of the day. Don't feel condemned if your circumstances do not permit you to be alone with God until the day is well under way. He will be there waiting for you whenever you can make it.

The story is told of Susannah Wesley (the mother of John Wesley) that when she was deprived of privacy for her Quiet Time, she would lift her apron over her head, and for a few minutes commune in prayer with God. The children would whisper to each other, 'Hush, mother is having her Quiet Time.'

Try also to be alone when you have your Quiet Time. It is good for married couples to share together in prayer, but everyone needs to cultivate an individual relationship with him. Try to have some time alone with God at the beginning of the day. Those moments will provide you with a fountain in your heart at which you can slake your thirst throughout the day.

✣ *My Father and my God, help me not to take you for granted. My awareness of you will depend on how often I make contact with you. Help me cultivate a greater closeness. In Jesus' Name. Amen.*

Take it

FOR READING AND MEDITATION – PSALM 55:1–23
'Evening and morning and at noon I will pray, and cry aloud,
and he shall hear my voice.' (v. 17: NKJ)

We need a daily time when we can cultivate a closeness with our Lord. In all the years I have been a Christian, I have never met anyone who told me that they enjoyed a deep and constant sense of God's presence who did not have fixed and regular times of prayer and contemplation. I have met many who told me that after being baptised in the Holy Spirit, they felt such a keen sense in their lives that they no longer needed to spend fixed times with him in prayer. One man put it like this: 'Before I was filled with the Spirit I used to have some pretty dull Quiet Times. Now I have a constant and continued Quiet Time every moment I am awake. I no longer need to get alone with God in prayer or spend so much time in the Bible. I am more alive to God than I ever thought was possible.' I warned him what would happen if he neglected fixed times with the Lord in prayer, and it was no surprise to hear that he had become spiritually cold and indifferent.

Living in a state of strong spiritual awareness without definite times for prayer and contemplation will lead to the loss of both. It is as senseless as hoping to live in a state of physical nourishment without taking fixed times to eat. The times we set aside to cultivate an awareness of God result in a state of continual awareness of God.

O God, teach me how to fix the habit of daily prayer and contemplation, for I see that the benefits of this far exceed the difficulties I may experience in establishing it. For Jesus' sake. Amen.

The best way to begin

FOR READING AND MEDITATION – PSALM 119:97–112

'Your word is a lamp to my feet and a light to my path.' (v. 105: NKJ)

We said yesterday that it is a mistake when people feel they can enjoy a constant sense of God's presence without taking fixed times for prayer and contemplation. The New Testament tells us that Jesus felt the need of three simple habits: (1) he went into the synagogue to read 'as his custom was'; (2) he went up a mountain to pray 'as his custom was'; (3) he taught the people 'as his custom was'. These three simple habits – reading the Scriptures, spending time in prayer and sharing with others – are as basic to the Christian life as 'two and two make four' is to mathematics.

But how are we to make the best of our daily or regular times of prayer and contemplation? There can be no fixed rules – only suggestions. Experience has shown that the best way to begin a Quiet Time is by reading the Scriptures. This is why I began writing *Every Day with Jesus*. Prior to that people used to say, 'But I don't know what to read.' You cannot know the joy it gives me to know that thousands of people who hitherto had no daily Quiet Time now begin their day by reading the Word of God, followed by these devotional thoughts. My words may help people, but through the Scriptures Life speaks to life. God has gone into his Word and so, when we read it – God comes out of it.

O Father, I am so thankful for the Scriptures and for the inspiration and power that flow through them. Help me to love your Word and delight daily in it. For your own dear Name's sake. Amen.

Who talks most?

FOR READING AND MEDITATION – 1 SAMUEL 3:1–19

'… if he calls you … say, "Speak, Lord, for your servant hears" ' (v. 9: NKJ)

We continue looking at how to make our Quiet Time effective. Another suggestion is that after the reading of Scripture, one might sit quietly in the Lord's presence and say, 'Father, have you anything to say to me?' Sometimes God may have something special and personal to say to you arising from your reading of his Word. Wait and see what he might have to say to you before moving on. A lady I know who practices this approach, told me that when she says, 'Father, have you anything to say to me?' the Lord sometimes responds, 'No, nothing more than I have already said in my Word. But what have you to say to me?'

God not only delights in talking to us, but he is delighted also when we talk to him. This is what prayer is – a conversation with God. So talk to him. Tell him the things that are on your mind – the joyful things as well as the difficult things. If your mind wanders or gets distracted when you are praying, then pray about the thing to which your mind has wandered.

Another suggestion is to have a notebook and a pen at hand during your Quiet Time in case God says something to you. A notebook can be a sign of faith – it says, 'Speak, Lord, for your servant hears.'

✎ *O God, forgive me that so often my prayer life is built around the phrase: 'Listen, Lord, your servant speaks,' rather than 'Speak, Lord, your servant hears.' Help me to change things – starting today. Amen.*

The Secret Companion

FOR READING AND MEDITATION – JOHN 15:1–11

'... live in me, and let me live in you ...' (v. 4: TLB)

We turn now to look at another suggestion to increase and sharpen the awareness of God's presence in our lives – order your day on the basis of a divine partnership. I got this idea many years ago from an old Welsh miner who told me that he would think of what he had to do that day and visualise the Lord as being involved in every moment of it. 'I am in partnership with God,' he said, 'and I have learned to think of the responsibilities of the day not as "mine" but as "ours".'

He went on to tell me that as he thought ahead into the issues of the day, he would talk to God about them in the same way that a man would talk to a business partner: 'What shall we do about this matter, Lord? There's another issue that will be coming up later in the day ... how shall we handle that?'

The chief merit of this approach is that it highlights one of the greatest truths of Scripture – the divine-human partnership. Can you think of anything more wonderful than the fact that the almighty God, the Creator of the universe, takes an active interest in every single detail of our lives and is willing to team up with us? 'Christianity,' said a missionary to China, 'is a secret companionship.' Just think of it – you need not go into any day alone, but arm in arm with that Secret Companion.

✎ *O God, help me survey every day, not from my perspective but from our perspective. Without you I don't want to take one step over the threshold. But with you – I can go anywhere. Amen.*

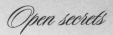
Open secrets

FOR READING AND MEDITATION – PSALM 32:1–11

'I will instruct you and teach you in the way you should go;
I will counsel you ...' (v. 8: NIV)

Some object to the idea of ordering our day on the basis of the divine partnership – that it makes us over-dependent. 'God,' they say, 'has designed us to think for ourselves, and if we depend on the Almighty to do our thinking for us, we will not become free, self-determining, creative personalities.' There is some truth in this, of course, but as so often happens, if we take part of a truth and do not consider the other parts, we will come out with wrong conclusions. Truth out of balance becomes error. Partnership with God does not mean that he dominates our personalities; his purpose is to guide – not override.

The Almighty relates to us in a way that is helpful and supportive, yet, at the same time, taking care not to snuff out our initiative and creativity. E. Stanley Jones describes the divine-human partnership in this way: 'God comes close to his children in a way that leaves them free to think and act, yet in a way that awakens the personality to aliveness and alertness of mind and spirit. His guidance is always sufficiently obvious to be found, but not so obvious that it does away with the necessity of thought and discriminating insight.' His secrets are always 'open secrets' – open, yet sufficiently secret to make us think. This kind of partnership – to guide us without overriding us – is a task that only divine wisdom can accomplish.

✎ *Gracious Father, I am so grateful that you love me in a way that does not dominate me but develops me. You guide but do not override. Amen.*

What kind of partner is God?

FOR READING AND MEDITATION – HEBREWS 2:5–18
'Since the children have flesh and blood,
he too shared in their humanity ...' (v. 14: NIV)

To go into every day on the basis of a divine-human partnership, it might help to think about God's qualifications for this important role. We ask can the eternal God really understand the pressures and difficulties of living in the realm of time? Is he really able to enter into our human feelings? The answer, of course, is 'yes'. In the Person of his Son, God has worn our flesh, measured its frailty and knows exactly how we think and feel. A quaint old preacher was praying and thanking God for the Trinity, and when he came to Jesus, he said, 'O God, even you couldn't do better than he did.'

There is no need to wonder what kind of partner God makes, for all you have to do is look at Jesus. He is 'God's highest character reference'. Firstly, he was a person of immense courage: not the excited, desperate courage of the battlefield, but quiet courage in the face of growing opposition and certain crucifixion. Does the day ahead look as if it needs special courage and determination? Are you facing a situation that requires greater strength and confidence than you feel you are capable of? Then take heart – in Christ you have a Partner who knows precisely how you feel and will, if you ask him, stamp his quiet courage and determination deep into your soul this very hour.

Lord Jesus Christ, stamp your courage and confidence into the warp and woof of my being, so that I shall do what has to be done. For your own dear Name's sake I ask it. Amen.

What better partner?

FOR READING AND MEDITATION – PSALM 73:13–28

'Whom have I in heaven but you? And there is none
upon the earth that I desire besides you.' (v. 25: NKJ)

What kind of partner does God make? Can the Creator really understand what goes on in the hearts and minds of finite human beings? The good news is that the incarnate Jesus does. However difficult our day might be, we have in Christ a Saviour and a Partner who knows and understands our deepest needs. He is able to provide the exact measure of strength and courage we require to meet what lies ahead. He is a trustworthy and reliable partner.

He cares! When he was here on earth, he cared more about the needs of others than he did about his own needs (see John 4:34). He gives! When people consider entering into partnership, they usually want to know how much their partner is willing to give. The true test of partnership is not just the giving of time, money, words, attendance at meetings – but the giving of oneself. Jesus Christ gives himself (see Gal. 1:4). He empowers! The disciples, prior to Pentecost, were afraid that they might not be able to continue the work Christ had committed to them – but after receiving the power of the Spirit, they were like men ablaze. Peter was conscious that Christ had teamed up with them, for he said, '… what I do have I give you …' (Acts 3:6). You cannot give what you don't have. You have Christ and he has you. What better partner could you find?

✎ *My Father and my God, that you should team up with me seems too good to be true. Yet it is too good not to be true. I know you will never default on your end of our partnership – help me to do the same. Amen.*

Every reason to praise

FOR READING AND MEDITATION – PSALM 22:1–11, 19–28

'But you are holy, who inhabit the praises of Israel.' (v. 3: NKJ)

Let's examine another way in which we can sharpen the awareness of God's presence in our lives – by cultivating a praising heart. Our text for today reminds us that the Almighty delights to dwell in the midst of his people's praise. Rest assured that the more you cultivate a praising heart, the more deeply you will feel the Lord's presence in your life. Some might dislike my phrase 'cultivating a praising heart' on the grounds that praise must be spontaneous and not something called up from within the soul. It might be helpful to begin by differentiating between praise and thanksgiving.

Although thanksgiving is a close relative of praise they are quite distinct and separate in their meaning. We thank God for what he does – we praise him for who he is. The psalmist declared, 'I will bless the Lord at all times; His praise shall continually be in my mouth.' (Ps. 34:1, NKJ). But can we truly be expected to praise the Lord at all times? Surely it means 'most times'? Or 'almost all times'? The prime purpose of praise is to honour and glorify God and because he never changes, praise of him is always appropriate. Some may feel they have little for which they can give thanks, but no one, no matter how poor, deprived or downcast, has any excuse not to praise.

✎ *My Father and my God, give me a clear insight to see that because of who and what you are, I am never without a reason to praise. May my lips and my life combine today to praise and glorify your Name. Amen.*

Praise is a choice ...

FOR READING AND MEDITATION – PSALM 42:1–11

'O my God, my soul is cast down within me;
therefore I will remember you ...' (v. 6: NKJ)

Praise begins not so much in the feelings as in the will. We can choose to praise the Almighty whether we feel like it or not. The psalmist, in today's verse, is obviously feeling sad and seems to find nothing in life for which he can be thankful. But look at how he deals with his doleful condition. Firstly he admits to feeling downcast. He doesn't stay too long with his feelings, but he is careful not to deny them. The teaching in some Christian circles is that we must never admit to feeling down, for once we do we have given the devil the right to take over control in our lives. To me this is sheer and utter nonsense.

After acknowledging his feelings, the psalmist makes a choice: 'I will remember you from the land of the Jordan, and from the heights of Hermon, from the Hill Mizar' (v. 6: NKJ). He chooses to focus his thoughts on the goodness of God in bringing his people into the Promised Land. In the final verse of the Psalm, he affirms a truth: 'Hope in God; for I shall yet praise him, the help of my countenance and my God.' So whenever you feel sad or depressed, acknowledge your feelings and then decide by an action of your will to focus your thoughts upon the goodness of God. It will save you from prolonged periods of gloom in the future.

✎ O God, I see that I can go through more times of sadness and gloom than I need to if I do not know the correct way to deal with them. Help me learn this lesson and learn it well. For Jesus' sake. Amen.

Inner health made audible

FOR READING AND MEDITATION – PSALM 92:1–15

'It is good to give thanks to the Lord, and to sing praises to your Name,
O Most High.' (v. 1: NKJ)

We continue meditating on the importance of cultivating a praising heart. A doctor once told me that the happiest and healthiest
people are those who are quick to praise. Then the thought came to
me: if this is true in the natural realm, then how much more true
will it be in the spiritual realm? Dr Clyde Narramore defines praise
as 'inner health made audible'. What does he mean? He means that
there is a connection between a readiness to praise and the state of
our physical health. If there really is this connection, then how can
it be explained?

One answer is that we are made in our innermost beings for
praise. God designed us to be praising beings. There is no surer
way of completing and fulfilling ourselves – when praising, we are
doing what we were designed for. If we decide not to make it our
chief occupation to praise God, inevitably we will suffer some spiritual and physical deprivation. A Christian physician says, 'When I
go through my day praising God, my blood flows better in my
veins.' Praise is good for you – it makes you a better person. You
will feel better, think better, work better, relate to others better and
sleep better. Try it and see.

✏ *Gracious and loving Father, these words of the hymnist express everything that is in my heart: 'Fill thou my life, o Lord my God, in every part with
praise, that my whole being may proclaim Thy being and thy ways.' Amen.*

Making praise a habit

FOR READING AND MEDITATION – PSALM 150:1–6
'Let everything alive give praises to the Lord!
You praise him? …' (v.6: TLB)

We remind ourselves that there are many reasons why we should praise God. How is this so? Because the Lord inhabits the praises of his people. Praise is the ramp down which God comes running into our hearts. He delights so much in praise that when we reach out to him in adoring worship, he just cannot stay away. Can I ask you to determine right now that you will make it a daily habit to spend some time in praise of God? Once you make that commitment, then go further and decide how you will carry it out. Don't leave it to the vagaries of feeling.

A friend of mine has the kind of watch that can give out a bleep every hour, and he uses the time signal to prompt him to focus his thoughts on praising God. Another friend who does a lot of driving uses the moments when he is brought to a halt by a red traffic light in direct praise of God. You might say that is mechanical. My friends tell me that it only sounds mechanical – they have found it to be medicinal. We pick up bad habits all too quickly. What is wrong with setting up a habit that enables us to turn our minds toward the Lord and give him the praise that he so wondrously deserves?

O God, teach me how to develop my praise of you into an art form. Show me how to salvage the spare moments of my life – moments that otherwise would be lost – in adoring praise of you. In Christ's Name I ask it. Amen.

Truth in the inner parts

FOR READING AND MEDITATION – 2 CORINTHIANS 13:1–14

'For we cannot do anything against the truth, but only for the truth.' (v. 8: NIV)

We move on to consider yet another step we must take in order to make sure that the awareness of God's presence in our lives is sharp and clear – break decisively with all known sin. Nothing dulls or blunts the awareness of God's presence in our lives so much as continuing to think or act in ways of which God cannot approve. The harbouring of moral wrong makes God unreal. I knew a man once who seemed to carry the sense of God's presence with him. People would often say that to spend a few minutes with him was a spiritual tonic. While visiting him one day, I asked him to share with me the secret of his deep spirituality. He told me that although he had a daily Quiet Time, early every Sunday morning he would get alone with God and examine his life in the light of five pointed questions: (1) Have I been truthful and honest? (2) Have I been impure? (3) Have I allowed bitterness to take root in my heart? (4) Has love been my motive in everything? (5) Have I sought God's glory – or my own glory?

How do you and I stand in the light of that first searching question today? You see, truth is inviolable. The early Christians, standing before tribunals, their lives in the balance, could have told a lie and their lives would have been saved. They refused, for they knew that truth was inviolable. They could die but they could not lie. Can you be depended on to tell the truth – no matter what?

✎ *O God, my Father, make me a transparent person, with nothing covered, nothing which I must conceal from myself or others. In Jesus' Name. Amen.*

Make me pure – but not yet

FOR READING AND MEDITATION – 1 CORINTHIANS 6:12–20
'You were bought at a price. Therefore honour God with your body.' (v. 20: NIV)

Let's think about honesty: have I been truthful and honest? How easy it is to lie – even for a Christian; the willingness to twist a meaning to gain a point; to misquote if the misquotation serves an end; to exaggerate in order to impress. What is at the base of this looseness with the truth? It is often the fact that we believe a lie is justifiable. But the truth is inviolable.

Let's look at my friend's second question: have I been impure? The question of purity is fundamental; if life sags now, it will probably sag all down the line. Have we victory or defeat at this point?

I remember having to confront a church official on one occasion with some evidence of serious impurity, and as he threw himself down into the chair in front of me, he said, 'I may be guilty, but I am still a decent man. I am not a man of the gutter.' Not of the gutter? The gutter was *in* him! Those of us who have put ourselves under the authority of Christ must watch our tendency to excuse ourselves when caught up in some wrong. Look into your heart and ask: am I a pure person? Do I allow my mind to dwell on the things that blunt the awareness of Christ's presence in my life? If so, then surrender it now. Don't adopt the attitude of St Augustine, who once prayed, 'Lord, make me pure, but not right now.'

Lord Jesus, I surrender my whole being afresh to you today. Cleanse the festering places of my heart and make it a place in which you can be at home. For your Name's sake. Amen.

Christ and bitterness – incompatible

FOR READING AND MEDITATION – HEBREWS 12:12–29

'See to it that no one misses the grace of God,
that no root of bitterness grows up …' (v. 15: MOFFATT)

We continue looking at the questions asked. (3) Have I allowed bitterness to take root in my heart? Of all the things that choke spiritual growth, bitterness is probably the most effective. Christ and bitterness are incompatible. If you hold on to bitterness, you have to let go of Christ, and vice versa. Each of us must ask ourselves: am I a bitter person? Do I hold grudges? Do I find it hard to forgive? If so, then surrender it now into the hands of Christ. Give up your bitterness before it gets you down.

(4) Has love been my motive in everything? All the motives of life, if they are to be sound, are reduced to one – love. And this love is not a general love, but a specific one – the love of Christ. Paul, one of the greatest Christians of all time, said, 'The love of Christ controls us …' (2 Cor. 5:14, RSV). This cuts deep. It is possible to be controlled by the love of achievement, of success, of a cause. To be controlled by the love of Christ is different, in degree, in kind and quality. When we do everything for the love of Christ, it transforms the menial into the meaningful, the sordid into the sacred. Perhaps this makes the presence of God alive in our hearts. The apostle John says, 'Now he who keeps his commandments abides in him, and he in him' (1 John 3:24, NKJ).

❧ *O Father, help me to face the challenge of loving and forgiving which has been presented to me today. Show me that I must do more than hear – I must obey. Help me, dear Father. In Jesus' Name. Amen.*

A little girl's first lie

FOR READING AND MEDITATION – 1 CORINTHIANS 10:23–33

'… whatever you do, do it all for the glory of God.' (v. 31: NIV)

The last question we look at is this: have I sought God's glory – or my own glory? What prompts your actions – self-interest or Christ-interest? In the deepest citadel of your spirit, who has the final word – you or Christ? The issue is this – if you dominate your life, then Christ cannot dominate it. You will not feel his presence as strongly in your heart. You will be more self-conscious than Christ-conscious. What is important, is that we are willing occasionally to engage in some form of self-examination or spiritual check-up – not just examining ourselves, but deciding to do something about the things we discover are blunting the edge of our spiritual awareness.

A minister's little daughter went into a guest's room and stole some sweets. When challenged by her mother as to where she got them, she told her first lie. The broken-hearted mother put her on her lap and told her what it all meant. The little girl wept bitterly and the mother said, 'I'm glad to see you are sorry – now take the sweet out of your mouth and throw it away.' The little girl looked at her mother through her tears, clamped her mouth shut and said, 'No, I am enjoying it too much.' After admitting she did wrong and showing remorse, she omitted the final necessary step of giving it up.

✎ O Father, save me from just identifying the things that dull the awareness of your presence in my life, but help me to give them up. In Christ's Name I pray. Amen.

Some things we need not ask for ...

FOR READING AND MEDITATION – PSALM 107:1–22

'Let the redeemed of the Lord say so ...' (v. 2: NKJ)

We look now at another way we can sharpen the awareness of God in our lives. It may come as a new thought to some and may be resisted. The suggestion can best be summed up in the phrase 'praying the affirmative way'. Praying the affirmative way is not asking for something to be so, but affirming it to be so; it is proclaiming to oneself that a matter or an issue is exactly the way God has decreed it. There are some things in the Christian life that we do not need to ask for at all – they are part of our Christian commitment. The promise of God's continued presence is one of them. Listen to what the Almighty says: 'I will never leave you nor forsake you' (Heb. 13:5, NKJ). And again: 'When my father and my mother forsake me, then the Lord will take care of me' (Ps. 27:10, NKJ).

Once we surrender our lives to God and are his committed sons and daughters, we have the guarantee that his presence will be in and around us every moment of the day. So do not ask for it, affirm it. Instead of praying, 'O God, be with me through every moment of this day,' say, 'Thank you, Father, that you are with me right now.' You may withdraw from him, but he will never withdraw from you.

✎ *Gracious Father, every day I need to learn something more of the Christian way. If there is something in this that I need to discover, then let there be an inner witness in my heart. In Jesus' Name I ask it. Amen.*

Affirming God's presence

FOR READING AND MEDITATION – PSALM 91:1–16

'We live within the shadow of the Almighty ...' (v. 1: TLB)

We said yesterday that there are some things in the Christian life that are part and parcel of our Christian commitment. The continued presence of Jesus Christ in our lives is one of them. About some things in life we would have to say in all honesty that we are not sure whether we know the mind of God about them. Thus we pray and petition God for light and illumination before we can proceed. No Christian needs be unsure of God's promise to dwell in the hearts of his children. He has put the issue beyond all doubt by assuring us that he is ever with us. Why, then, do we find ourselves so often praying for God to be with us, instead of simply affirming it?

One reason could be that we have a concern not to take the blessings and favours of God for granted. I suppose most of us are aware that we tend to take the blessings of God more for granted than with gratitude; so to avoid doing this, we lean the other way and concentrate on asking God to give us something which he has already vouchsafed – namely his continued presence. This is a kind of compensation in which we go to one extreme to avoid another. Someone has described it as 'leaning backward to avoid tipping forward'. It may sound very 'spiritual' to ask God to surround us with his presence, but we may find that we ask it because we do not really believe his promise in the first place.

✎ *Gracious and loving Father, I do not want to rationalise your promises; I want to realise them. Help me to examine my motives and see whether, deep down, I really believe what your Word tells me. Amen.*

Petition and affirmation – the difference

FOR READING AND MEDITATION – PSALM 139:1–12

'Where can I go from your Spirit? Where can I flee from your presence?' (v. 7: NIV)

To ask God to give us his companionship may seem 'spiritual', but could be a guise for our unbelief. We must be careful not to rationalise spiritual issues; it is far better to acknowledge that this may be a possibility, and consider it, rather than dismiss it out of hand. So ask yourself now: do I believe that Christ's presence is with me every moment of the day? If your answer is 'Yes', then ask yourself: then why do I not more frequently affirm it?

Secondly, we do not pray the affirmative way, because we do not clearly understand the difference between petition and affirmation. The difference is this: petition is asking God for something, affirmation is acknowledging that we have it. There are times when it is right to petition God, and there are times when it is wrong. Where is the dividing line? It centres on two things: (1) that God wants to give us what we ask for, and (2) that it is his perfect time. When both of these are in agreement, we need no longer ask – we simply believe it. Let's apply these suggestions to the question of God's presence. Do we know he wants to give it to us? 'Yes, we do.' Is it dependent on a certain time? 'No – he has pledged never to leave us.' We need not ask for God's presence – just affirm it.

I see, dear Father, that I do not have to ask for your presence: I already have it. In you I live and move and have my being. Thank you that you are with me everywhere I go. I am eternally grateful. Amen.

Growing in faith

FOR READING AND MEDITATION – MARK 11:12–25

'… whatever things you ask when you pray, believe that you receive them,
and you will have them.' (v. 24: NKJ)

We look again at the difference between the prayer of petition and
the prayer of affirmation. The truth is we need not petition him at
all. It doesn't mean that we take his presence for granted without
gratitude. We are simply taking God at his word. Some will say,
'What does it matter how we frame our prayers? God knows what
we mean. After all, a loving earthly father would not get upset with
a child who phrases his statements incorrectly.' That is quite true,
but the issue needs to be looked at.

   The statements of Scripture demand of us a degree of faith,
and faith is not something we are very good at displaying. We
would much prefer not to have to exercise faith and believe that
God means what he says by praying in such words as: 'Lord, help
me to believe that your presence is with me everywhere I go.' I
know full well that there are times when we have to pray like that,
when we are going through a hard and difficult time. But what I am
advocating is exercising our faith so that more and more we begin
to take God at his word. If we can't affirm the thing which the Lord
has made crystal clear in the Bible – his constant and continued
presence – then how are we going to grow in faith so that we can
affirm those things which are not so clear?

*O Father, forgive me that so often I shrink from the challenge to expand
my wings of faith. It is so much easier to ask for things than to believe for
them. But I want to grow. Teach me to affirm. Amen.*

The breath of God

FOR READING AND MEDITATION – JOHN 20:19–31

'... he breathed on them and said, "Receive the Holy Spirit." ' (v. 24: NKJ)

Another way in which to sharpen the awareness of God's presence is by establishing simple daily practices that help to remind us of the fact that he is constantly and continually with us. Now I want to talk about establishing some habits that will help remind us of the nearness of our Master's presence. These practices might not appeal to everyone, but those who follow them say they have greatly helped in bringing about a sharper awareness of God's presence in their lives.

Dr Frank Laubach, a medical practitioner, says that some of the most popular ones are these: walking on the inside of the pavement and visualising the Lord walking on the kerb side; playing the game of 'Minutes', in which you see how many times during an hour you think of God, then counting the number of minutes that you thought about him; taking a breath and saying, 'As this physical breath I am taking is filling my whole body with life-giving oxygen, so the breath of God, when I take it in, strengthens and sustains my inner life.'

Can I suggest that you take a moment right now to sit quietly in God's presence, breathing deeply as a physical focus to remind yourself that the Almighty is closer than the very air you breathe, and say the following prayer:

✑ *My Father and my God, as this physical breath I am taking is cleansing the blood in my lungs from all impurities, so your breath, as I take it within my being, purifies my inner life. I am so very, very grateful. Amen.*

Having 'elevenses' together

FOR READING AND MEDITATION – LUKE 24:13–35

'... Did not our heart burn within us while he talked with us ...
and while he opened the Scriptures to us?' (v. 32: NKJ)

Another daily practice some people use as a reminder of God's continual presence is to leave a vacant chair at a table or at the bedside and imagine Christ sitting there. A minister suggested to a lonely Christian woman: 'Every morning, when you have your coffee, pull up a chair and imagine that the Lord is sitting with you. Talk to him. Tell him everything – your joys, your sorrows and so on.' At first she reacted strongly against his advice, classifying it as 'unhelpful and unspiritual', but later she did as he had suggested. When the minister visited her some weeks later, he found a transformed woman. She said, 'That advice has helped me more than you will ever know. I have my Quiet Time early in the morning when I read God's Word and pray, but I also enjoy so much those moments when the Lord and I have our 'elevenses' together. Precisely at 11:00 I pull up two chairs at my kitchen table, pour out two cups of coffee and then we enjoy a lovely chat together!' A missionary who lived alone and had a strong tendency to worry used to pull up a chair alongside his bed at night and imagine Christ sitting there. Someone once asked him, 'John, what does the Lord say to you in those closing moments before you go to sleep?' He replied, 'He says, "You go to sleep now, John, and I'll stay up."'

Lord Jesus Christ, I am so thankful that you, who used so many visual aids in your earthly ministry, understand better than anyone that physical things can trigger spiritual understanding. Thank you, dear Lord. Amen.

Staying alert

FOR READING AND MEDITATION – PROVERBS 25:11–25

'Like cold water to a weary soul is good news from a distant land.' (v. 25: NIV)

We ended yesterday with the thought that our Lord Jesus Christ understands better than anyone how physical things can trigger off deeper spiritual awareness and understanding. I viewed some of the habits and practices as nothing more than 'crutches' for those who would not give priority to daily Bible reading and prayer. As I have talked with devout Christians about their spiritual lives, however, I have had to change my mind about this, for I have seen how the establishing of a simple daily habit has made their relationship with God even more meaningful.

We look now at another habit which some people practise in order to remind themselves of God's continuing presence in their lives – being alert and watching for anything interesting or unusual that happens during the day, and immediately bringing God into it. One woman I know, who practices this, says, 'Whenever something unusual or unexpected happens in my day, such as bumping into an old friend I haven't seen for years, receiving an unexpected phone call or a surprise gift, I immediately thank God for arranging my day in that way. This habit immediately focuses my mind on his all-pervading presence.' Stay alert and let the unusual and unexpected trigger in you an awareness of God's presence.

⊲ Gracious and loving heavenly Father, I see there are many things I can do to increase and sharpen the awareness of your presence in my life. Help me to choose the ones that are best for me. In Jesus' Name. Amen.

Another fixed habit

FOR READING AND MEDITATION – COLOSSIANS 3:1–17

'… whatever you do in word or deed, do all in the Name of the Lord Jesus, giving thanks to God the Father …' (v. 17: NKJ)

Another daily practice that can be used as a reminder of our Lord's presence in our lives is to let every completed task become a trigger for approaching God and thanking him for the gift of his presence. Some years ago, a woman who was seriously depressed came to me and told me that the cause of her depression was her husband's lack of interest in their home – and in her personally. 'I can clean the house from top to bottom,' she said, 'and my husband will not notice a thing. This makes me so angry, but nothing seems to change him.' I suggested to her that the next time she cleaned the house, she should get down on her knees and say, 'Lord, thank you for this home you have given me. I have cleaned it from top to bottom for you, for you are with me in everything I do.' When she cleaned the house a few days later, she did that and was amazed to hear the Lord say to her, 'Well done.' Those two words wiped out her depression.

I cannot promise, whenever you finish a task and turn to God in prayer, that you will hear his voice so clearly, but I can promise that he will find some secret stair into your soul. God delights in our response to him and his eye is quick to detect an appreciation for his presence.

My Father and my God, show me how to develop fixed habits that will assist me in becoming more spiritually established. I want to be fixed – not 'in a fix'. Help me. In Jesus' Name I ask it. Amen.

Practising the presence of God

More aware than ever ...

FOR READING AND MEDITATION – PSALM 46:1–11
'Be still, and know that I am God ...' (v. 10: NIV)

We pause at the beginning of another month to consider what practising the presence of God means. It is the fixing of the soul's gaze upon God, the savouring of him, the remembering of his unimpeachable promise that 'I will never leave you nor forsake you'. Brother Lawrence defines it in this way: 'The unbroken attitude of mind which envisages God within, the hearer of all speech, the monitor of all thoughts, the judge of all actions.' We easily lose sight of the fact that God is with us in everything we do. We need to pause and direct our thoughts and our gaze toward him.

Biblical meditation is one way of practising his presence. Regrettably it is one that is little understood and little used. David Ray, an American minister and author, says, 'I used to look with suspicion on people who talked about Bible meditation as being out of touch with reality. Then someone showed me how to take a verse such as Psalm 46:10 and allow it to soak into my thoughts. Within days, I became more aware of God's presence in my life than ever before.' May I suggest that you begin right now to practise the art of Bible meditation by letting this same verse lie on your mind throughout the day. Think about it, probe it, contemplate it – and draw out of it all that God has put into it.

O God, I see that if I am going to take up this challenge, it is going to take up some of my time. But help me see that when I give you time – you give me eternity. Amen.

The missing ingredient

FOR READING AND MEDITATION – PROVERBS 12:14–28

'The lazy man does not roast his game ...' (v. 27: NIV)

Today we ask ourselves: what exactly is Bible meditation? It is the process of holding a verse of Scripture in the mind, pondering it, continually contemplating it, dwelling upon it, viewing it from every angle of the imagination until it begins to affect the deepest parts of one's spiritual being. Do not confuse this with other types of meditation, particularly those that come from the East. Other forms of meditation focus on emptying the mind; Bible meditation focuses on filling it with the truths and insights of Scripture. It continues to surprise and astonish me, that although the Bible has so much to say about meditation, only a small minority understand and practice it. Research conducted among Christians in the US showed that comparatively few knew how to meditate. What percentage do you think it was? One in ten? No. One in a hundred? No. One in a thousand? No. Only one in ten thousand knew how to meditate. Now get this, for it could mean a watershed in your Christian experience. You can read the Bible, memorise and study it – but unless you know how to meditate on it, you will not get the best out of it. The Christian who does no more than read the Bible, memorise it and study it is like a person who chews his food but doesn't swallow it. Look at our text for today once again – that's what we are like when we fail to meditate.

✎ O God my Father, help me overcome any inertia I might feel in responding to the challenge to commit myself to meditating on your Word. I don't just want the good – I want the best. In Jesus' Name. Amen.

A more excellent way

FOR READING AND MEDITATION – PSALM 1:1–6
'But his delight is in the law of the Lord,
and in his law he meditates day and night.' (v. 2: NKJ)

One synonym for the word *meditate* is *ruminate*. Many animals, such as sheep, goats, antelope, camels, cows and giraffe are called ruminant animals. This is because they have stomachs with several compartments – the first of which is called the rumen. They digest their food by first bolting it down and then later regurgitating it from the rumen back into its mouth, where it is chewed again to extract further nourishment from the food. This process of rumination – or chewing the cud – enables the food to be thoroughly digested, whereupon it is absorbed into the animal's bloodstream, so becoming part of its life. Rumination and meditation are parallel words. When a Christian takes a text or phrase of the Bible and quietly and continuously contemplates it, the power and energy that is contained in the Word of God is absorbed into the spirit, the most important part of us. Truth held in the mind must become assimilated by the spirit if it is to have its greatest influence and effect. The more we contemplate and meditate on Scripture, the more speedily, effectively and powerfully truth is impressed into our spirit. Just as through rumination the animal gets the most nourishment out of the plants, so through meditation a Christian extracts from Scripture the life and energy God has put into it.

✥ *O Father, I see that if I am to get the most out of the Bible, then I must give myself to the practice of meditation. Help me to push aside any obstacles that may stand in the way of my achieving this. Amen.*

A day of decision

FOR READING AND MEDITATION – JOHN 15:1–11

'… if you live your life in me,
and my words live in your hearts …' (v. 7: J.B. PHILLIPS)

Take the text at the top of this page and begin to practice the art of meditation today. First memorise it. If you have difficulty in remembering a verse of Scripture, write it on a card, keep it in your pocket, and refer to it as often as you can throughout the day. Now begin meditating on it. Bring it into the central focus of your mind at different times throughout the day. Think about what it is saying and probe it with questions such as these: 'If you live your life in me' – what does it mean to live in Christ? What life is the Lord talking about here – natural life or spiritual life? What more ought I to be doing to 'live' in him? Then go on to the next phrase: 'And my words live in your hearts.' What does that mean? What words? How many 'words' of Christ do I know? How many have I memorised? Contemplate the next phrase: 'You can ask for whatever you like and it will come true for you.' 'Whatever you like' – does that mean I can get anything I like out of God? No, for if his Word is living in my heart, then I will only ask for those things that are in accordance with his will; I will only want what he wants. I can guarantee this – if you take a verse of Scripture each day of your life and meditate on it, then, other things being equal, you will never have to wonder why you can't feel God's presence in your heart and life.

✎ *Gracious and loving Father, what is being asked of me today is more than I can rise to in my own strength. I bring my weakness to you now – give me in its place your divine enabling. In Jesus' Name I ask it. Amen.*

The benefits of Christian fellowship

FOR READING AND MEDITATION – MATTHEW 18:15–20

'For where two or three come together in my Name, there am I …' (v. 20: NIV)

We now consider a way of practising the presence of God that all believers follow – except, of course, those who are housebound by reason of sickness or infirmity. I refer to the matter of meeting together in fellowship with other Christians. All of us do this, but not all of us understand the power and significance of what happens when we meet together in our Lord's Name. Although the presence of Christ is with every Christian individually, when we meet together corporately for prayer and worship, the presence of the Lord seems to be more intensely felt within ourselves individually. It is as if, in the physical presence of other Christians – praying together, singing together, sharing together – something is triggered that opens one's spirit more to God.

C.S. Lewis once expressed a similar thought: 'God can only show himself as he really is … to men (and women) who are united together in a body, loving one another, helping one another, showing him to one another … consequently the only really adequate instrument for learning about God is the whole Christian community, waiting for him together.' The closer we get to one another, the closer we will get to God, and the closer we get to God, the closer we will want to get to one another.

✎ Father, I am so grateful for the fellowship and relationship I have with my fellow Christians. Help me to cherish that and to enjoy its benefits in my personal life and experience. For Jesus' sake. Amen.

What makes a fellowship?

FOR READING AND MEDITATION – JOHN 17:20–26

'... I pray also for those who will believe in me ...
that all of them may be one ...' (vv. 20–21: NIV)

Meeting together with other Christians is one of the most effective ways of practising the presence of God. The more we open up to one another, the more we open up to Christ. We ought to pay more attention to this in the contemporary Christian church. If we do not take the necessary steps to experience true Christian fellowship, we inevitably deprive ourselves of the joy of his corporate presence. God can only mediate his presence in and through a community of his people to the extent that they are open to him and to one another. I know a number of churches where the people belong to a common tradition, subscribe to a common creed, share a common form of doctrine, but do not belong to one another. They think that sharing common beliefs makes them a living fellowship – it doesn't. What makes a group of Christians a living fellowship is their desire and willingness to open up to one another and share on the deepest levels of their personalities. What is it like in your church? Is it a place where you feel you really 'belong' – belong not just to Christ, but to one another? If so, rejoice in it. If not, begin by sharing yourself with your brothers and sisters as deeply as you are able. A church where people have no true relationship with one another blocks the way for the mediation of God's corporate presence.

O Father, I see that a local church whose members are not in harmony with one another restricts and limits the power of your presence. Bless my own fellowship this day and make us truly one. Amen.

The things that hinder us

FOR READING AND MEDITATION – 1 CORINTHIANS 11:23–34

'For if we searchingly examined ourselves …
we should not be judged …' (v. 31: AMPLIFIED)

A church that does not pay attention to the need for deepening their relationships with one another will not experience a keen sense of God's presence in their midst. He can only mediate his presence to the degree that his people are willing to open themselves up to him and to one another. The only exception I know to this is during times of revival, when God flows into a group of people in such terrible and awesome power that he sweeps aside all obstacles and hindrances. A church where the leaders and the congregation, recognising that they were not experiencing the degree of Christ's presence in their meetings that they should, got together on a Saturday for self-examination. They shared openly with one another. It was obvious there were many barriers between them. They were courageous enough to identify and make a list of them: fears, suspicions, jealousies, resentments, guilts, self-preoccupations, a desire to have one's own way, resistance to God-given authority and so on. The list was put up on an overhead projector: 'These are the things that keep us from one another.' In small groups they took several hours a week to start building better relationships. It was a very cleansing process – a catharsis. God made his presence felt powerfully in their midst and moved them to a new dimension of spiritual authority and power.

O Father, I pray that around your world today your children might come to see the importance of being more open to one another and to you. Begin with me, dear Lord. Amen.

What gives a congregation cohesion?

FOR READING AND MEDITATION – HEBREWS 10:19–39

'Not forsaking or neglecting to assemble together as believers …
but … encouraging one another …' (v. 25: AMPLIFIED)

We must not get the impression that all we need to do to realise
Christ's presence in a corporate way is to relate with one another.
This would put the focus on us, and not on him. One of the problems that can arise in churches where there is a strong relational
focus is that of concentrating more on the horizontal relationship
than on the vertical relationship. We must never forget that it is in
Christ's Name that we meet, not in our own name. After all, what
gives a Christian congregation cohesion? What holds it together? It
is not just the presence of Christ, but the Person behind the presence – Christ himself. When I was pastor in Yorkshire and used to
visit my flock, an old lady would always remark as I bade her
farewell, 'I will see you at the next meeting, for I don't want to miss
meeting him.' Most people would have said, 'I will see you at the
next meeting,' but her focus was not just on meeting with her fellow Christians – 'them'; it was on meeting with her Lord – 'him'.
She loved 'them', but she loved 'him' even more. Our priorities in
our times of Christian fellowship together must be in that order –
first 'him' and then 'them'. Whenever we link ourselves with 'him'
and 'them', we have one of the greatest means of practising the
presence of God that we can ever know.

✎ *My Father and my God, help me not to get this out of focus and make
more of meeting with my brothers and sisters than of meeting with you. In
every meeting I want to meet you. Amen.*

The Spirit makes Christ real

FOR READING AND MEDITATION – EPHESIANS 5:8–20

'… be filled with the Spirit.' (v. 18: NIV)

We continue our consideration of the options that are open to us for increasing our awareness of the presence of God in our lives. I use the word 'options', because we can take them or leave them; God will not force them upon us. He makes himself available to us, and when we make ourselves available to him, the result will be a deep and continuous sense of his presence in our hearts. Another way of experiencing God's presence is, as our text for today puts it, to 'be filled with the Spirit'. One of the ministries of the Holy Spirit is to make God and his Son, Jesus Christ, real to us: 'He (the Holy Spirit) will glorify me, for he will take of what is mine and declare it to you' (John 16:14, NKJ). Therefore, the more we allow the Holy Spirit to have sway in our lives, the more aware we will be of the divine presence.

Now the question will be asked: what does it mean to be filled with the Spirit? Does not every Christian possess the Holy Spirit? The answer is 'Yes', for Scripture teaches that every Christian has the Holy Spirit from the moment of their conversion. For example, 'Unless one is born of water and the Spirit, he cannot enter the kingdom of God' (John 3:5, NKJ). However, although all Christians have the Holy Spirit, the Holy Spirit doesn't have all Christians. In the light of this, let us face this question before going further: I have the Holy Spirit, but does he really have me?

✎ *O God, help me not to dodge or evade this question. You have given all of yourself to me – help me give all of myself to you. In Jesus' Name I pray. Amen.*

The three prepositions

FOR READING AND MEDITATION – JOHN 14:15–27

'… But you know him, for he lives with you and will be in you.' (v. 17: NIV)

If every Christian has the Holy Spirit, then why do we have this continuous debate among ourselves about such phrases as 'the baptism of the Spirit', 'being filled with the Spirit', 'walking in the Spirit', and so on? It was not until I was shown the three different prepositions which Jesus used in relation to the Holy Spirit that the matter became clear to me. Someone has said, 'A preposition can alter a proposition,' and nowhere is that more true than in relation to the teaching on the Holy Spirit.

The three prepositions Jesus used when talking of the Holy Spirit are 'with', 'in' and 'upon'. What did Jesus mean when he said the Holy Spirit was 'with' the disciples? He meant, so I believe, that the Spirit was accompanying them, was working with them on the outside. He most certainly was not in them, for Christ clearly indicated that that phase of the Spirit would be at some point in the future: 'He will be in you.' This is how the Spirit worked in our lives prior to our conversion. He was with us in order to convict us of sin and to persuade us of the fact that without Christ our eternal future was one of gloom and despair. Wonderful and awesome though it may be to have the Spirit with us, there can be no real radical change in our lives until the Holy Spirit moves within us.

✎ O Father, how can I sufficiently thank you for the change your Spirit has brought about in my life since the day I let you come in. If I want anything more, it is more of what I have. Thank you again, dear Father. Amen.

When were the disciples converted?

FOR READING AND MEDITATION – JOHN 20:19–31

'… he breathed on them and said, "Receive the Holy Spirit."' (v. 22: NIV)

We ended yesterday with the statement, 'Wonderful and awesome though it may be to have the Spirit with us, there can be no real radical change in our lives until the Holy Spirit moves within us.' This brings us to the question: when did the Holy Spirit enter into the disciples to bring them the new birth? Many will say it took place at Pentecost. I do not think so. Our passage today depicts that glorious post-resurrection meeting of Christ with his disciples in which, after commissioning them, he proceeded to breathe on them, saying, 'Receive the Holy Spirit.' What did the disciples receive at that moment? Obviously – the Holy Spirit. But if that is so, then what happened on the Day of Pentecost? This is where our prepositions help. Here in the Upper Room – so I believe – the disciples' hearts were regenerated by the power of the Holy Spirit. He who had been 'with' them, now came 'in' them to convert them. Although the disciples belonged to Christ prior to the Cross and resurrection, they could not have actually experienced the regeneration power of the Spirit, for that could only have been conveyed to them following Christ's conquest of Satan on the Cross and his victory over the grave. It is interesting that the first thing Jesus does when meeting his disciples after coming back from the dead is to impart to them the Holy Spirit. Now, because of the Cross and resurrection, he who had been with them was able to come into them.

✎ *O Father, once again I bow before you in deepest gratitude for the fact that your Spirit is not just 'with' me, but 'in' me. I am so grateful. Amen.*

The Day of Pentecost

FOR READING AND MEDITATION – ACTS 1:1–14

'… you shall receive power when the Holy Spirit has come upon you …' (v. 8: NKJ)

We look now at the third preposition: 'You shall receive power when the Holy Spirit has come *upon* you.' This was a prophetic reference to a day not far distant – the Day of Pentecost – when the Spirit would once again have a part to play in their lives. So now we ask: what happened at Pentecost? The Holy Spirit, who had been 'with' the disciples prior to the Cross and resurrection, and came 'in' them in the Upper Room, would now come 'upon' them in all his fullness to saturate them with divine power and turn them from timid, vacillating disciples into men and women who were ablaze and invincible. When the Spirit came in fullness at Pentecost, the disciples who hitherto, though converted and committed to Christ, were somewhat frightened and dispirited, began to feel his personal presence in a way that transformed them within. Now they had no doubt that Christ was actually living in their lives and, feeling his presence, they went out and began to turn the world upside down.

What does this mean to you? The Spirit has been 'with' you in order to bring you to Christ and is now 'in' you through the work of regeneration, but you experienced your own personal Pentecost. Is the Spirit enduing you with divine energy and power? Bottom line is this – is he a dynamic force or merely a doctrine?

✎ O God, save me from being satisfied with just an intellectual understanding of the doctrine of the Spirit. In this 'upper room' where I am now – give me what you gave those first 120 disciples. Amen.

He seems ashamed of his body

FOR READING AND MEDITATION – ROMANS 12:1–13

'... I urge you ... to offer your bodies as living sacrifices,
holy and pleasing to God ...' (v. 1: NIV)

Another aspect of practising the presence of God, is keeping the physical body in good health and order, as far as possible, for some are handicapped with a poor physical frame. Even so, perhaps it can be made better – even well. Our physical body is the house in which the soul lives, and if, through neglect or abuse, we allow that house to fall into disrepair, it might well have an adverse effect upon the soul. What goes on in the soul influence and affect the body. What goes on in the body influence and affect the soul. There have always been those who have looked on the body as the enemy of the soul. They see it as something that has to be continually suppressed, sometimes mutilated, and they go through life thinking their soul is imprisoned in a body. A Christian once said that another seems to be ashamed that he inhabits his body. Not one word in Scripture leads us to have a morbid view of our bodies. On the contrary, the passage before us today exhorts us to present our bodies as a living sacrifice. Note the word 'living'. While we are here on earth, we live in a body, whether we like it or not and we have to ensure that, as far as we are able, our bodies become a well-kept temple in which the presence of God can effectively dwell.

✎ O God of my mind and my body, I want both under the control of your redemption and guidance. Help me pass on the health of my mind to my body and the health of my body to my mind. Amen.

Divine service is held here ...

FOR READING AND MEDITATION – HEBREWS 10:1–22

'... sacrifice and offering you did not desire,
but a body you have prepared for me.' (v. 5: NKJ)

We said yesterday that there is not one word in Scripture that leads us to have a morbid view of our physical bodies. The Bible teaches, of course, that the body has been affected by the Fall and that the curse which fell on the earth has greatly affected our physical functioning, but it encourages us, nevertheless, to respect our bodies and view them as a temple in which the presence of God dwells. Jesus accepted his body as a gift from God: 'A body you have prepared for me' (Hebrews 10:5, NKJ). His body and soul were attuned. He neither neglected his body nor pampered it – he offered it as the vehicle of God's will and purpose. It is Jesus Christ, and not sick or infirm saints (no disrespect intended), who must be the pattern of how we are to act toward our bodies. Just enough sleep to make us fresh, and a little less than that which would make us lazy. Just enough food to keep us fit and not make us fat. Just enough physical exercise for fitness and not so much that we become so preoccupied with it that it drains higher interests. If we keep our bodies fit like a well-tuned violin, then the music of God will be able to come forth from every fibre of our being. When tempted to ignore the needs of the body, say to yourself, 'My body is a temple of the Holy Spirit and deserves the highest concentration and interest.'

✎ *Holy Spirit, I am amazed that you should want or be willing to inhabit my physical frame – yet it is so. Help me to care for it in such a way that we will both be comfortable in it. In Jesus' Name I pray. Amen.*

A good weight-reducing technique

FOR READING AND MEDITATION – 1 CORINTHIANS 6:12–20
'You were bought at a price. Therefore honour God with your body.' (v. 20: NIV)

Another pointed question: if, as we have seen, the body is the temple in which God dwells, then what can we do to make it a fit habitation for the Almighty? I am not going to refer here to emotional things, but to things that are purely physical. It is true that our emotions and attitudes greatly affect our physical functioning, but my concern now is to focus purely and simply on the matter of physical care. First, if you have not done so for a long time, have a physical check-up to see if there are any structural problems in your body. If there aren't, then you know that you can give yourself to some of the other things that I am going to mention in a disciplined way. Second, make sure you have plenty of physical exercise. When you maintain a regular programme of physical exercise, you work better, think better and concentrate better. Third, control your appetite. A traveller tells of how he watched a man on board ship, pacing up and down like a caged tiger, irritable because his breakfast had not come on time. He didn't just have an appetite; the appetite had him. And in addition to that the man was fifty pounds overweight. If you are overweight, then try this as an exercise – put your hands on the table when you are halfway through a meal, and push so hard that your chair moves away from the table. It's one of the best weight-reducing exercises that I know.

✎ My Father and Creator of my body, I desire this physical frame of mine to be at its best. You have made me for health and rhythm. Help me to keep fit for you. Amen.

Relaxing in God's presence

FOR READING AND MEDITATION – 1 TIMOTHY 4:1–12

'Bodily fitness has a limited value,
but spiritual fitness is of unlimited value …' (v. 8: J.B. PHILLIPS)

We spend another day looking at ways in which we can ensure that our bodies are fit temples for the Holy Spirit. Fourth, learn to relax. This is what I do whenever I feel tense and under stress: I lie down on a bed, close my eyes and say to all the organs of my body in succession, 'Brain, you are now in the presence of God. Let go and listen. He wants to touch you. Receive his peace. Eyes, you are weary through looking at many distracting things. You are now in the presence of the One who made you. Receive his peace. Nerves, you who are the intelligence department of my being, strained and torn by living in a world of chaos, you are now to report better news. God is coming to you with the news of calmness and tranquillity. Receive his peace.' I go over my whole body like this, which takes about ten or fifteen minutes. Often I rise as if made anew. Fifth, build into your life periods of recreation – activities that leave you physically rejuvenated and toned up. Only creation and no recreation make 'Jack', and everyone else, a dull boy. Life is made for work and play. Recreation, whether it is a physical game or a mental game, must leave you with a sense of heightened vitality in the total being. And remember, any recreation into which Christ cannot be taken is not for a Christian.

⬧ *Father, I ask for wisdom in dealing with this instrument, my body. Help me to make it the best it can be. Amen.*

Feelings that come from nowhere

FOR READING AND MEDITATION – PSALM 23:1–6

'He restores my soul; he leads me in the paths
of righteousness for his name's sake.' (v. 3: NKJ)

We looked at keeping our physical body in good order, so that it does not adversely affect our spiritual sensitivity. Now we'll look at the realm of the mental and emotional. Did you know that wrong mental attitudes and unhealed hurts can reverberate inside you to such a degree that they can sometimes effectively suppress the sense of God's presence within your soul? I have found that despite my theological training, there are some people whom I cannot help. They say things like, 'I know I am a Christian, but there are times when God's presence seems to leave me, and I only feel deep loneliness and sadness. I have not committed sin and I know of nothing in my life that is dishonouring to God. These feelings seem to come out of nowhere and without any apparent reason. I do not know what to do about them. Can you help me?' Many of these people feel this way because of some unhealed hurt of the past, some disturbing memory that had been repressed, or some wrong attitude that had never been corrected. These things rise up from time to time within the soul and blunt their spiritual sharpness and sensitivity. If you have ever experienced what I am talking about, then I hope that what I am going to say over the next few days may help you to control this problem whenever it occurs again.

✎ *My Father and my God, help me to come to you that I might learn not only to keep my body under control, but also my mind and my emotions. I ask this in Christ's peerless and precious Name. Amen.*

Can Christ heal our inner wounds?

FOR READING AND MEDITATION – PROVERBS 18:1–14

'A man's spirit sustains him in sickness,
but a crushed spirit who can bear?' (v. 14: NIV)

Some people's awareness of God is occasionally blunted by strange, even terrifying feelings that arise within the soul and affect their spiritual sensitivity. They can be walking along the street with a deep awareness of Christ's presence in their lives when a dark cloud descends upon the soul and dampens their spiritual delight. One of the major causes of this is that something out of the person's past – a repressed fear, unhealed hurt or a deep rejection – has intruded into the present, taking its toll on the personality. Someone told me, 'There are times when I feel God's pre-sence surrounding me so closely that I feel like dancing with joy, and then suddenly, for some reason, I feel incredibly lonely.' A few pointed questions brought us both to see that in that person's spi-rit was a wound that had never been healed. But what is a wounded spirit? These wounds are some-times deeper and more painful than a physical wound. The wounds I am talking about here usually arise from two things – deep hurts and deep horrors. The hurts come from rejection or deprivation of love. The horrors come from having experienced deep trauma, bru-tality, violence and physical abuse. Can Christ really sympathise and help us with our deep inner wounds? He can! He can!

❧ Lord Jesus, it was said of you that you were 'wounded in the house of your friends'. Now your wounds speak to my wounds. Heal me of any inner hurt or horror that may be reverberating within. Amen.

Emotional healing – not automatic

FOR READING AND MEDITATION – PHILLIPIANS 1:1–11
'Being confident of this, that he who began a good work
in you will carry it on to completion …' (v. 6: NIV)

In some Christian circles – thankfully, not all – whenever the problem of past problems intruding into the present is mentioned, the objection is raised, 'Are you denying the power and reality of conversion? All those things are dealt with at the moment a person is converted – why harp back to the past?' The teaching that conversion instantly resolves all our emotional problems has caused great difficulty in the Christian church. At conversion we have the potential for dealing with all our emotional problems, and at conversion some people have been healed of all their emotional problems, but it is definitely not true that it happens automatically. We cannot begin to help one another until we are willing to face reality and deal with issues, not as we would like them to be, but as they are. But how is a wounded spirit healed of these wounds from the past that intrude into the present? First we have to face the fact that these things are going on within us. Don't say, 'All this was dealt with at my conversion and I am just deceiving myself that I have a problem.' This kind of difficulty cannot be dealt with by wishful thinking. Acknowledge it to yourself. If you can, share it with another Christian – preferably a counsellor. Many Christians miss out on healing because they are unwilling to share something with another person.

✎ *O Father, in this quest for health – inner health as well as outer health – make me completely realistic, facing up to everything. Amen.*

Stop blaming others

FOR READING AND MEDITATION – JOHN 5:1–15
'When Jesus saw him lying there … he said to him,
"Do you want to be made well?" ' (v. 6: NKJ)

When things out of our past intrude into the present we ought to accept some responsibility for the way we are. But you say, 'I was the one who was rejected, deprived and subjected to the most terrifying trauma.' That may be true, but in every situation we face in life we have the choice to respond by forgiving or resenting. It might sound hard and insensitive, but, no one can be freed of these things from the past until they stop blaming others and accept responsibility for their present attitudes. If there is any resentment in your heart toward others for some hurt or failure toward you, then you must forgive. Third, do you really want to be healed and delivered? Jesus asked the man who had been ill for thirty-eight years, 'Do you want to be made well?' You see, it is possible that past problems serve a purpose for us. We might use them as a crutch so that we can walk with a limp and thus get the sympathy of others or we could use the hurts as an excuse to hurt others. Fourth, bring whatever is troubling you to God and ask him to heal it. If you go through the other three steps carefully, this last step will be a very easy one. If nothing happens, then go over the first three steps again – something is being missed. Whenever we do our part, God never fails to do his.

✎ *Yes, Lord, I want to be whole. Help me renounce all my wrong choices and wrong attitudes. Sweep through me and deliver me from all that binds me to the past. Amen.*

Sharing – an inherent impulse

FOR READING AND MEDITATION – 2 CORINTHIANS 5:12–21

'... the love of Christ constrains us ...' (v. 14: NKJ)

Another way to sharpen the awareness of God's presence in our lives is to ensure that we give out what God puts in. I call this the discipline of sharing. Discipline yourselves to share by word and deed what you know of God as we do to pray and read the Scriptures. Many do not do this. They are earnest and regular in their Quiet Times, but they have never disciplined themselves to share – it happens more by accident than by choice a question of whim rather than a question of will. The natural impulse of a heart in which God's love and presence dwells is to radiate that love and presence to others. You might have heard the story of the man who, finding a little dog with a broken leg by the roadside, took it to his house and attended to it until it was well. It began to run around the house and then, one day, it disappeared. The man had grown to love the little dog and felt somewhat disappointed and let down. But the next day there was a scratching at the door. The little dog was back again, but this time there was another little dog with it – and the other little dog was lame! The impulse in that little dog's heart was natural and right – it was the impulse to share with others what it had received. Does God's love and presence abide in you? Good. It will get even deeper and richer as you take the initiative in sharing his love and presence with others.

✍ O Father, who can feel your love and power stirring in their hearts and not want to share it? The impulse is there – inherently. Help me not to choke it. Amen.

No freedom without law

FOR READING AND MEDITATION – PSALM 119:1–16
'Happy are they who follow his injunctions,
giving him undivided hearts.' (v. 2: MOFFATT)

If it has not occurred to you already, then the point must be made now – the practice of the presence of God involves discipline. I suggest deliberate and concentrated effort. It is much easier to relax and let things happen of their own accord, but in my experience it is the disciplined who get the best results. There are those who will object and say, 'We are made for freedom – all this talk about discipline is foreign to Christianity.' But freedom can only come through disciplined obedience. I am free from pressure by the police only as I obey the law; within the framework of the law they represent, I am free. Someone has put it like this: 'I am free to swing my arm, but my freedom ends at the tip of your nose.' There is no such thing as absolute freedom – freedom, if it means anything at all, must be controlled by law. And it is a law of the kingdom of God that what goes on in the soul must pass through the soul. Intake must result in outflow. God is not interested in just living in us; he is interested in living through us. The joyous thing about sharing with others what God has put inside us is that we become all the better for the sharing. As we give, so we receive. And not only do we become better – we become better off. We experience his presence in a more real and wonderful way.

◆ *O Father, I have taken discipline from too many things. I have obeyed this and that. The result is that I have become this and that – nothing. Help me to be a disciplined person. In Jesus' Name I pray. Amen.*

Don't be a hearer only

FOR READING AND MEDITATION – REVELATION 22:1–21

'The Spirit and the bride say, "Come!"
And let him who hears, say, "Come!" ' (v. 17: NIV)

Over the years, both in letters and in private conversation with fellow – Christians, I have been asked, 'I have known the presence of God in my life in a real and vital way, but now for some reason it seems to have ebbed away. Why is this?' There could be many reasons, but I have often found that a major cause for this is a failure to share with others what they know of God. Without outflow, the inflow automatically stops. It is a law of life that whatever is not used, dies. Professor Henry Drummond, in his book *Natural Law in the Spiritual World*, talks about some fish caught in the dark waters of the Mammoth Caves in Kentucky, USA. Although they had eyes, they could not really see. No one knows how they got into the caves, but in the darkness eyesight became superfluous. 'Nature,' said Professor Drummond, 'adopted the position: what you don't use, you don't need.' Now, of course, we must not push this too far and suggest that if we do not work at sharing God's love and presence with others, we will lose our salvation, because that is not what Scripture teaches. It is a fact, however, that the more we share what we have received: the more we will have to share. In my teenage years the Spirit challenge me, 'You have been a hearer – now say "Come"'. I went out and won my first soul to Christ.

✎ O God, I want all my channels to be wide open today. If they are clogged, then show me how I can be free. I, who have been a 'hearer', am now going to begin to say, 'Come'. Help me. Amen.

Four steps in helping others

FOR READING AND MEDITATION – JOHN 1:35–51

'Philip found Nathanael and told him, "We have found the one
Moses wrote about … Jesus of Nazareth …" ' (v. 45: NIV)

Many people hesitate to share the love and presence of God
because they do not know how to. I dislike exceedingly the idea of
'selling religion' – it smacks of commercialism and makes Christ
appear to be a commodity. Nevertheless, I have noticed that some
sales people get a lot of customers, while others get none. The ones
who make an impression usually do so because of two basic
things. One, they act as though the thing they are selling is of great
importance to them, and two, they do not push too hard, for they
know this might produce an unfavourable reaction. A sales man-
ager gave four steps in presenting a commodity: (1) What is it? (2)
What will it do for you? (3) Who says so? (4) How can you get it?
Use these four steps when sharing with others what God has
shared with you. What is it? First clear away misconceptions and
point out what it is not. It is not being joined to a religion, but being
joined to a Person – Christ. What will it do for you? You will find
forgiveness, freedom, reality, a sense of inner unity and of 'coming
home'. Who says so? Christ does – through his Word and through
the testimony of multitudes of his followers. How can you get it? By
repenting of sin – not just wrong habits and actions, but the basic
sin of self-dependency – depending on self rather than on God.

*My Father and my God, I hear all around me, on radio and television,
the witness to false gods – the gods of money, materialism and so on. Help
me to witness all the more clearly for you. Amen.*

Everything works our way

FOR READING AND MEDITATION – JAMES 1:1–12

'... count it all joy when you fall into various trials,
knowing that the testing of your faith produces patience.' (vv. 2–3: NKJ)

My final suggestion on how to sharpen the awareness of God's presence in your heart is to willingly and joyfully open the door of your life to any trials and tribulations that may knock upon it. This will be difficult for many to accept, but it is firmly rooted in Scripture. Look at the *J.B. Phillips* paraphrase of today's text: 'When all kinds of trials and temptations crowd into your lives, my brothers, don't resent them as intruders, but welcome them as friends! Realise that they come to test your faith and to produce in you the quality of endurance.' Can you see the tremendous truth that is contained in these words? They are saying that when we open the door to trials and temptations, they serve not to demean us, but to develop us.

Scripture is telling us there is a better response than our natural response to slam the door shut – open wide the door and welcome trial and temptation in as you would a long-lost friend. How strange. Why does Scripture tell us to do this? Because trials and temptations will, if we respond correctly, cause us to rely less on our own and more on Christ's strength. The difficulties become the doors through which his presence flows more powerfully into our lives.

Father, if ever I needed insight and understanding, it is now. You know how I shrink from facing the trials and temptations of life, but help me lay hold on this tremendous truth that in you everything contributes. Amen.

Isolation becomes revelation

FOR READING AND MEDITATION – REVELATION 1:4–20

'I, John, your brother and companion … was on the island of
Patmos because of the word of God …' (v. 9: NIV)

Trials and temptations can, if we respond correctly, help us to experience the presence of God more powerfully in our lives. The apostle John says, 'I … was on the isle called Patmos, (banished) on account of my witnessing to the Word of God …' (AMPLIFIED). He experienced one of the greatest trials that anyone could endure – banishment and isolation. He was bereft of the presence of his Christian friends and companions – but was he bereft of the presence of God? 'I was in the Spirit – rapt in his power – on the Lord's day, and I heard behind me a great voice …' (v. 10: AMPLIFIED). Shut off from men, he was open to God. Do you experience a trial of banishment and isolation? I don't mean a lonely island in the middle of the ocean, but a situation where you feel bereft of Christian fellowship. Take heart – the island of isolation can be an island of revelation. God will not fail you – he will, if you do your part by accepting your circumstances, make his presence so vital and real to you that you will emerge from this experience realising the truth of Paul's great words in Rom 8: 'Neither death nor life, nor angels nor principalities nor powers, nor things present nor things to come … shall be able to separate us from the love of God which is in Christ Jesus our Lord' (vv. 38–39: NKJ).

✎ *Father, I see that when you abide by me, then I can abide by anything. And not only abide by it, but experience an even deeper sense of your presence in it. I am so thankful. Amen.*

The presence of Christ

FOR READING AND MEDITATION – 2 CORINTHIANS 12:1–10

'... My grace is sufficient for you,
for my strength is made perfect in weakness ...' (v. 9: NKJ)

It is probably safe to say that one of the reasons why we may not experience a rich and satisfying sense of God's presence in our lives is due to our unwillingness to face life's trials and temptations and, then we will never experience the deep power of Christ's compensating presence in the midst of those trials and temptations. If only we could grasp the truth that, in Christ, nothing can work successfully against us – it can only work for us. In trials we experience even more deeply and keenly the sustaining power and presence of our Lord Jesus Christ. They serve a divine purpose by opening us up to knowing Christ's presence. A man who was informed that he had terminal cancer, went into a state of shock for a few days. When he came out of it, he said to himself, 'All right, if this is so, then by life and death – I want to glorify the Lord.' He set about re-establishing his priorities and focused on how he could best minister to people during his last few months on this earth. By the time you read these lines, if the prediction of the doctors is correct, and the Lord does not heal him, he will be in heaven. When I asked him what was the one thing above all else that he could be thankful for, he replied with tears in his eyes, 'The presence of Christ.'

O God my Father, I see that I need not whine or complain at anything that happens. Through you, I can make music out of misery, a song out of sorrow and experience the deepest joy in the midst of the deepest pain. I am eternally thankful. Amen.

The way the dawn comes ...

FOR READING AND MEDITATION – LUKE 22:39–53

'And there appeared to him an angel from heaven,
strengthening him in spirit.' (v. 43: AMPLIFIED)

We spend one more day discussing the importance of facing all
our trials and temptations in the knowledge that they serve only to
open us up to knowing more of God. A guide and an inexperienced
climber had to spend all night in the Pyrenees; they couldn't make
it back. Toward dawn, as a tempestuous wind twisted the trees and
rocks rolled down the mountain, the climber was terrified. The
guide reassured him, 'Don't worry, this is the way the dawn usually comes up here in the Pyrenees.' Sometimes our dawn comes
through the storms of trials and temptations – John Wilhelm
Rowntree tells how when he left a doctor's office after being told
that his advanced blindness could not be halted, he stood by some
railings for a few minutes to collect himself. 'Suddenly,' he says, 'I
felt the love of God wrap me about as though an invisible presence
enfolded me, and a joy filled me such as I had never known before.'
That presence will manifest itself when most needed. Christ went
into the Garden of Gethsemane and endured such agony that an
angel was sent to strengthen him. In the hour of his greatest need
he experienced the greatest strengthening. You may be called on to
face a 'Gethsemane' experience today. If so, remember you can
come out of it as did Jesus, with a deeper sense of God's strengthening presence than you ever knew before.

*O Father, help me see that my fear of losing the sense of your presence in
the midst of my trials is groundless and invalid. Amen.*

Practice makes perfect

FOR READING AND MEDITATION – PSALM 16:1–11

'... you will fill me with joy in your presence,
with eternal pleasures at your right hand.' (v. 11: NIV)

On our last day together, we ask ourselves: what are some of the benefits that flow from an increased awareness of God's presence in our lives? First it makes our faith stronger. The more we realise that by a simple act of memory we can sharpen the awareness of God's presence in our hearts, the more easily we will be able to put our faith into operation in the bigger issues. Secondly it strengthens hope. 'Hope,' says E.M. Blaiklock, 'grows in proportion to our knowledge, and according as our faith penetrates through this holy exercise (reminding ourselves that God's presence is constantly with us) into the secrets of the Divine ... our hope grows and strengthens itself, and the grandeur of this good which it seeks to enjoy, and in some manner tastes, reassures and sustains it.'

A third benefit is that it makes us stronger in love. The more we gaze upon God, the more we will love him, and the more we love him, the more we will gaze upon him. The more we practise his presence, the more perfectly we will feel his presence. At the time of seeming aloneness, he is closer to you than you realise. But do not take his presence for granted – practise it. Like all things in life – practice makes perfect. Go out now, then, and practise the presence of God.

✏ *O God, help me to put into practice the things you have taught me. Help me to beautify the hours as they come and go by experiencing your presence in my life in a way I have never known before. In Jesus' Name I ask it. Amen.*

The true Lord's Prayer

FOR READING AND MEDITATION – JOHN 17:1–26

'… Jesus … looked toward heaven and prayed:
"Father, the time has come." '(v.1: NIV)

'There is no better way to prepare our hearts for the Easter season,'
said famous Welsh preacher Dr Cyndyllan Jones, 'than by a serious
contemplation of the prayer of our Lord in John 17.' Usually we refer
to the prayer which Christ framed for his disciples in Luke 11 as 'The
Lord's Prayer', but that was not a prayer the Saviour used himself –
at least not in its entirety. Christ would not have prayed 'Forgive us
our sins', for he had no sins to forgive. This is why some people
describe the prayer here in John 17 as the true Lord's Prayer, prayed
in the shadow of the Cross, just before he left the Upper Room and
went with his disciples into the dark valley of the Kidron. Some people regard it as the greatest prayer ever prayed – an opinion I share.

We can tell a lot about people by the way they pray. Often something they would say would be like a window into their soul. Reve-
rently I ask the question: what do we learn about our Lord as we
listen to him pray in this great intercessory moment before stepping
on to the Cross? We learn that here is someone who is Man, yet more
than a man, apprehensive, but not afraid. His thoughts are on the
events about to overtake him, yet his foremost concern is the wellbeing of his disciples. The prayer reveals the prayer.

꙾ *Gracious and loving Father, unfold to me by your Spirit the riches and
depths of this, my Saviour's prayer. New light always breaks out from your
Word. May that be my experience as I meditate on it day by day. In Jesus'
Name. Amen.*

The first true note

FOR READING AND MEDITATION – LUKE 11:1–13

'He said to them, "When you pray, say: Father …"' (v. 2: NIV)

The true Lord's Prayer opens with the words, 'Father, the time has come.' Our Lord taught his disciples in Luke 11 that their prayers should begin by focusing on God as their Father. Why is this important? It turns our minds away from ourselves to our Father in heaven. Only then can we get the right perspective on things. Our biggest failures in prayer begin when we rush into God's presence and start presenting our petitions without any regard to who God is. It only keeps our attention on what is already troubling us and increases our awareness of our lack. When we begin by focusing on God as our Father and take a slow, calm, reassuring gaze at him – the first thing we receive in prayer is a calm spirit. The tendency to plunge into a panicky flood of words leaves us, and we begin to see that there is an entirely different way of looking at things.

Another consequence of focusing on God as Father is that it reminds us that when we come to God in prayer we are not talking about God but talking to him. We are not engaging in a theological dialogue; we are talking to a Father. Prayer essentially is a relationship. Praying cannot be praying in the New-Testament sense unless we understand that when we talk to God we talk to him as a child talks to a loving father. This is the first true note in prayer.

Father – with what joy I say the word. Help me never to forget that prayer begins with adoration, not with supplication, with the focus on you, not on me. Forgive me for so often getting things the wrong way round. In Jesus' Name. Amen.

Prayer's first principle

FOR READING AND MEDITATION – 2 CORINTHIANS 6:1–8

'I will be a Father to you, and you will be my sons and daughters ...' (v. 18: NIV)

We saw yesterday that our Lord not only taught his disciples to begin their prayers by focusing on God as their Father, but he set the example by doing so himself in the famous prayer recorded in John 17. 'Father,' he said, 'the time has come.' Prayer ought always begin with the acknowledgement of God as Father. When we do this, it immediately eliminates such concepts that characterise the prayers and petitions of those who do not have any real relationship with him.

Prayer is to a Father with a Father's heart, a Father's love and a Father's strength. The very first principle of prayer is that we come to such a Father. We must come to him as a child in trust, simplicity, and with frankness. A father is a person, not a machine. A father is able to hear – not aloof and insensitive. A father responds – he is interested and concerned. Six times in John 17 our Lord addresses God as Father. The late Dr Martyn Lloyd-Jones pointed out that Christ used the term 'Father' so often in his prayer because that was the way he instinctively looked upon him. God, of course, is all-powerful, all-present, and all-knowing, but the most wonderful thing about him is that he is our Father. When we think of him in this way we are drawn to talk to him.

Gracious and loving God, the thought that you are my Father and I am your child fills me with a joy I am not able to describe. Once I thought of you as God; now I think of you as Father. As I hold that thought, let it also hold me. In Jesus' Name. Amen.

The high-priestly prayer

A root problem

FOR READING AND MEDITATION – PSALM 89:14–29

'He will call out to me, "You are my Father, my God,
the Rock my Saviour." ' (v. 26: NIV)

I have tried to help many people over the years with the problems of prayer, and I have usually found that the root problem is that they do not have a clear concept of God as Father. Those who know God in this way are the ones who are most eager to come into his presence and to speak with him often. And let us resist the modern-day trend to accommodate those who substitute human reason for divine revelation and insist on addressing God as Mother. The greatest authority on God is the Son, and he commands us when we pray to address God as 'Father'. There is no-thing sexist about this.

Clearly there is femininity in God. Scripture says, 'God created man in his own image ... male and female he created them' (Gen. 1:27). But, as C.S. Lewis puts it in *That Hideous Strength*, 'God is so masculine that everything else seems feminine in comparison.' This is not to demean femininity, but simply to state what is fact. The thought behind fatherhood is that of initiation, movement, and it is in this capacity that God most often reveals himself in Scripture. It is as Father that God chooses to be addressed when we speak to him in prayer. How can we claim to know better than God?

✎ *Gracious and loving God, clear out of my heart any misconceptions I have concerning you, and help me see you as you are, not as I wish you to be. May I be true to Scripture even though it goes against modern-day trends. Amen.*

Right on time

FOR READING AND MEDITATION – ROMANS 5:1–11

'You see, at just the right time, when we were still powerless,
Christ died for the ungodly.' (v. 6: NIV)

Let's look now at the next words in our Lord's high priestly prayer: 'the time has come'. 'This is not the same,' comments Ray Stedman, as saying 'my time has come.' 'My time has come' has about it an air of resignation; 'the time has come' is more suggestive of realisation. Our Lord is referring here to a brief concentrated period. At the wedding at Cana when our Lord's mother pressed him to do something about the lack of wine, he said, 'My time has not yet come' (John 2:4). He meant that even though he would eventually do what his mother suggested, it would not have the results she had anticipated, again, when his disciples upbraided him for not going to the feast at Jerusalem, he said, 'The right time for me has not yet come' (John 7:6). Then, as he got closer to that predetermined hour for which he had come into the world, he announced, 'The hour has come for the Son of Man to be glorified' (John 12:23).

Once Jesus had embarked upon his ministry his eye seemed constantly to be turned upward. Everything he did appeared to be regulated by the tick of its pendulum. Wherever he went and whatever he did, he was always right on time. Even as he draws near to the hour of his death, his feet do not drag. As ever, he is right on time.

༄ O Father, as I reflect on what a punctual God you are, help me understand that you are governing the affairs of my life with the same amazing precision. Your purposes are never realised too soon or too late. What comfort I draw from this. Amen.

The guided life

FOR READING AND MEDITATION – JOHN 7:25–44

'... but no one laid a hand on him, because his time had not yet come.' (v. 30: NIV)

At what point in his life did our Lord become aware that he was destined to die for the sins of the world? And did it dawn upon him slowly or did it come like a lightning flash? We cannot tell. What is clear, is that early in his ministry Christ was aware that he was moving toward a powerful and pivotal hour. This passage gives us insight into this as it shows how the Jews sought to arrest him in the temple. But they were unable to effect their evil purpose because, as the evangelist explains, 'his time had not yet come'.

I heard of a man who persuaded himself that as he was a child of God, he would be protected from any harm if his time had not come. He presented his idea to Dr J. Vernon McGee and said: 'I am so convinced that God is keeping me that I think I could step right out into the midst of the busiest traffic at noontime and, if my time had not come, remain perfectly safe.' Dr McGee said, 'Well, if you stand in the middle of traffic at noontime, brother, your time *has* come.' It is important to observe that our Lord never took the matter of divine protection for granted. He got his instructions from his Father through waiting upon him in prayer. Perhaps if we spent more time in prayer and thus lived more *guided* lives, we might have fewer reasons to rue the calamities that seem to befall us.

🔖 *O Father, I long more than anything to walk, as Jesus did, in the very centre of your will, taking nothing for granted but everything with gratitude. Help me know you better, for only then can I live a guided life. In Jesus' Name I pray. Amen.*

When God laughs

FOR READING AND MEDITATION – PSALM 2:1–12

'The One enthroned in heaven laughs; the Lord scoffs at them.' (v. 4: NIV)

The hour that produced the cross is the pivotal point of history. Our Lord came to earth for that very hour, an hour that was divinely determined, and the greatest hour the world has known. The thought that God foreknows all matters and appoints certain critical hours in history to be turning-points is something that we ought to find tremendously reassuring. As we read Biblical history we see times when it looked as if events were out of control and then, suddenly, a particular occurrence turned the whole situation around. When God's time arrives, he intervenes, and the situation is seen as contributing to his purpose, not anyone else's. Sometimes we get depressed as we look at the state of the world. But we must learn that God's hand is upon the situation and a divine plan is being worked out.

The psalm before us today reminds us that at any moment God can arise and confound his enemies. Why 'laughs'? Because as he sees the little people of this earth strutting so arrogantly through their days, he knows that at a word he can destroy them all. But he won't, for divine purposes are being worked out. We must not let the problems of the day blind our eyes to the fact that everything runs according to God's schedule. How different life would be if we could learn to look at it through God's eyes rather than our own.

✎ O Father, give me the divine perspective on everything. Take the veil from my eyes so that I might see – really see. Show me that your will ultimately prevails, no matter that appearances may be to the contrary. Amen.

God is to be glorified

FOR READING AND MEDITATION – PSALM 86:1–17

'… I will glorify your Name for ever.' (v. 12: NIV)

Our Lord continues his prayer in John 17 with these words: 'Glorify your Son, that your Son may glorify you' (v. 1). He is not concerned about being glorified for his own sake, but that through his being glorified, the Father may be more greatly glorified. Christ's over-whelming desire in everything he did was to glorify his Father. He lived for that one purpose alone. We will never really understand the reason for us being on this earth until we see that the whole purpose of our salvation is to glorify the Father. What a difference it would make to our lives if we could fully grasp this.

We are all guilty of tending to think that God is here for our benefit, not we for his. We think more in terms of God glorifying us rather than us glorifying him. Once I was in a meeting where an evangelist asked, 'What do you want God to do for you?' A man stood up and said, 'I can think of a dozen things I would like God to do for me, but shouldn't we be more concerned about what we can do for him?' I felt sorry for the evangelist as he seemed to have no reply. Our Lord lived exclusively for the Father's glory – and so must we. One of the greatest signs of our maturity as Christians is whether our all-consuming desire is for God's glory rather than our own.

Father, help me understand that in glorifying you I do not impoverish myself. For I am made to glorify you, and the more I do, the more my inner being is drawn to health. Your glory is my glory. Thank you, my Father. Amen.

The greatest sin

FOR READING AND MEDITATION – DANIEL 5:17–31
'But you did not honour the God who holds in his hand
your life and all your ways.' (v. 23: NIV)

As Christ was on earth to glorify the Father, so also are we. But we are so taken up with wanting things from God that we forget what God wants from us. A few theologians asked, 'What is the chief end of man?' The answer: '… to glorify God and to enjoy him for ever.' The purpose of our salvation is not simply to deliver us from the snares of the devil, but that we might worship God. If we fail to understand this, we will often get our emphasis wrong.

Why do respectable people in our churches have a struggle to believe they are sinners? Because they are under the impression that sin consists in vices such as drunkenness, adultery, dishonesty, and so on. They haven't committed any of these evils, so they do not think of themselves as 'sinners'. But the essence of sin is *the failure to glorify God,* and anyone who does not glorify God is guilty of the worst kind of sin. Our preaching and teaching ought to focus on this – we ought to make it clear that even though a person may not get drunk, commit adultery, or live dishonestly, what makes them sinners is *living for themselves and their own glory.*

Belshazzar's greatest sin was not that he desecrated the holy cups and filled them with wine for his own enjoyment, but that he did not glorify God. Perhaps that may be our greatest sin, too.

꙳ *O God, forgive us for getting things out of perspective. We think of sin as doing wrong deeds, but it consists also of not doing the right things. My purpose on earth is to glorify you. I do so – gladly. Amen.*

What's in it for me?

FOR READING AND MEDITATION – COLOSSIANS 3:1–17

'Set your minds on things above, not on earthly things.' (v. 2: NIV)

I find it deeply moving that immediately prior to the Cross our Lord's one desire was this – that he might glorify the Father. He was saying in effect, 'Father, I have come to this earth to bring glory to your Name; strengthen me so that I will be able to do that.' How different are our attitudes when called upon to face a crisis. We are more concerned with how we will come out of it than how much God will be glorified.

Why is it that we are so far off beam in today's church? I think it is because we are being brainwashed by a world that is filled with self-interest and self-concern. Here in Britain pastors tell me that people are so used to asking such questions as 'What will the government do for me now I am unemployed?' or 'What will the social services do for me as a single parent?' that when they are invited to come to Christ, their first thought is: 'What will salvation do for me?' How far removed we are from the days when people cried out, 'What must I do to find salvation?' If we can't change the questions people ask when they come into the church, we ought to be able to change the questions they ask once they are there. Is this where the church is failing? Brainwashed Christians need washing by the water of the Word (Eph. 5:26).

✎ O God, we ask your forgiveness once more that we have allowed ourselves to be brainwashed by the world. We are more concerned for our own comfort than we are for your glory. Wash us by the water of your Word. In Jesus' Name we pray. Amen.

Saved in eternity!

FOR READING AND MEDITATION – EPHESIANS 1:1–14

'And he made known to us the mystery of his will …
which he purposed in Christ …' (v. 9: NIV)

The next sentence of the prayer of our Lord in John 17 is this: 'For you granted him authority over all people that he might give eternal life to all those you have given him' (v. 2). These words imply that at some point in the past Christ, the second Person of the Trinity, was placed in a position of authority and assigned the task of giving eternal life to as many as God foreordained. This raises a host of questions in our minds: At what point in the past was this authority vouchsafed to the Son? If Christ is equal with God, why does he need to be given authority? And where does the Holy Spirit, the third Person of the Trinity, figure in all this?

Christ, in referring to it here, does so not because he thought that the Father might have forgotten it, but that together they might rejoice in it. It is a matter not only for the Trinity to rejoice over, but also for us. Our salvation is a planned salvation. It is not an afterthought, but was conceived in the mind of the Trinity long before time began. Can you see what this means? Our salvation is safe! It is not stretching the truth to say, as Dr Martyn Lloyd-Jones so often did, 'We were saved in eternity!' As one Welsh preacher quaintly put it, 'God thought it, Christ bought it, the Spirit wrought it, and though the devil fought it – *thank God I've got it.*'

✑ *O God, how can I ever sufficiently thank you for including me in the glorious plan of salvation? I cannot understand it, but I can stand on it. All honour and glory be unto your wondrous Name. Amen.*

Jubilant praise

'He came and took the scroll from
the right hand of him who sat on the throne.' (v. 7: NIV)

It is impossible to understand the meaning of Scripture or the plan of salvation unless we look in on the meeting of 'The Eternal Council', where the three Persons of the Trinity planned the creation of the world and, in anticipation of the Fall, its new creation also. Here the Son, the second Person of the Trinity, was appointed as the One through whom the purposes of God for humanity should come to pass. Though God, Christ and the Holy Spirit are co-eternal and co-equal, there is a distinct order in the Trinity. The Father is seen as first, the Son second, and the Holy Spirit *third*.

One of the first items on the divine agenda was the entry of sin into the world and what should be done about it. It was agreed that the Son should deal with this matter. With the agreement of the other two members of the Trinity he was made responsible not only for the inanimate creation but the world of men and women also.

In today's passage John is perplexed that no one is great enough or strong enough to open the books of history. Then the Lion of the tribe of Judah steps forward and all heaven breaks out in jubilant praise. Why? Because Jesus Christ is the Lord of history. Indeed, as it is often said – history is *his*-story.

✦ *My Father and my God, what confidence it gives me to know that the final authority for all things lies in the hands of your Son. May the wonder of that cause your church also to break out in worshipful and continuous praise. Amen.*

Marked out in eternity

FOR READING AND MEDITATION – JOHN 6:25–40

'All that the Father gives me will come to me…' (v. 37: NIV)

We pause now before the profound truth that the Father handed over to the Son not only the world and all its people but a special group of people also: 'that he might give eternal life to all those you have given him' (John 17:2). Notice it does not say he was given authority over all people so that he might give eternal life to all, but *to all those you have given him*.

Time and again we find in Scripture that before the foundation of the world God the Father gave to Christ a special group of people who are destined to enjoy the blessings of salvation and live with him forever. God chose them and draws them. It is as if the Father said to the Son: 'I am giving you a special group of people and I want you to save them for me.' Does this mean a group of people were chosen at random back in eternity and appointed for salvation? Or does it mean that God, foreseeing a certain group of people would genuinely repent and accept Christ as their Saviour, marked such people as the possessors of salvation? Great theological debates have raged over these questions. One thing is sure – our salvation was forethought, foreseen and foreordained. We were 'saved in eternity'. What a thought! Let the wonder of it wrap itself around your soul.

✣ *O Father, how secure I feel when I realise it is not as the result of a chance occurrence that I am saved. I did not 'accidentally' come to you. I came because I was drawn – drawn by a Power that reached out to me from eternity. I shall be eternally grateful. Amen.*

What is a Christian?

FOR READING AND MEDITATION – JOHN 10:22–42

'I give them eternal life, and they shall never perish ...' (v. 18: NIV)

A question often asked by people in the world is this: what exactly is a Christian? *A Christian is someone who has eternal life.* This is the primary reason why God sent his Son into the world: 'that he might give eternal life to all those you have given him'. In John 17:3 our Lord explains just what eternal life is: 'This is eternal life: that they may know you, the only true God, and Jesus Christ, whom you have sent.' Eternal life, then, consists in knowing God.

There are certain basic facts associated with the gospel which, if understood, will affect not only our daily living but our ability to make the gospel known to others also. We have all been taught them, but it will do us no harm to be reminded of them before moving on. Everyone who comes into this world, is spiritually dead. They may be alive to the world, but they are dead to God. No one can produce the life of God in his or her soul by self-effort, and thus no one can make himself or herself into a Christian. Salvation is a gift, not something we merit or earn. There is only one Person who can give us this gift – Jesus Christ himself. Those who attempt to generate the life of God in their souls without coming to Christ are fools. Eternal life is knowing God, and God can only be truly known when we approach him through his Son, Jesus Christ. It's so simple, yet so sublime.

✣ *O God, awaken your church worldwide to the need of presenting these simple facts of the gospel. How can we share the faith if we don't really understand the faith we share? Help us, dear Lord. In Jesus' Name. Amen.*

No place for idols

FOR READING AND MEDITATION – 1 JOHN 5:1–21
'Dear children, keep yourselves from idols.' (v. 21: NIV)

We saw yesterday that a Christian is someone who has received the gift of eternal life. Being a Christian is not a matter of degree but a matter of pedigree. We are either children of 'wrath' (Eph. 2:3) or children of God. Now let's consider our Lord's next phrase in John 17:3: 'That they may know you, *the only true God*'. By using the words *true* and *only*, it is obvious that Christ is cautioning us against idols and false gods.

The apostle John ends his first epistle with a similar caution. Why? Because both Jesus and John knew the tendency in all our hearts toward divided loyalty. We usually associate idols with a low-level expression of religion – the idols of pagan faiths. But idolatry is the tendency to substitute something in the place of God. Anything that becomes a centre of love greater than the love we give to God, is an idol. Idolatry is – the substitution of the lesser for the greater. There is nothing worse than Christian idolatry, when we don't go as far as to reject God; we simply put something else at the centre and God is then marginalised. There he can only faintly influence our lives – and the result is weakness and immaturity. To know God in the way Jesus knew him we must serve him in the way Jesus served him – with no divided loyalty.

✑ O God, when I have you I have all I need – and more. Help me to give myself to you, as you give yourself to me – entirely. There is no divided loyalty in you. Let there be none in me. In Christ's Name I pray. Amen.

That one dear face

FOR READING AND MEDITATION – HEBREWS 1:1–14
'The Son is the radiance of God's glory and
the exact representation of his being …' (v. 3: NIV)

Every word in John 17 has significance. Listen once again to the verse we are considering: 'This is eternal life: that they may know you, the only true God, and Jesus Christ, whom you have sent' (v. 3). Here our Lord puts himself on the same plane as the only true God. People deny this. Their interpretation is that Jesus claimed that there was only one true God and that he (Jesus) was on a lesser level than the great Creator. They fail to see that the One who said the words 'the only true God' immediately went on to put himself in the same position as God: 'the only true God, and Jesus Christ, whom you have sent'. They further argue that to worship Jesus is to make him into an idol. Is Jesus an idol? The question to ask about an idol is: Is God like this in character and life? An idol misrepresents God; Jesus represents him. Is Jesus like God in status, character and life? Fully and truly like him? The answer is an unqualified 'Yes'. Jesus fulfils the chief desire behind most forms of idolatry – to have God near and understandable. We have in Jesus a God with a face. 'Is your face towards me Daddy?' asked a little boy to his father when afraid. 'Yes,' replied the father, 'it is.' The little boy then fell asleep. Jesus gives God a face and that face is towards us – always.

O God my Father, I am so grateful that in Jesus I have a God with a face. And when I look into that face I see what you are like – wholly and exactly. Keep your face ever turned towards me. In Jesus' Name I ask it. Amen.

A secret of success

FOR READING AND MEDITATION – JOHN 19:28–37

'When he had received the drink, Jesus said, "It is finished." ' (v. 30: NIV)

We look now at our Lord's words in John 17:4: 'I have brought you glory on earth by completing the work you gave me to do.' Suppose you knew that your life would come to an end in a few days and you wanted to sum up for someone what you felt were the abiding values in your life – what would you say? This is the situation in which our Lord finds himself here. At this point in his prayer he reviews his thirty-three years of ministry on earth, and gathers it all up in one tremendous statement. Let's look at the words *you* and *me*. First the word *you*. 'I have … [completed] the work you gave me to do.' There were many things the disciples (and others) wanted our Lord to do which he steadfastly resisted. He did so because his main concern was to follow his Father's agenda, not the agenda of others. Is not this the secret of spiritual success?

One of the reasons why we get spiritually run down and, anaemic is because we spend our lives responding to what others want us to do rather than finding out what God wants us to do. Early in my ministry I had a breakdown. It is only because I began to apply myself to doing what God wanted me to do that I have survived. Our Lord glorified the Father because he got his job description directly from the Father's hand. So must we.

✎ *Father, I simply must learn this lesson – to listen more to what you want me to do and less to the demands and needs of others. I realise this will not make me less of a person, but more. And maybe I will even achieve more – by doing less. Amen.*

Christ's finished work

FOR READING AND MEDITATION – JOHN 8:1–12

'As long as it is day, we must do the work of him who sent me.' (v. 4: NIV)

Today we focus on the word *me* in this verse. There is a belief abroad in some parts of the Christian church that the sole purpose of Christ coming into the world was to be our example – the divine ideal to which we all must strive. In a sense this is true, but it was not the primary purpose of his coming to earth. As one preacher put it, 'Our Lord Jesus Christ did not come into the world merely to tell us what we have to do; he came to do for us what we could never do for ourselves.' What then was the 'work' that he had come to do? It was the work of *reconciliation* – of bringing sinful but repentant men and women into relationship with a pardoning God. Only as we keep this in mind will we be able to explain the work that the Father sent him to do.

Four great facts, define the gospel: 'A Baby in a cradle, a Man upon a cross, a Body in a tomb, a King upon a throne'. Christ's work involved an incarnation, a death by crucifixion, a resurrection, and a final ascent to the eternal throne. No one but Christ could do this work, and *the beginning of Christian faith is the acceptance of these facts*. The proof that we are Christians lies in our belief that only Christ could effect the work of reconciliation with God, and we can do no other than rest upon that finished work.

✎ *O Father, help your church to see that the work your Son did here on earth is the full and final payment for our salvation. Nothing we do can add to it, and nothing can be taken away. May we rest on that finished work. In Jesus' Name. Amen.*

Homesick for heaven?

FOR READING AND MEDITATION – ISAIAH 42:1–13

'I am the Lord … I will not give my glory to another …' (v. 8: NIV)

We come now to John 17:5: 'And now, Father, glorify me in your presence with the glory I had with you before the world began.' Our Lord is looking ahead to what lies before him and seems to be saying to his Father, 'Has not the time now come when I can come back to you? I have completed the work you gave me to do and now I look forward to returning to where I was before.' No other human being could ever have spoken those words. Our Lord was the only One who could look back to a time of being with the Father before the world was made. Isaiah reminds that God does not share his glory with anyone less than himself. But here is One who shared the Father's glory before the world was made, and who recognises that it was properly his.

I often wonder to myself how much of the former glory Christ was able to remember when he was here on earth. Could he recall all the great scenes of eternity, or only some of them? We do not know. One thing we do know, however, is that our Lord voluntarily surrendered for the period of thirty-three years the right to be worshipped, the right to the glory that belonged to God. Do we sense here in the Saviour a homesickness for heaven? Perhaps. I'm glad, though, that his desire to return to heaven was not as great as his determination to complete the work his Father had given him to do.

❧ *Lord Jesus Christ, heaven would have welcomed you at any time, but you stayed here on earth and agonised on a cross so that I might one day join you in glory. Blessed be your wondrous Name for ever. Amen.*

No attitude problem

FOR READING AND MEDITATION – PHILIPPIANS 2:1–11
'Your attitude should be the same as that of Christ Jesus ...' (v. 5: NIV)

We continue with the thought we reflected on yesterday, namely that when our Lord was close to the end of his work here on earth, he looked forward to returning to the glory that he had with the Father before the world began. We must not forget that our Lord's life here on earth was characterised by a continual self-emptying – a laying aside of glory. Ray C. Stedman says, 'It was not merely what Jesus *did* which glorified the Father. It was his willingness to be always available, to be for ever giving of himself, that glorified God.'

The words of the apostle Paul bring this point into focus. He was great by what he did, but he was great also by the attitude with which he did it. Throughout his life he had a heart that was ready to obey, an ear that was ready to hear, and a will that was ready to be subject to the Father. When John baptised him in the River Jordan, a dove descended from heaven, and the voice of God declared from the skies: 'This is my Son, whom I love; with him I am well pleased' (Matt. 3:17). Christ had not done anything yet, but for thirty years he had delighted the Father's heart. Jesus did not set out to draw attention to himself in John 17:5 he put his finger on the essence of that which glorifies God – self-giving love. Does the same attitude lie behind all that we do for God?

✒ *O Father, help me get hold of this truth, too, that it's my attitude that determines my spiritual altitude. I go up only in proportion to my willingness to go down. May I be as self-giving as Jesus. In his Name I ask it. Amen.*

God – a Christlike God

FOR READING AND MEDITATION – JOHN 1:1–18

'No-one has ever seen God, but God the One and Only,
who is at the Father's side, has made him known.' (v. 18: NIV)

Let's look at the second section of our Lord's prayer in John 17: 6 –19. Our Lord's high-priestly prayer can be divided up into three main sections. In the first section (vv. 1–5) our Lord prays for himself. In the second section (vv. 6–19) he prays for his immediate followers. And in the third section (vv. 20–26) he prays for all who would come to believe in him. Let's focus on verse 6: 'I have revealed you to those whom you gave me out of the world. They were yours; you gave them to me and they have obeyed your word.' Consider first the opening four words: 'I have revealed you …' Who could have made such a statement apart from Jesus? To reveal God one must be God. Why was it necessary for Jesus to reveal God to us? If Jesus had not revealed God to us we would never have known what God was really like. Our misconceptions would have kept us away from him. All the other ways in which God has revealed himself are somewhat limited. They reveal God, but not perfectly. However, I look up to God through Jesus and I know what God is like – perfectly. He is a Christlike God – good and trustworthy. E. Stanley Jones put it rather daringly: 'If God wasn't like Jesus, I would not be interested in him. For the highest I know in the realm of character is to be Christlike.'

✎ *O God my Father, I need not wonder if you are like Jesus, or Jesus is like you, for you are one in nature and one in purpose. My soul rejoices in this union, for through your mercy and forgiveness I am part of it, too. Amen.*

Out of the world

FOR READING AND MEDITATION – JOHN 15:18–27

'... you do not belong to the world,
but I have chosen you out of the world ...' (v. 19: NIV)

Yesterday we looked at the fact that Christ was the perfect revelation of God, John 17:6 continues: 'I have revealed you *to those whom you gave me out of the world*'. Clearly our Lord is thinking here of his immediate disciples and the point he focuses on is that they had been given him *out of the world*. The first thing it says is that a disciple of Christ is someone who does not belong to this world. If we are of the world we are not of Christ, and if we are of Christ we are not of the world.

We have tended to divide society into three classes – lower class, middle class and upper class. It is fair to say that nowadays these classes are being broken down. God, however, does divide humanity perpendicularly. On one side are those who are of the world, and on the other those who are of Christ. When we die it will not make the slightest difference what political party we belong to, or whether we are rich, poor, educated or uneducated. I know we open ourselves to criticism from non-Christians when we say we are not of the world. They condemn us. But this is what salvation is all about – being *in* the world but not *of* it. We must be careful, however, that this does not become a matter of pride. We should not look upon ourselves as better than others, even though we may be better off.

✒ *Father, help me examine myself in your presence right now to see how much of the world's attitudes are still in me. You have taken me out of the world, now take the world out of me. In Jesus' Name I ask it. Amen.*

A Great High Priest

FOR READING AND MEDITATION – HEBREWS 4:1–16
'For we do not have a high priest who is unable
to sympathise with our weakness …'

We continue examining John 17:6: 'They were yours; you gave them to me and they have obeyed your word.' Yesterday we said that a Christian is someone who is not of this world. The second characteristic of a Christian is that he or she is someone who receives God's Word and keeps it. Our Lord is drawing a contrast here between those who had accepted God's Word and those who had rejected it. There were those in his day who argued with everything he said – the Pharisees. About his own disciples our Lord says, 'They have obeyed your word.' What a statement. Is Christ being over-generous with his praise? Hadn't the disciples been a bit obtuse over some of the things he had said? Did they not say on one occasion: 'This is a hard teaching. Who can accept it?' (John 6:60). Yes, they had, but there was a strong sense of commitment among them. Peter summed up their position when he made the great statement: 'Lord, to whom shall we go? You have the words of eternal life' (John 6:68).

The disciples could not always understand the Master, but they stayed with him through thick and thin. To *obey the Word* does not mean we will never have times of doubt and struggle, but that we hold on to it nevertheless.

✎ Lord Jesus Christ, what insight this gives me into your heart. You could have criticised your disciples over many things, but instead you overlooked their flaws and deficiencies and prayed for them. Teach me to do the same with fellow-believers. For your own dear Name's sake. Amen.

A day for decision

FOR READING AND MEDITATION – MATTHEW 16:13–20
' "Who do you say I am?" Simon Peter answered, "You are the Christ,
the Son of the living God." ' (vv. 15–16: NIV)

Our Lord continues his prayer, 'Now they know that everything you have given me comes from you. For I gave them the words you gave me and they accepted them. They knew with certainty that I came from you, and they believed that you sent me' (vv. 7–8). Christ, in praying for his disciples, is reminding the Father that they knew that the word which he had brought them had come from God, and they were certain about who he was. This suggests to us an important aspect of being a follower of Christ – *we must be clear as to who Jesus is.* We fool ourselves when we look at people who live good moral lives and describe them as Christians. However, the first mark of being one of Christ's disciples is to be convinced that Christ is the Son of God and to know why he came.

True Christians believe that the Word was made flesh and dwelt among us. They do not say, 'The important thing is to live a good and godly life in this world.' Am I talking to some right now who believe themselves to be Christians simply because they go to church? More is required. Are you certain that the Lord Jesus Christ is the Son of God, born of the virgin Mary, and that he suffered and died for your sins on Calvary?

O God, I come to you now through your Son. Thank you for sending him into this world to live and die for me. Forgive every one of my sins and make me one of your disciples. I ask this in Christ's Name. Amen.

A long prayer session

FOR READING AND MEDITATION – HEBREWS 7:18–28

'…he always lives to intercede for them.' (v.25: NIV)

As Jesus prepared to leave his disciples and move on to the Cross, no doubt they felt baffled and bewildered by what was taking place. Thus, as they overheard his words, 'I pray for them' (John 17:9), how it must have brought consolation to their hearts. And as he continued, 'I am not praying for the world, but for those you have given me, for they are yours,' they would have gained even more comfort. He was praying as their Mediator, their Advocate, their Great High Priest. Today's passage tells us something even greater – *now in heaven he is interceding for you and me. The Amplified Bible* makes it even more clearer: 'He is always living to make petition to God and intercede with him and intervene for them.' Just think of it – at this very moment our Lord is interceding for you and me. If we could let this thought occupy us more than it does, it would make a tremendous difference to the way we face our days.

One of the delights of my life is the knowledge that many people are praying for me. Yet, what fills my heart with even greater delight is the knowledge that Christ is praying for me. But not just for me – he is interceding also for you. And he has been engaged in this task of praying for his people since he arrived on the throne over 2 000 years ago. This makes it the longest prayer session in history!

✎ *O Father, how humbled I am by the knowledge that Jesus intercedes for me before your eternal throne. I know that his is a voice you would never fail to heed. What joy fills my soul! Amen.*

I'm praying for you!

FOR READING AND MEDITATION – LUKE 22:24–38
'Simon, Simon, Satan has asked to sift you as wheat.' (v. 31: NIV)

We ended yesterday with the thought that Christ prayed for the disciples during their hour of bewilderment, and is interceding for us before the royal throne. We said also that it would make a tremendous difference to our ability to face and handle life's problems. Murray McChene tells in one of his books how he attempted to counsel a timid young Christian. 'I'm so afraid of people,' said the young man, 'so shy and nervous. People terrify me. How can I overcome this problem?' McChene asked him, 'What if you could hear the Lord Jesus Christ praying for you in the next room – and praying for you by name? What do you think it would do for you?' 'I don't think I would ever be the same again,' replied the young man. 'Well, he is praying for you,' said McChene, 'not in the next room, but on the royal throne.' That idea so overwhelmed the young man and made such an impact on him that was transformed.

Did you notice that Jesus mentions Simon's name twice? I can't imagine Christ praying for him without mentioning his name, can you? Are you feeling battered and beaten by the adverse circumstances of your life at this moment? Do you wonder where your next ounce of strength is coming from? Then listen … listen … your Saviour is interceding for you on the throne. He is praying, not for the world, but for you. And by name!

✎ *Lord Jesus Christ, Priest, take the truth that I have been focusing on today and burn it deeply into my spirit until it makes me a transformed person, too. For your own dear Name's sake. Amen.*

A little means a lot

FOR READING AND MEDITATION – JOHN 15:1–16

'You did not choose me, but I chose you
and appointed you to go and bear fruit …' (v. 16: NIV)

The next statement we come to in our Lord's high-priestly prayer is 'All I have is yours, and all you have is mine. And glory has come to me through them' (John 17:10). Jesus first rejoices in the fact that he and the Father belong to one another and that they share the same essence and attributes. Then he continues: 'And glory has come to me through *them*.' How had glory come to him through his disciples? Was there not constant rivalry and jealousy among them? Hadn't they constantly misunderstood his sayings and failed to comprehend his purposes? Yet, here our Lord is saying quite categorically: '… glory has come to me through them.'

The only way I can unravel this paradox is by considering the great high-priestly ministry of Christ. Christ is loving, sympathetic and understanding. His gaze penetrates beyond our flaws and frailties to the innermost of our being. An observer watching the disciples over a period of time might have concluded that they were quarrelsome, jealous, dull and blundering. But Jesus saw that deep in their hearts they were definitely committed to him, and had already brought him glory by their obedient trust. Compared to what it might have been, their commitment was perhaps little. But to Jesus the little meant a lot.

✎ *Lord Jesus Christ, how grateful I am that your gaze penetrates beyond all my flaws and deficiencies and sees what is in my heart. May the love and commitment that is in my heart bring glory to you also. Amen.*

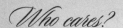

Who cares?

FOR READING AND MEDITATION – MATTHEW 6:25–34

'If … God clothes the grass of the field …
will he not much more clothe you …?' (v. 30: NIV)

As we continue, we come to his first direct petition on behalf of his disciples: 'I will remain in the world no longer, but they are still in the world, and I am coming to you. Holy Father, protect them by the power of your Name – the Name you gave me – so that they may be one as we are one' (John 17:11). It is surely impossible to read these words without feeling something of the gripping reality and practicality of the Saviour's request. He was about to leave the disciples to go to the Cross, but he pauses to pray that they will be protected and kept. How reassuring they must have found those words.

The focus of Christ's petition is found in the two words *protect them*. There were many other things Christ could have prayed for at this moment in the life of his disciples. He could have prayed 'use them', 'teach them', or 'guide them'. But as he is about to leave them to go to the Cross he puts into one brief phrase his heart's greatest desire – that they might be divinely protected. How this highlights the love and concern our Lord has for his people! Oh, if only we could get hold of the fact that our Lord's concern for us is greater than the concern we have for ourselves.

✂ *O Jesus, let the truth of your concern for me be more than mere theory. Let it grip me, impact me – even stagger me. You care for me far more than I care for myself. May that thought release something deep inside me this day. Amen.*

The knowledge of God

FOR READING AND MEDITATION – HEBREWS 2:10–18
'I will declare your name to my brothers …'

We saw yesterday that our Lord's first petition for his disciples was that they might be protected and kept 'by the power of your Name'. What is the 'Name' our Lord is referring to here? Is it his earthly Name – Jesus? No, that is not what the Saviour has in mind here. John 17:11 in *the Amplified Bible* gives us a clue to what he means: 'Holy Father, keep in your Name [in the knowledge of yourself] them whom you have given me …' Note the phrase *in the knowledge of yourself*. Names in the Bible are definitions. A name in Scripture does more than identify someone; it tells us what kind of person they are – their character, their essential nature. It truly reveals the person. In the Old Testament God revealed his nature to us through many different Names. For example, Abraham knew him as El-Elyon – God Most High, El-Shaddai – God Almighty, the Everlasting God, and Jehovah-Jireh – the Lord provides. In fact, when God entered into a new relationship with his people or disclosed another aspect of his character, he revealed a new Name.

The more we know his Name the more we know of him. But God's revelation through his Names was limited, that is, until Jesus came. Christ revealed through his life and works the nature of God in a way that no name could possibly do. It is that knowledge of God which only his Son could truly unfold that Jesus refers to here.

Father, I see that unless Jesus had come, I could never have known you as you really are. The more I consider this, the more gratitude rises within me. For gratitude is the only adequate response. Thank you, my Father. Amen.

One Name, one way

FOR READING AND MEDITATION – JOHN 10:22–42

'Jacob said, "Please tell me your name." ' (v. 29: NIV)

We continue meditating on the petition we looked at yesterday: 'Holy Father, protect them by the power of your Name ...' The greatest need of people in every age is to know the Name of God. For when we know his Name, we know him and come to an intimate understanding of him. In today's passage we hear Jacob saying to the man, 'Tell me your name.' Jacob knew that once he was aware of the man's name he would have a clearer understanding of the nature of his opponent. The Father sent the Son into the world to declare his Name, to unfold his character, to reveal his essential nature. The revelation brought by the Son has done more to explain the mystery of who God is than anyone or anything else. In Christ we have an understanding of God, and a knowledge of God which can come no other way. In praying that the disciples might be protected by the power of God's Name, Jesus is asking that they might be kept in that knowledge and in that understanding; that they might be protected by the special awareness they had of God as revealed through his own Person.

Let it be absolutely clear – there is no true knowledge of God except through his Son, Jesus Christ. Those who try to come to God some other way are described in John 10:1 as 'thieves and robbers'. To bypass Christ to get to God is to rob Christ of his glory.

O God, how grateful I am that in Jesus you offer me your all. In him dwells the fullness of the Godhead bodily. And in him, I find what I need most – redemption. All honour to his precious Name. Amen.

Jesus is God

FOR READING AND MEDITATION – JOHN 10:22–42
'I and the Father are one.'

We have one final section of John 17:11 to examine before we move on: '... protect them by the power of your Name – the Name you gave me – so that they may be one as we are one.' Christ is praying here that the same unity that exists between himself and his Father might be known also among his disciples. What a staggering thought it is that the Carpenter of Nazareth is one with the Father – God in human form. I was struck by this thought on the very first day of my conversion and I have not been able to get over it since. Some years ago, when talking to a Jehovah's Witness about the nature of Jesus Christ, I turned him to this verse: '... that they may be one as we are one'. He countered: 'But Jesus did not mean one in essence; he meant one in purpose.' I then drew his attention to the passage in John 10 and asked him if he believed the same about John 10:30. 'Yes,' he replied, 'there again Jesus was claiming to be one with God in purpose.' 'It's a strange thing,' I said, 'that the men who actually heard those words understood Jesus to be claiming equality with God and picked up stones to stone him. Yet you, standing here close on 2 000 years later, have a different interpretation. I think I would rather believe the first-century witnesses than the twentieth-century ones.' Be staggered by it if you will, but never let go of it. Jesus Christ is God.

My Father, help me understand that a Saviour who is less than God is like a bridge broken at one end. I rejoice that because Jesus is both God and Man, he is a safe access from here to eternity. Thank you, my Father. Amen.

The big picture

FOR READING AND MEDITATION – EPHESIANS 3:1–21

'… may have power … to grasp how wide and long
and high and deep is the love of Christ …' (v. 18: NIV)

We pause today to remind ourselves of why so long ago our Lord died upon a grisly cross. Let me turn you to what I call the 'big picture'. Aeons ago, the great God of the universe settled on having a people for himself who would be his joy through all eternity. Once he had marked out those who were to be his, he gave them to Christ. A covenant was then drawn up between the Father and the Son to the effect that the Father would give the Son all those whom he had chosen for himself before the foundation of the world so that the Son might make them a people fit for God's special possession and enjoyment. Jesus' entrance into the world by way of the virgin birth was the first step in the carrying out of that plan. He came because God had handed to him the people whom he had foreordained in eternity, and said, in effect, 'They are not fit for heaven as they are; they would not enjoy me nor I them, so I give them to you, to save and to sanctify. Make them a people in whom I can have the greatest pleasure.'

The Lord Jesus Christ came from heaven to do just that. This is the whole purpose of his incarnation, his temptation, his agony in the garden, his death upon the cross, his resurrection, indeed everything he did. See the big picture.

O God, help your church today to see the big picture. May we comprehend in a deeper way than ever before the length and breadth and depth and height of our great salvation. In Jesus' Name I ask it. Amen.

Forsaken by all

FOR READING AND MEDITATION – MATTHEW 26:47–56

'Then all the disciples deserted him and fled.' (v. 56: NIV)

On this day it seems appropriate that we think about how the disciples must have felt when they knew their Master had died. Did they chide themselves for deserting him in the hour of his greatest need? Were they fearful that they, too, might be sought out and brought before the authorities? Did their thoughts go back to the moment when they heard Christ pray for them in the words now recorded for us in John 17? We have no way of knowing exactly what occupied their thoughts in those dark days, but it is clear from what we read that they were caught up in a deep spiritual crisis.

'Glory has come to me through them,' Jesus had said, '… they have obeyed your word.' Would Jesus have revised his prayer if he had prayed it following their act of desertion? No, Christ knew his disciples would forsake him, but he knew also that despite their fears, their hesitancies, their denials and their doubts, in their hearts they would be undergirded by the conviction that what he said would come to pass. I am sure of that because I am aware that the same thing happens to me whenever I am in a crisis. Deep down there is a conviction that despite all appearances to the contrary, God is in control.

O God, how thankful I am that something has been deposited in me by you that will eventually rise to the surface even in the most critical of situations. Doubts are temporary, but faith is permanent. All honour and glory be to your Name. Amen.

New life for everyone!

FOR READING AND MEDITATION – MATTHEW 28:1–5

'He is not here; he has risen, just as he said.' (v. 6: NIV)

We think this day of those glorious words: 'He is risen!' What Christian does not thrill to that most marvellous of statements? The story is told of Dr W.E. Sangster, the famous Methodist, that he found himself one Easter Sunday morning without the ability to use his voice. He wrote a note to his family that said, 'It is terrible to wake up on Easter morning and have no voice with which to shout, "He is risen!" But it would be more terrible to have a voice, and not want to shout.'

We said the other day that the incarnation, temptation, agony, crucifixion and resurrection were all part of God's plan to make us fit for heaven and fit to enjoy heaven. But we must also remember that it would all have been nothing unless our Lord had broken through the grave and came back from death. The empty tomb is the proof that God's plan had worked. A Sunday-school class was asked to bring to church on Easter Sunday something that would speak of new life. One brought a tiny flower, another a stone with moss on it, another an egg. Stephen, a boy who was slightly retarded, brought an empty tin. 'Have you forgotten something to put in this tin?' asked the teacher. 'No,' said the little boy, 'my tin is the tomb in which Jesus lay and *because it's empty, it means new life for everyone.*' It does!

✎ *O God, I feel like echoing the words of the angel and shouting them from the rooftops: 'He is not here; he has risen!' Let your church worldwide proclaim the truth. In Christ's Name I pray. Amen.*

We are kept

FOR READING AND MEDITATION – 1 PETER 2:13–25

'… but now you have returned to the Shepherd
and Overseer of your souls.' (v. 25: NIV)

We return now, after the Easter period, to the words of our Lord in
John 17:12: 'While I was with them, I protected them and kept them
safe by that Name you gave me.' These words reveals the Saviour's
intense concern and care for his disciples. The thought in the mind
of our Lord as he utters these words is this: 'Father, while I was with
my disciples, I kept them in the knowledge and worship of you.
Now that I am going away, I am handing that task over to you.'

How did the Master keep and protect his disciples while he
was with them? One way was by his personal petitions on their
behalf. On one occasion (as we saw) he said to Simon Peter: 'Satan
has asked to sift you … but I have prayed for you' (Luke 22:31–32).
Another way was by his frequent warnings and caution, for example when people were bringing little children to him to have him
touch them, but the disciples rebuked them. 'When Jesus saw this,
he was indignant. He said to them, "Let the little children come to
me, and do not hinder them …"' (Mark 10:13–14). He kept them
also by teaching them about the world and its subtlety, about sin
and its enticements, about the devil and his blandishments. In the
same way he keeps us.

❧ Lord Jesus Christ, I shudder to think where I might be today were it not
for the fact of your wondrous keeping power. You pray for me, guide me, confront me, uphold me and comfort me. Whatever I am, it is all because of you.
Thank you, my Saviour. Amen.

A son of hell

FOR READING AND MEDITATION – JOHN 6:68–71

'... Jesus replied, "Have I not chosen you, the Twelve?
Yet one of you is a devil!"' (v. 70: NIV)

We come now to the most perplexing statements in our Lord's prayer in John 17: 'None has been lost except the one doomed to destruction [son of hell, TLB] so that Scripture would be fulfilled' (v. 12). Clearly he is referring to Judas. In context the thrust of his remark is this: 'I have kept and guarded all those given to me by the Father, but Judas was not one of them.'

Why does Jesus refer to Judas in this way in his prayer? There are at least three reasons. First, that the disciples should know beforehand what Judas was going to do so that they would not be too bewildered by his betrayal. Second, that they should gain a glimpse of the Saviour's foreknowledge and be even more convinced of his deity. Our Lord knew exactly what Judas was going to do. He drew attention to it in John 6:64, in John 13:11, and again here in his prayer in John 17. Third, that the disciples might understand more clearly the power and authority of Scripture. The treachery of Judas was prophesied in Psalms 41 and 109, and our Lord is saying in effect, 'The prophets saw this coming centuries ago, and Judas, "the son of hell", is going to fulfil their predictions to the letter.' We will never fully understand why Jesus allowed Judas to be one of the disciples, but we know enough to trust him.

🖊 O Father, help me to deepen my trust in you and your Son so that when faced with unanswerable questions, I will not struggle to resolve them, but simply rest in thee. In Jesus' Name I pray. Amen.

Judas the thief

FOR READING AND MEDITATION – JOHN 12:1–11

'He did not say this because he cared about
the poor but because he was a thief ...' (v. 6: NIV)

We spend another day on the subject of Judas Iscariot, the man whom Jesus described as 'a son of hell'. One of the most debated issues in the Christian church is the matter of eternal security, or as some put it: once saved, always saved. Personally I have never been able to make up my mind on this issue. Some Scriptures, like the ones in Christ's prayer in John 17, seem to suggest this is so, while other scriptures suggest otherwise. I am convinced, however, that Judas Iscariot was not a true disciple of Christ. John 6:70 reveals that Judas was a child of the devil and a tool of Satan. The original Greek suggests that Judas was dominated by the devil, blinded by him, inwardly controlled and motivated by him, so that he could not see the truth. He walked with the Lord day by day, sat and listened to him teach, heard the most amazing truth from his lips, but he never comprehended or took it in.

He was also a man of base character – a thief. His dishonest act was not done on the spur of the moment; it was premeditated and contrived. Finally, it was predicted of Judas that he would be lost. The Old-Testament Scriptures point clearly to this fact. In his prayer our Lord is careful to point out that he is not praying for Judas – but for those whom the Father had given him, those who belonged to God.

Father, help me be clear on this one point – my trust is to be in you and not in myself. I am kept by your power, not my own. Thank you, Father. Amen.

'Ask and you will receive, and your joy will be complete.' (v. 24: NIV)

The next issue we focus on as we move through our Lord's high-priestly prayer, is this: 'I am coming to you now, but I say these things while I am still in the world, so that they may have the full measure of my joy within them' (John 17:13). I direct your attention to just two words – 'my joy'. The Saviour wants his disciples to be partakers of his own deep joy. Jesus often referred to the subject of joy. The word leaps out from almost every page of the Gospels, particularly the Gospel of John. It fairly bulges in the epistles too. Joy is not a truth that occasionally appears here and there in the New Testament – it is a theme of the New Testament.

Some think that joy is a matter of temperament – or even the condition of the liver. I heard a man once comment about another who was full of life and laughter, 'What a fine liver he must have!' But the joy our Lord longs for his disciples to possess has nothing to do with temperament, or one's liver; it is a joy that comes directly from him. 'My joy.' This joy does not depend on physical or psychological conditions. It is not self-generated – we cannot reach down into the depths of our being and pump it up. Christ possesses it in all its fullness, and when we live in him, he gives it to us. It is as simple as that. Permit me to ask the question: Do you have this kind of joy?

O Father, however much of it I have I still ask for more. Fill me with your joy and fill me to overflowing. For the world is sad and I do not want to add to its gloom. In Jesus' Name I ask it. Amen.

A little bit of heaven!

FOR READING AND MEDITATION – HABAKKUK 3:1–19

'... yet I will rejoice in the Lord, I will be joyful in God my Saviour.' (v. 18: NIV)

The issue of joy in the Christian life is very important. I detect in the writings of a few well-known Christian authors a tendency to turn the attention of their readers away from the present to the future. There is, of course, value in this. We cannot have heaven in all its fullness now, but unless we are careful and get the balance right, we will lose out on the fact that we can get a little bit of heaven here on earth. To put it bluntly, we are fools if we think that we cannot get something of the joys of heaven in the here and now. There is more available here – more joy, peace and happiness – than many would have us believe.

A question often asked, is this: Why are Christians so solemn and serious? Many unconverted people think that if they become Christians it will make them miserable. They think that life in Christ is less and less, rather than more and more, and that they will be asked to give up the things that make glad the heart of man. A person has to be serious to become a Christian, but once we are Christians we are inheritors of a deep and abiding joy. Jesus was a serious yet joyful Man. Perhaps the reason why there is so little joy in the lives of some Christians is because they do not take him seriously.

Father, I see that joy, your joy, is my birthright. However much awaits me in heaven, I know I can have some of it now. Fill me with joy and help me spread it wherever I go. In Jesus' Name. Amen.

Hated by the world

FOR READING AND MEDITATION – ROMANS 12:1–8

'Do not conform any longer to the pattern of this world ...' (v. 2: NIV)

The next verse of John 17 that engages our attention, is this: 'I have given them your word and the world has hated them, for they are not of the world any more than I am of the world' (v. 14). We saw earlier that one of the first marks of a Christian is that he or she does not belong to this world. Our Lord refers to this fact several times in his prayer because it is very important. We can't get very far in the Christian life unless we remember that we and the world are going in different directions. We must recognise the fact that once we come over on to the side of Christ, the world hates us.

Listen again to our Lord's prayer: 'I have given them your word and the world has hated them.' We should not be surprised about this, for, as Jesus told the disciples in John 15:18–19: 'If the world hates you, keep in mind that it hated me first. If you belonged to the world, it would love you as its own.' Does the world hate us as it hated our Lord? I doubt it – at least not here in the West. Ought we then to go out of our way to court opposition, or to antagonise people so that they might persecute us? No, for love of persecution is unhealthy – it is masochism. The world did not hate Jesus because he was deliberately antagonistic. It hated him because of his sheer purity and holiness. It will be the same with us.

Father, can it be that we your people reflect so little of your purity and holiness that the world does not notice us? If so, forgive us. Make us more like you – come what may. In Jesus' Name we ask it. Amen.

Why Christians are hated

FOR READING AND MEDITATION – 1 JOHN 3:11–24

'Do not be surprised, my brothers, if the world hates you.' (v. 13: NIV)

We continue with the point that the closer our relationship to Christ, the more likely the world will hate us. The world never hates the imitation of Christianity, but it hates the real thing. I used to wonder why people of the world never hated those who were merely moral, but they would hate a true Christian. Then I read this by Dr Martyn Lloyd-Jones: 'The world in a sense likes the moral man. It never hates him because it realises that he is acting in his own strength, and in that way he is paying a compliment to fallen human nature. The world hates the true Christian because Christ himself and the true Christian condemn the natural man in a way that nobody else does.'

In a strange way non-Christians detect in Christians that they are not depending on their own strength and ability but on the strength and ability of Another – and that runs counter to their pride. The problem with the human heart is pride. A poor sinner who is 'down and out' never hates Christ as much as the one who is 'up and out'. The self-centred moral person hates Christ because they sense that he is going to condemn their self-effort. Scripture teaches us that 'all have turned away, they have together become worthless; there is no one who does good, not even one' (Rom 3:12). Those who are unwilling to give up their pride, cannot stand such condemnation. So they hate the true Christian as they hated Christ.

O God, help me be more like Jesus and less like the world. In his Name I ask it. Amen.

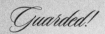

Guarded!

FOR READING AND MEDITATION – 2 TIMOTHY 1:1–18

'... I ... am convinced that he is able to guard
what I have entrusted to him ...' (v. 12: NIV)

The next statement we come to in our Lord's petition for his disciples, is this: 'My prayer is not that you take them out of the world but that you protect them from the evil one' (John 17:15). Some have thought it strange that Christ should present this petition in such a negative way and have even suggested that the Father might have been considering taking the disciples to heaven straightaway along with Christ, following his resurrection.

When I was a young Christian, I myself wondered why God didn't take his people to heaven immediately after their conversion. Pondering it, I came to understand why: if Christians were taken from the world to heaven immediately they were converted, who would preach the gospel? And who would act as salt and light in the world? We must be careful that we do not read too much into the negative aspect of this part of our Lord's petition. He is saying in effect: 'It would be helpful for them if they were taken out of the world, but that is not the best for them or you, Father. So, as they have to remain in the world in order to fulfil your purposes, keep them and protect them by your power.' Christ knew better than anyone the evil that was in the world, and he knew also the weaknesses of his disciples.

✠ *O God, may I never forget that my arrival in heaven will not be a testimony to my self-sufficiency, but to divine sufficiency. I provide the willingness; you provide the power. My gratitude knows no bounds. Amen.*

Influence or intelligence?

FOR READING AND MEDITATION – I PETER 5:1–14

'Your enemy the devil prowls around like
a roaring lion looking for someone to devour.' (v. 8: NIV)

Now we look at the last phrase of John 17:15: '… protect them
from the evil one.' Our Lord saw very clearly into the nature of life
as it is, the nature of reality. He knew that his disciples faced not
only an evil influence but an evil intelligence. That evil intelligence
we know as the devil. We do not see the devil, for he keeps himself
behind the scenes and thus has helped to create the myth that he
doesn't exist. I sometimes meet Christians who say they don't
believe in a personal devil. My response is usually, 'You may not
believe in the devil, but I assure you – the devil believes in you.'

Christ makes clear in his prayer that it is not only the world
that is against those who follow him; it is also 'the god of this
world', the devil himself. Satan has a great variety of strategies
which he uses to attack Christ's disciples, but his chief weapon is
doubt. It was doubt concerning God's goodness that led to the first
sin. Doubt is not an evil in itself, but when allowed to linger and
not firmly ejected, it can soon lead to a loss of confidence in God.
Oswald Chambers said, 'The root of sin is the belief that God is not
good.' Though you may occasionally doubt the goodness of God,
bring those doubts to the cross. There doubt is inevitably extin-
guished.

✎ O God, I am so grateful for the cross. It proves your love in a way that lies
beyond all doubt. Help me understand that I do not have to fight doubt; I
simply have to bring it to Calvary. There it dies of its own accord. Amen.

A change of citizenship

FOR READING AND MEDITATION – PHILIPPIANS 3:1–21
'But our citizenship is in heaven.' (v. 20: NIV)

Our Lord makes much of the fact that his people are 'not of the world' in his prayer in John 17. He repeats it in verse 16: 'They are not of the world, even as I am not of it.' Once I stepped into a church one Sunday and heard a minister preach from this text. Obviously he was a liberal, because he proceeded to say, 'Here Christ was stretching the truth at love's demand. The real truth was that the disciples were quite deeply steeped in the world and all its ways.' Was he right? I don't believe so. The disciples may well have displayed worldly attitudes from time to time, but because of their relationship with Christ, they had received a change of citizenship. Just as Christ belonged to the eternal kingdom, so did they. Because of their allegiance to him, they had been given new passports, so to speak, that brought them under a new authority, into a new culture and a new kingdom. Of course they still displayed some of the characteristics of the old 'culture' – newly-converted Christians can get discouraged when they occasionally find themselves resorting to worldly ways and attitudes. They think because they do not always act in a wholly Christian manner they cannot be true Christians. If you come across someone like that, help them understand that though they may have lost their way, they have not lost their address.

❧ *Gracious Father, thank you for reminding me that I am a citizen of heaven – a new country and a new culture. Help me break free of any 'pull' the old country may have on me. In Jesus' Name I pray. Amen.*

Changed from the inside

FOR READING AND MEDITATION – THESSALONIANS 4:1–18

'It is God's will that you should be sanctified …' (v. 3: NIV)

In his first petition for his disciples Christ prayed that they might be kept and guarded from the world (John 17:11). His second petition was that they might have the full measure of his own joy (v .13). His third petition is this: 'Sanctify them by the truth; your word is truth' (v. 17). In the first petition our Lord's desire is that his disciples might be kept. Then, that they might be filled with his own joy. Next, he shows us how they are to be kept and filled with perpetual joy – by being sanctified.

What does our Lord mean by *sanctified*? The word *sanctify* has various meanings in Scripture, but basically two main meanings: first, to be set apart for God's use, and second, to be made fit for God's use. There is always a double aspect to this primary meaning of the word – it involves both dedication and purification. 'The Christian life,' said one preacher, 'is all about sanctification; it is becoming more and more like Jesus every day.' In John 17:17 we begin to see more clearly why our Lord prayed that his disciples should not be taken out of the world. He had in mind something better – that the world should be taken out of them. We can't stop the world being outside us, but we can stop it being inside us. God doesn't necessarily want changed circumstances for us – he longs for us to be changed from the inside out.

Father, help me understand that sanctification is basically a relationship. The more I get to know you, the more I become like you. Dwell still more deeply in me, Father. In Jesus' Name. Amen.

The power of God's truth

FOR READING AND MEDITATION – PSALM 119:1–16

'How can a young man keep his way pure?
By living according to your word.' (v. 9: NIV)

Sanctification, we said yesterday, is being set apart from the world and for God. But how does it take place? God uses two main resources to sanctify us: the Holy Spirit and the Word – what Jesus describes in John 17:17 as 'the truth'. The Spirit is not mentioned, simply because he had not 'yet been given' (John 7:39). Sanctification is primarily and essentially God's work in us. The very way the Lord words his prayer implies this: 'Sanctify them by the truth; your word is truth.' In sanctification God takes his Word and by the power of the Holy Spirit brings it back to us, opens our understanding of it, enables us to comprehend and apprehend it. The great debate among Christians regarding sanctification is whether it is instant or continuous. Initially I used to think that sanctification was something instant because I had an experience of the Holy Spirit that was tremendous and powerful. But I have come to see that I still needed to know the continuous flow of the Spirit and the Word to develop and grow. Whatever great experiences God may give us through the power of the Holy Spirit, we must never use them as a substitute for taking the truths he shows us in his Word and applying them to our lives. Reading the Word and applying the Word – that is how God works to bring us sanctification.

O Father, help me become a more avid reader of your Word, for I see that it is there that I find the power to change. May I be a wholly sanctified Christian. In Jesus' Name I ask it. Amen.

What are we to believe?

FOR READING AND MEDITATION – 1 PETER 3:8–22
'But in your hearts set apart Christ as Lord.'

We spend one more day on this important subject of sanctification. When Jesus prayed to his Father, 'Sanctify them,' he meant, 'Enable these men to fulfil the ideal that you have had for them from before the foundation of the world. Let them find the reason for their existence, the reason why they were born. Bring them to the place where they discover your purposes and programme for their lives.' How? By the truth: 'Your word is truth.' But how do we enter into the sanctifying purposes of God? By acquainting ourselves with the truth, by apprehending it, believing it, and by applying it.

Although the theory of sanctification is not difficult to understand, the application of it seems to give many great difficulty. It is because we are used to believing our feelings more than we believe God's Word. People have said to me, 'I try hard to believe the Word, but somehow I end up believing my feelings.' When as a young man I shared this concern with my pastor, he replied, 'Yes, it takes time to overcome that kind of problem; just make sure it does not take you more time than it ought to.' Over the years, whenever my feelings have contradicted the Word, I have learned to say, 'God, it's my feelings that need disbelieving, not your Word. What I see in your Word is fact. Inevitably so.'

O my Father, I stand in awe of your goodness. You have given me the Word. Help me to trust it, even when my senses may be screaming otherwise. In Jesus' Name. Amen.

Everyone an evangelist!

FOR READING AND MEDITATION – JOHN 20:1–23

'As the Father has sent me, I am sending you.' (v. 21: NIV)

Our Lord's next statement in his great high-priestly prayer is this: 'As you sent me into the world, I have sent them into the world' (John 17:18). The *Authorised Version* translation of John 20:21 confirms the idea of an equation: 'As my Father hath sent me … so send I you.' 'As' – 'so'. This is what I call 'the divine equation'. In an equation one side has to balance the other. Christ has fulfilled his half of the equation – and now the disciples are expected to fulfil their half, too.

If we look a little more closely at how Christ fulfilled his half of the equation, we will be able to get a clearer picture of what was expected of the disciples. As – so. Our Lord was sent by the Father for the express purpose of being his representative in the world. If Christ had not come, then we would never have known the purposes that lay in God's heart for us. It was through Christ – the sent One – that God's purposes were made known and the Name of the Father glorified. Now our Lord tells the Father that he is sending the disciples into the world in the same way. The Saviour is to be glorified through the witness and work of the disciples. We must never forget that the only way people in the world can learn of Christ is from what we show and tell them – first by our lives, then by our lips. For this reason – every Christian is an evangelist.

O God, I begin to see more clearly why you have such a prayerful concern for your disciples. If we fail to let the world know of the Father, then he will remain unknown. Help us, dear Lord. We dare not fail. Amen.

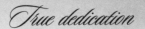
True dedication

FOR READING AND MEDITATION – HEBREWS 10:1–18
'I have come to do your will, o God.' (v. 7: NIV)

We now examine the last statement made by our Lord in the section of his prayer concerned with the needs of his disciples. 'For them I sanctify myself,' says the Master, 'that they too may be truly sanctified' (John 17:19). Does this mean that the Saviour was suddenly conscious of a need to be cleansed and purified? No, for he was perfect, without blemish and without sin. He is using the word *sanctify* here in its primary sense of dedication. He refers to the fact that he had set himself apart for the special task which had been given him by the Almighty, and that he was continuing in that task with a joyful commitment. He means that every part of him was dedicated to the task of bringing glory to God. He is saying that all he has, and is, he is now giving entirely and utterly to God so that his disciples may in turn be truly sanctified.

If we were to paraphrase his words, they would read something like this: 'For their sake I dedicate the whole of my being to you.' One commentator says of verse 19, 'The whole of the Christian gospel is summed up in these words.' The Son of God has devoted himself utterly to our redemption, and has given himself to it with unswerving devotion. Has there ever been a dedication more wonderful?

✎ *O God, forgive us that we are content to offer you a lesser dedication than the one presented to you by your Son. Help us exclude everything that does not contribute to your purposes and serve you with unswerving devotion. Amen.*

Saved to serve!

FOR READING AND MEDITATION – MATTHEW 28:16–20
'Therefore go and make disciples of all nations …' (v. 19: NIV)

We come now to the part of the high-priestly prayer where our Lord prays for all those who would come to believe in him: 'My prayer is not for them alone. I pray also for those who will believe in me through their message, that all of them may be one, Father, just as you are in me and I am in you' (John 17:20). Note the words *through their message*. Clearly our Lord is confident that his followers would spread the gospel throughout the world. What confidence our Lord shows in his followers. Despite the disinclination of some to witness for Christ, because of this prayer we may be assured that the work of evangelism will always go forward.

Years ago a poll was taken among a group of British evangelists as to which illustrations they found most effective in their preaching. This text headed all the lists. Soon after the resurrection, when Christ had returned to heaven, the angels inquired of him: 'Master, what plans do you have to ensure your gospel will be preached throughout the world?' The Lord explained that he had left the task completely in the hands of his followers. The angels seemed surprised at this, and one of them said, 'But Master, your disciples are so fickle and unreliable, what if they fail? What other plan have you made?' Solemnly the Lord said, 'None, this is the only way my gospel can be made known. I have no other plan!'

✎ *Father, nothing could be clearer – we are not saved merely to be safe but saved to make others safe. We are saved to serve! May my lips and my life speak forth your praise day by day. In Jesus' Name. Amen.*

Our model for unity

FOR READING AND MEDITATION – PSALM 133:1–3

'How good and pleasant it is when brothers live together in unity!' (v. 1: NIV)

The thrust of this part of Christ's prayer (John 17:21) has to do with the unity of his people: 'That all of them may be one, Father, just as you are in me and I am in you.' Our Lord is asking that the same unity which exists between him and his Father might be seen also in all his followers. Unity is often confused with words such as union, uniformity, unanimity, etc. When some Christians talk about unity, they're really talking about *union* – churches joining together to form one fellowship. But you can have union and still not have unity. Others think of unity in terms of uniformity – everyone worshipping in the same way and following the same kind of church order. But again, you can have uniformity without having unity. Still others think of unity as being unanimity – everyone thinking the same way about everything. Yet this, too, is not unity. Unity is the bonding of one believer to another, an overriding sense of belonging to the same family, a disposition of oneness that is so deeply ingrained, it brings its influence to bear on all thinking, all decisions, and all actions. We are talking about the same kind of unity that the Son has with the Father. Does that kind of unity characterise the relationships of the church of today? If not, why not?

✎ Lord Jesus, forgive us that despite your prayer for unity we still struggle over the meaning of the word. The unity between you and your Father is the kind of unity we crave. Help us arrive there. For your own dear Name's sake. Amen.

Why ecumenicism fails

FOR READING AND MEDITATION – ROMANS 15:1–13
'May … God … give you a spirit of unity among yourselves
as you follow Christ Jesus …' (v. 5: NIV)

Unity is bonding, an overriding sense of belonging. Only true Christians can talk about spiritual unity, because it begins with understanding what it means to be a Christian. A Christian is someone who knows that his or her salvation was planned in eternity, has entered into it through faith in Christ, is utterly different from the world, and enjoys a continuing relationship with the Lord Jesus Christ. Many of the ecumenical movements come to nought in their efforts to bring about unity because a significant number of the leading proponents are religious but have no clear testimony of being converted. Unity is not something that can be imposed upon the church by simply getting together; unity has to be exposed from within the Body of those who know without doubt that they belong to Christ. The first unity to get straight is our unity with God. Disunity here results in disharmony. A problem in the church of today is that we are trying to relate to one another without relating to God. When we live in unity with God, we take on the significance of the One to whom we are united. When Peter was rightly related to God, 'he stood up with the Eleven' (Acts 2:14). Previously he had stood against them (Luke 22:24). Unity with God made the difference.

✎ *Father, drive this truth deep within the hearts of all your children that unity is something exposed. May your people be so one with you that they will inevitably become one with one another. In Jesus' Name. Amen.*

Four Biblical 'unities'

FOR READING AND MEDITATION – EPHESIANS 4:1–16

'… so that the body of Christ may be built up
until we all reach unity in the faith…' (vv. 12–13: NIV)

This might surprise some, but the unity for which our Lord prayed in John 17:21 is already existing among those who are truly his. In Scripture several types of unity are seen. There is the unity between the three Persons of the Trinity: 'I and my Father are one.' There is the unity that exists between Christ and his people: 'I in them.' Then there is the unity of faith. This unity is something that we are bidden to move towards: 'until we all reach unity in the faith'. There is another unity, the unity of the Spirit: 'Make every effort to keep the unity of the Spirit through the bond of peace' (Eph. 4:3). This unity is a spiritual unity – the kind of unity our Lord was thinking of in his prayer in John 17.

The moment we come into the church, we become part of a Body that is united by the power and energy of the Holy Spirit. Our task then is not to 'make' unity, but simply to maintain it. It is a unity of people who have become spiritual – born again. We belong to Christ and we realise that because of this we belong to everyone else who belongs to Christ. The closer the church gets to Christ, the less we will talk about unity and the more we will see of it.

✎ O God, forgive us that so often we are more interested in knowing what denomination someone belongs to rather than rejoicing in the fact they are our brother or sister. Shake us out of these carnal and unspiritual attitudes. In Jesus' Name. Amen.

Effective evangelism

FOR READING AND MEDITATION – 2 CHRONICLES 30:1–20

'… the hand of God was on the people to give them unity of mind …' (v. 12: NIV)

This subject of Christian unity is so important, it requires one more day. The unity Christ prays for in John 17 is analogous to the mystical unity enjoyed by the Father and the Son. It is unity of Persons, yet there is separateness. 'You … in me' and 'I … in you' (v. 21). The Father and the Son were gloriously united, but yet each kept his separateness. Each gave himself to the other in total surrender, yet each maintained his own personality. It is this our Lord has in mind when he continues in his prayer, 'May they also be in us so that the world may believe that you have sent me.'

When we give ourselves to the Persons of the Trinity, they give themselves to us. Martin Luther described this as 'the divine exchange'. Giving ourselves to God, Christ and the Holy Spirit is the easy part; the difficult part is giving ourselves to one another. Yet, the more we give ourselves to the Trinity, the easier it will be to give ourselves to one another. We draw out love from them and share it with our brothers and sisters. The Lord's other statement is quite staggering: '*that the world may believe that you have sent me*'. Our Lord says it is the unity of believers that will convince men and women of his mission to this world. The visible unity of believers is therefore the greatest form of evangelism. What a rebuke this is to the groundless and often bitter divisions among Christians.

✎ *O God, how your heart must be grieved by the divisions evident among us. And how, too, we hinder the work of evangelism by our fragmentation. Forgive us, renew us, and unite us. In Jesus' Name we pray. Amen.*

The glory 'given'

FOR READING AND MEDITATION – HEBREWS 2:1–9

'… we see Jesus … now crowned with glory and honour …' (v. 9: NIV)

The first four verses of the final section of our Lord's prayer in John 17 (vv. 20–24) consist entirely of our Lord's concern for the unity of all his followers. He bears down on this point again in verse 22: 'I have given them the glory that you gave me, that they may be one as we are one.' What is this glory Jesus is talking about here? Some think it is the glory which he had with the Father before he came to the earth – a glory characterised by humility, service and love. Others think the glory is the presence of Christ's love among his disciples – a love which makes the unity of believers clearly visible. Still others believe he is referring to the glory given to him by God on the Mount of Transfiguration. The apostle Peter refers to it in 2 Pet. 1:17: 'For he received honour and glory from God the Father when the voice came to him from the Majestic Glory'. My own view is that our Lord is anticipating the glory he would receive in heaven and which in turn would be reflected in the lives of all his people. When Christ returned to heaven, he did not leave his humanity behind him, and thus he is now glorified and sits on the throne not only as God but the God-Man. This, I believe, is the peculiar glory he speaks of in John 17:24.

✎ O Saviour, what joy it gives me to know that my humanity is represented on the eternal throne. It is wonderful to think of you as God, but even more wonderful to think of you as the God-Man. All honour and glory be to your Name. Amen.

Two indwellings

FOR READING AND MEDITATION – JOHN 3:1–21

'… God (sent) his Son into the world … to save the world through him' (v. 17: NIV)

We are now just a few verses away from the end of our Lord's great high-priestly prayer. He says in verse 23, 'I in them and you in me. May they be brought to complete unity to let the world know that you sent me and have loved them even as you have loved me.' There are two indwellings spoken of here: 'I in them and you in me.' The first is the dwelling of the Son in his followers, and the second is the dwelling of the Father in the Son. Note that it is only because of the latter that the former can take place. This is the only formula for complete unity. Note again the emphasis on an evangelistic aim: 'To let the world know that you sent me and have loved them even as you have loved me.' This time it is connected with the mission of Jesus and God's love for his people and for his Son.

We have already spoken of spiritual unity being a tremendous force for evangelism, but we must not run away with the idea (as some do) that if we could get rid of all our denominations, it would immediately cause the whole world to turn to Christ. The purpose of this unity is not that the world might believe, but that the world might *know*. The whole world is not going to believe. Our task is not to save people, but to let them know they can be saved. We are to spread the gospel by our lives and by our lips; it is God's great task to save.

Father, you never fail to fulfil your task, but so often we, your people, fail at ours. Renew us and refresh us, dear Lord, that we might be the people you want us to be. In Jesus' Name we ask it. Amen.

United in love

FOR READING AND MEDITATION – COLOSSIANS 2:1–23

'My purpose is that they may be encouraged
in heart and united in love ...' (v. 2: NIV)

The phrase *complete unity* which we looked at yesterday is so significant that we continue to explore the issue of Christian unity. We are constantly being told that one of the greatest scandals in the world is a disunited church. Some hold the idea that if we could get rid of all our denominations and have one world church, the world would be deeply impressed. The result, they say, would be the greatest surge forward in evangelism since the days of the apostles. This is quite unrealistic. Is it really our denominations the men and women in the world are troubled about, or our denominationalism?

I think what God is concerned about is not so much taking us out of a denomination, but taking the denomination out of us. It is denominationalism that works against the spirit of Christian unity – arrogant attitudes that put the interests of denominations before the interests of God. I think the dismantling of denominations could be a good thing, but that in itself will not produce unity. When people in the world see we are sustained, empowered and united by that love – that will impress and affect them. The more the world sees us as dependent rather than independent, the more it will be affected by the gospel. This is the unity that will shake the world.

✑ *O God, once again we plead with you to save us from the central wrong of living independently of you. Open our eyes to the fact that without you we can do nothing. Unite us around that truth so that we might be a powerful witness to the world. Amen.*

Our Lord's last will

FOR READING AND MEDITATION – JOHN 12:20–36

'… and where I am, my servant also will be.' (v. 26: NIV)

As we near the end of the great high-priestly prayer, we come to the verse which has been described as 'Christ's last will and testament'. This is what the Saviour prayed: 'Father, I want those you have given me to be with me where I am, and to see my glory, the glory you have given me because you loved me before the creation of the world.' The words *I want* can equally be translated *I will*. His will for us is that we might be with him and to see his glory. It's always a wonderful thing to be included in someone's will. But to be included in Christ's will is something that stretches credulity. Yet it is true. It is his *will* that we be with him in eternity and behold and participate in his glory. And nothing, *nothing*, can stop the Saviour's last will and testament being executed in the manner he desires.

What is going to happen to us when we die? Where do we go when we stop breathing? We are going where Christ is … as Paul puts it: to 'be with Christ, which is better by far' (Phil. 1:23). And notice that we are not just going to be with Christ, but we are going to see his glory. Clearly the Saviour is looking forward to this day. It is as if he is saying, 'They have seen me in my humiliation – a Man of sorrows and acquainted with grief. Now I long for that time when they will see me in my glory.' I can hardly wait!

✎ *O Father, what a prospect that one day I am going to see Jesus in all his glory! I feel like saying with the poet, 'O day of rest and triumph, delay not thy dawning.' Even so, come Lord Jesus! Amen.*

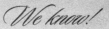

We know!

FOR READING AND MEDITATION – JOHN 17

'… the Father himself loves you because you have loved me …' (v. 27: NIV)

As the Saviour draws to the close of his prayer, he uses a form of address which appears nowhere else in the New Testament: 'Righteous Father, though the world does not know you, I know you, and they know that you have sent me' (John 17:25). There is probably some connection between Christ addressing God as righteous Father, and the words that follow, 'The world does not know you.' The words emphasise the great difference between the Father and the world. The Father is righteous; the world unrighteous. Once more Jesus draws attention to the fact that he came to make known the Father. It is one of the central truths of our faith.

We note that again the main concern of our Lord in this verse is not for the world but for his predestined people. 'They [the elect] know that you have sent me.' These words do not mean that Christ has no love for those who will not come to him. He still provides them with the benefits of what theologians call 'common grace' – the blessings of life, such as air to breathe, food to eat, and so on. God loves all his creation, but the fact has to be faced, he has a special love for those who come to know him through Christ. We who are his children must not gloat over this fact, but glory in it. We can be sure we are Christ's when we are able to look into the face of the Father and say, 'We know that you have sent him into the world.' We know.

✎ *Father, though I doubt many things in this world, I do not doubt this. No knowledge rejoices my heart more than the knowledge that you sent the Son to be my Saviour. Thank you, my Father. In Jesus' Name. Amen.*

A magnificent obsession

FOR READING AND MEDITATION – JOHN 17
'… the glorious riches of this mystery,
which is Christ in you, the hope of glory.' (v. 27: NIV)

The final statement of our Lord in his high-priestly prayer is: 'I have made you known to them, and will continue to make you known in order that the love you have for me may be in them and that I myself may be in them' (John 17:26). Christ says that not only has he made the Father known, but he will continue to do so. There is no sense of the Saviour saying, 'Well, I have finished my task, now I can sit back and let the third member of the Trinity – the Holy Spirit – take over.' Whichever member of the Trinity you come across in Scripture, you never get a sense that he is performing merely from a sense of duty.

At this point our Lord is just about to go to the Cross and to die one of the most fiendishly cruel deaths ever devised by man, yet his thought is not of himself but of continuing in the task God had given him. He closes his prayer: '… that I myself may be in them'. William Law said of this phrase: 'This is the whole gospel, the birth of the holy Jesus within us; his conquering life overcoming our inward death.' It is, of course, a wonderful thing to be 'in Christ'. Paul uses 'in Christ' or its equivalent no less than 164 times in his writings. It was, as someone put it, his 'magnificent obsession'. But for Christ to be in us, in me … is equally wonderful – perhaps even more so.

✎ O Father, it is no exaggeration to describe this concept of 'Christ in me' as the essence of the gospel, for I see that a Christ not in me is a Christ not mine. May the wonder of it thrill my soul hour by hour, and day by day. Amen.

A final summary

FOR READING AND MEDITATION – JOHN 17:1–26
'My prayer is not for them alone.' (v. 20: NIV)

Today we look back over the last two months at the highlights of our journey through our Lord's great high-priestly prayer. Three things stand out. First, the fact that as Christians we are God's chosen people. Long before time began, the Trinity met in a kind of Divine Council to plan our salvation. The Father looked into the future, saw those who were destined for salvation, and marked them as his. His next step was to give them to his Son so that he might wash them, sanctify them, and bring them into the close fellowship of the Trinity as an eternal possession. Second, that on the eve of his agonising death on the cross our Saviour's foremost thoughts were not for himself but for those whom his Father had given him. Third, the more we allow the truths in this chapter to take hold of us, the less we will fall prey to anxiety and uncertainty.

I believe that if you were to reflect for five minutes at least once a day on the truths contained in this prayer of our Lord, you would never again be overcome by the negativism and darkness of the world. I am not surprised to learn that when the great reformer John Knox lay dying, he asked his wife to read to him John 17. Why did not this fiery preacher want her to read from Amos, Jeremiah or Hosea? It was where he cast his spiritual anchor. And so must we.

✎ O God my Father, thank you for what I have learned from this, my Saviour's high-priestly prayer. Burn its truths deep into my soul so that never again I will doubt the certainty and security of my salvation. In Christ's Name I ask it. Amen.

A counsellor par excellence

FOR READING AND MEDITATION – JOHN 14:1–17

'… I will ask the Father, and he will give you
another Counsellor to be with you for ever …' (v. 16: NIV)

We focus today on Christ's famous announcement of the Holy Spirit as the divine Counsellor (John 14:16). Let me set the scene. It is the night before Christ is to be crucified, and he is closeted with his disciples in an upper room in the city of Jerusalem. The Passover has been celebrated, Judas has just left, and suddenly Christ informs his disciples that he is soon to leave this world. When the disciples first heard these words, they were anything but calm. For over three years he had been their teacher, confidante and guide. He had comforted them when they were sad, inspired them in times of doubt, and encouraged them. He had been to them a counsellor *par excellence*. But now he was going.

How were they to handle things in his absence? What were they to do when they didn't know which course of action to take? Who was to be their inspiration and guide? Another Counsellor is to take his place – the blessed Holy Spirit. The Spirit came at Pentecost to be to the disciples all that Jesus was – and more. He has remained in the world to be our Counsellor, too. How often do we draw on his counsel? Sadly, all too seldom and too little.

✎ *O God my Father, forgive me if I treat your Holy Spirit as a Counsellor only in name, and lean more on my own understanding than on his. Show me how to avail myself increasingly of the resources of this divine Counsellor. In Jesus' Name. Amen.*

A permanent presence

FOR READING AND MEDITATION – JOHN 14:18–31

'I will not leave you as orphans; I will come to you.' (v. 18: NIV)

The statement, 'I will ask the Father, and he will give you another Counsellor,' is found in the section of John's Gospel known as 'The Upper Room Discourse' – chapters 14 to 16. Imagine how Christ's news that he was leaving the world to go to the Father would have been received by the disciples. For more than three years they had been inseparable. Now that was about to change – for ever. No more meals together, quiet talks around the camp-fire, shared laughter, deep spiritual discussions. Speaking of his departure from the world, our Lord used the word *orphans*, as we see from our text today. Why ? The disciples were adults, not children. But his departure would leave them feeling as bereft as a child who has lost both parents. Yet, his promise was *not* to leave them as orphans.

It must have been difficult for the disciples to believe at that time that they would ever get over the feelings they experienced as they heard their Master was going away, but when the Holy Spirit visited them at Pentecost, the dispirited disciples came alive again. They appeared to become twice the men they were when Jesus was with them. Why? Because Jesus had been *with* them, but the Holy Spirit was *in* them. There was no fear that he might go away. He would remain with them always. And with us also – he is a permanent presence.

Gracious God and heavenly Father, thank you that your Spirit has come not as a temporary guest but as a permanent one. Amen.

Glorious foreverness

FOR READING AND MEDITATION – JOHN 1:19–34

'… The man on whom you see the Spirit come down and remain …
will baptise with the Holy Spirit.' (v. 33: NIV)

When Jesus announced that the divine Counsellor would abide with his disciples permanently, keep in mind that it had never been like this before. But from now on … yes! Remember, too, that the pattern the disciples had of the coming of the Holy Spirit, as seen in the Old Testament, was of temporary endowments of power for temporary tasks. In other words, he came and went. Yet, in John 14:16–17, as we saw, Jesus announced the Holy Spirit's coming would be permanent. This foreverness of the Spirit was intimated in the passage before us today. Note the words *and remain*. The phrase used in John 14:16 – *to be with you for ever* – strikes the same note.

The idea of an occasional visitation is replaced by a permanent coming. The Holy Spirit is a Counsellor who is available every day, all day. No prior appointments are needed with the divine Counsellor. You can approach him any time of night or day. And you don't have to search for him – he is in your own heart. The Holy Spirit is a divine and dependable Counsellor, permanently available to you and me.

O God my Father, I am grateful for all that you have done for me through Christ, but I am especially grateful that your Spirit has taken up his permanent abode in my heart. Help me understand all the deep implications of this. In Jesus' Name. Amen.

Another Counsellor

FOR READING AND MEDITATION – ACTS 16:1–10

'Paul ... travelled throughout ... Phrygia ... having been kept
by the Holy Spirit from preaching ... in the province of Asia.' (v. 6: NIV)

Permit me to remind you again of our Lord's words which form the basis of our current meditations: 'I will ask the Father, and he will give you another Counsellor' (John 14:16). Note the word *another*. Without that word we have no point of comparison. Counsels us how? And to do what? He counsels us in the same way and with the same principles that Christ followed when he counselled his disciples. The Spirit's counsel was to be the same as Jesus' counsel.

Did you notice in today's reading that the terms *Holy Spirit* and *Spirit of Jesus* are used interchangeably: '... having been kept by the Holy Spirit from preaching the word' (v. 6), and 'the Spirit of Jesus would not allow them to' (v. 7). The Holy Spirit seemed to the disciples to be the Spirit of Jesus within them. They were one. The counsel given to every believer by the Holy Spirit will accord with the counsel given to the disciples by Jesus when he was here on earth. If God is a Christlike God, then the Spirit is a Christlike Spirit. When I meet a counsellor, I can usually tell what school of thought he or she belongs to by listening to that person talk. It is the same with the Holy Spirit. Having observed over the years how he functions in the lives of men and women, I can tell what school he comes from. It is the 'The Jesus school of counselling'.

O Father, I am so grateful that the counselling ministry of Jesus and of the Holy Spirit are one. This means that he will lead me in the same way that Jesus would lead me. I can trust him wholly – and I do. Amen.

The first thing

FOR READING AND MEDITATION – JAMES 1:1–11

'If any of you lacks wisdom, he should ask God …' (v. 5: NIV)

Today we face the question: How much do we avail ourselves of the Holy Spirit as our Counsellor? All across the world the Christian church is going through what has been called a *counselling explosion*. The danger with that is that we put our faith in human counsellors rather than in the divine Counsellor. I remember a time in the church when counselling was regarded by many as an unnecessary ministry. If you have a problem, it was said at that time, never look to others for help; instead, get down on your knees and talk to God about it – the Holy Spirit will show you what to do. That, of course, was an extreme position. Often it does help to talk through a problem with a Christian counsellor. As David Seamands puts it: 'A [Christian] counsellor is a temporary assistant to the Holy Spirit.'

The first thing we should do with a problem is to turn to the divine Counsellor and invite him to help us. If light does not, come then seek the help of a wise and godly friend. But seeking help from others should not be our first recourse; our first recourse should be to God. The Holy Spirit is a Counsellor *par excellence*. To seek counselling from another Christian is quite valid, but might be needed less if we depended on the Holy Spirit more.

✎ *O God, forgive me if my first thought when I am in need of help is not of you. If I have dropped out of the habit of opening my heart to you before I open it to anyone else, then help me recover that habit. In Christ's Name I pray. Amen.*

Grief in the Godhead

FOR READING AND MEDITATION – EPHESIANS 4:17–32

'And do not grieve the Holy Spirit of God …' (v. 30: NIV)

We spend another day on the need to avail ourselves more fully of the resources of the Holy Spirit, our divine Counsellor. In the midst of what is being called a *counselling explosion*, we're in danger of falling into the trap of taking our problems first to a Christian counsellor rather than bringing them straight to God. Why? Maybe we prefer a visible counsellor to an invisible one. Perhaps we are not sure how to establish contact with the divine Counsellor or how to recognise his voice when he speaks to us. Or possibly we are not quite certain that the divine Counsellor is interested in the likes of us. We can believe he guides such people as Billy Graham, Luis Palau or Mother Teresa – but ordinary people like us?

Let me lay this down in your mind right away: the services of the divine Counsellor are yours for the asking. If you are a Christian, then his resources are available to you – free and for the taking. It is customary for anyone charged with an offence in court to have a professional advocate to counsel them and plead their case. If they cannot pay one, one is provided for them – free of charge. As one of God's children, God does for you what any good government will do: he provides you with counsel. When we spurn the services of the divine Counsellor, we grieve him. For he is not merely an influence, he is a Person.

O God my Father, if I have been living too independently and relying on my resources rather than on yours then once again I humbly ask your forgiveness. Teach me how to be more God-dependent. In Jesus' Name I pray. Amen.

FOR READING AND MEDITATION – ACTS 13:1–12

'… The Holy Spirit said, "Set apart for me Barnabas and Saul…"' (v. 2: NIV)

We ended yesterday with the thought that the Holy Spirit is not merely an influence, but a divine Person. This is why we must refer to him as *he* and not *it*. Some Christians believe he is an impersonal influence, yet use personal pronouns such as *he* and *his* when referring to him. The Holy Spirit is not the personification of an influence, the sense of fellowship Christians share when they get together, or even spiritual enthusiasm. He is a Person with individuality, intelligence, hearing, knowledge, wisdom, sympathy, and so on. He can see, speak, rejoice, love, whisper, and when we spurn him by turning to other resources, or resist him when he seeks to work within us, he is grieved in the same way that a close friend would be hurt.

The Bible says he is God, with the very same attributes as God. In Job 26:13 he is seen as having the power to create. In Psalm 139:7 he is shown to have omnipresence – being everywhere present. In Hebrews 3:7 he is spoken of as issuing commands as only God can do. In 2 Corinthians 3:17 he is referred to as *Lord*. If you are a Christian, there is an unseen deity in your life – the Holy Spirit. He doesn't want to hide from you, and he doesn't want you to hide from him.

O God, before I go any further in these meditations, let this thought sink deep into my heart – the Holy Spirit is a Person with whom I can commune, and from whom I can draw resources. Help me become better acquainted with him. In Jesus' Name. Amen.

Who is the real you?

FOR READING AND MEDITATION – ROMANS 7:7–25

'What a wretched man I am!
Who will rescue me from this body of death?' (v. 24: NIV)

Before we move on to how the Holy Spirit's counselling helps us become the kind of person God sees that we can be, let's ask ourselves: To whom do we refer when we use the personal pronoun *I*? Is there anything in our personalities so constant and reliable that we can honestly refer to it as *I*? 'Human nature is so changeful,' said one philosopher, 'and so subject to swiftly alternating moods, that when I say *I*, I am not sure what *I* I am talking about.' Who is the real person? The man who sings heartily in church and then shouts at his wife and family on the way home in the car? The same person can be so many different persons. Whom do others mean when they say *you*, and whom do you mean when you say *I*?

Aristotle claimed there were six different Aristotles. Faust declared, 'Two souls, alas, dwell in this breast of mine.' Renan, the French author, admitted, 'I am two people; one part of me laughs while the other … cries.' Even Paul, in today's passage, talks about another self dwelling within him. Some might explain this as schizophrenia or 'dual personality', but the elements of what we are talking about are in us all. The real *you*, I believe, is not the person others see, not even the person you see, but the person God, Christ and the Holy Spirit see. Only they know the real you.

✎ *O Father, how consoling it is to know that the Trinity see me not only as I am, but as I can be. And you are all working to bring me up to my full height in Christ. Thank you, my Father. Amen.*

Double vision

FOR READING AND MEDITATION – JOHN 1:35–42

'Jesus ... said, "You are Simon son of John.
You will be called Cephas" (which ... is Peter).' (v. 42: NIV)

If the Holy Spirit is our Counsellor, then what are some of the ways in which he makes his counsel available to us? How does he go about this important task? When Jesus said, 'The Father ... will give you another Counsellor,' he meant that the Holy Spirit would counsel us in the same way he counselled his disciples. So, by looking at the way Jesus counselled them, we will have a clearer picture of how the Holy Spirit goes about counselling us.

One of the characteristics of a good counsellor is to have a clear vision of a person's potential so that they can encourage that person to move towards it. I mean not so much human potential, but our potential in Christ. Jesus looked at Simon and declared: 'You are Simon ... You will be called Cephas (which ... is Peter).' Jesus was really saying that he saw within Peter the potential to be a rock. Simon was the kind of vacillating character who could walk on the water with Jesus and yet 'followed afar off' when he was on the land. But Jesus had the insight, as do all good counsellors, to see people not just as they are but as they can be. This is a characteristic of the Holy Spirit also. He sees us as we are, yet loves us too much to let us stay as we are. Lovingly and gently he prods us toward perfection.

◁ O God, how grateful I am that you and the other members of the Trinity have double vision. You see me not just as I am, but as I can be. Continue your work in my life gently prodding me to perfection. In Jesus' Name. Amen.

How many Simons?

'... and you have been given fullness in Christ,
who is head over every power and authority.' (v. 10: NIV)

We continue looking at Simon, the brother of Andrew and the son of John, to emphasise the point that Christ saw him not as he was, but as he could be. Everything that Christ did in Simon Peter's life was designed to draw him up to his full height spiritually. This, too, is the way the Holy Spirit works with us.

Let's have a look at Simon. There were at least three: Simon as his friends saw him, Simon as he saw himself, and Simon as Christ saw him. What was Simon like in his friends' eyes? I can only conjecture, of course, that his friends might have described him as blustering, impulsive, loud-mouthed, but clearly endowed with leadership qualities nevertheless. What was Simon like in his own eyes? Certainly he did not perceive himself as the same man that his friends saw. We never see ourselves as others see us. When we look in a mirror, the image we see is always reversed. And mentally and spiritually it is the same: it is another self we see from within. The poet Robert Burns said, 'Oh wad some power the giftie gie us, to see ourselves as others see us!' That may be helpful, but much more helpful is to see ourselves as God, Christ and the Holy Spirit see us: not merely as we are, with dark marks on our soul, but as we can be – complete in the Godhead.

✎ O God, once again I want to confess my deep gratitude for the fact that though you see and love me as I am, you love me too much to let me stay as I am. I surrender to you to work with me to bring me to completeness. Amen.

False self-images

FOR READING AND MEDITATION – LUKE 4:38–44
'… Simon's mother-in-law was suffering from a high fever,
and they asked Jesus to help her.' (v. 38: NIV)

We never see ourselves as we really are. A minister tells of going to a children's home to give out Christmas presents. First he spent a little time with the matron in charge, and asked if the children had someone special who befriended them. She said that all did, except two. One of the two was a black boy called Philip. One day a chimney-sweep arrived. When Philip saw his black face, he started crying, 'There's a black man coming.' He had taken his ideas from the other children and, being small, he hadn't seen much of himself. After all, everybody else he saw was white!

We are quick to see in others what we so easily miss in ourselves. I wonder if Simon's picture of himself was also a flattering one? No doubt he thought of himself as a good judge of other people, a good husband, and perhaps even a good son-in-law. He also appears to have had a great concern when his mother-in-law was ill. If someone had asked Simon, 'Are you without fault?' He might have answered 'No', but I don't think he would have particularised his faults. Usually we don't until we are serious in the pursuit of holiness. Only then will we dig them out, itemise them and pray over them, 'This, this, and this is sin within me.'

O God, help me to become serious in the pursuit of holiness. If there are sins within me that I can't see, or even others can't see, then give me your light. For it is only in your light that I can see light. In Jesus' Name. Amen.

A reed turns into a rock

FOR READING AND MEDITATION – 1 PETER 2:1–10

'See, I lay a stone in Zion, a chosen and precious cornerstone …' (v. 6: NIV)

We look now at the two Simons Jesus saw. First, Simon as he was, and second, the Simon Christ could make him. The two were so different that they required a different name. Our Lord, looking at Simon, said, 'You are Simon son of John,' and then, envisaging the Simon he could make, said, 'You will be called a rock. That is the man I'll make you' (see John 1:42). What a change: Peter the reed, who could be shaken by even the gentlest wind, would under the counselling ministry of Christ become a rock. Through the combination of Christ's counselling and later the Holy Spirit's counselling, the impulsive blusterer became clear in judgment and firm in will. One commentator describes the changes that took place in him as follows: 'The man who could curse and swear and deny all knowledge of his best friend to save his own skin, became a valiant leader at Pentecost and the unshaken champion of the sect which was itself to change the world.'

In today's passage Peter speaks of Christ as the living Stone – rejected by men but chosen by God. It is interesting that Peter talks so much about Christ as being a Rock, for under the tuition of the 'Rock' he himself had become a rock. Not that Peter could be compared to Christ, but he had taken on the characteristics of his Lord which were foreign to his own nature.

✎ O God, if you could turn Peter the unstable into Peter the rock, then what can you do with me? Help me be open to all the changes the divine Counsellor wants to bring about in my life. In Jesus' Name. Amen.

Divine enticement

FOR READING AND MEDITATION – GENESIS 17:1–15

'No longer will you be called Abram; your name will be Abraham ...' (v. 5: NIV)

It is always a powerful moment when one person paints a picture for another of the kind of person they can be. I have often said to a husband who has told me he felt weak and inadequate, 'In Christ you have the potential to be the man who can strongly move into your wife's world, to be the kind of husband to her that Christ is to the Church – initiating, loving, and considerate.' I remember talking to a woman who had been raped in her teens and was finding it difficult to give herself fully to her husband: 'You believe deep down that because you were violated, you cannot now give your attractiveness to anyone. However, in the strength and power of Christ, your femininity which you now want to hide, can blossom into an attractiveness that will not only bring out your own inner beauty but his also.' Those God-inspired remarks changed those people's lives forever.

Our Lord's dealings with Simon Peter set a pattern the Holy Spirit follows in his counselling ministry with us. Have you ever been at prayer and caught a vision of what it would mean to be the person you longed to be? That was the divine Counsellor at work within you. He sees with double vision. Determine to spend more time with him.

✎ *Heavenly Father, my mind is made up. I will spend more time with you – beginning today. Show me how to manage my time to bring more of you into my day. For the more you have of me, the more I have of you. In Jesus' Name. Amen.*

Confined in a cage!

FOR READING AND MEDITATION – GENESIS 35:1–15

'God said to him, "Your name is Jacob, but you will no longer
be called Jacob; your name will be Israel." ' (v. 10: NIV)

Is the real you the person you yourself see? Positively no! You do
not know yourself. Psychologists and psychiatrists can be amazingly ignorant of themselves. Is the real you the person others see?
Definitely not. It may be an act of faith on my part, but I am ready
to assert that the real you is the person the Holy Spirit wants to
make you. You were not made to grovel, to be beaten and frustrated by sin. You were made for God himself, and seated deep in your
heart there are longings to know him and be like him.

Once in a zoo I looked at eagles in their cage. The sight hurt me.
The great birds were made for the skies and not to be confined to a
cage! So many of us are like that – made for higher things, but confined to a cage of doubt, fear, denial, perhaps even sin. When Jesus
looked on Simon the reed, he saw Peter the rock. The Holy Spirit
sees the part of you that is ineffective, beaten, cowed and fearful,
but he also sees that you can be confident, effective, sanctified and
strong, moving along the Christian pathway with great strides. If
only we could see ourselves as he sees us! If only we could move
closer to him and get that double vision – the vision of the people
we are and the people we might be. It is mainly our unwillingness
that stops us. If we're intent on getting closer, we'll find a way.

*O Father, help me to be willing. I know that my potential can never be
realised without spending time with you, but the cost of that is sometimes
more than I am willing to pay. Forgive me and help me. In Jesus' Name. Amen.*

The person God meant

FOR READING AND MEDITATION – 2 CORINTHIANS 3:7–18
'And we ... are being transformed into his likeness
with ever-increasing glory ...' (v. 18: NIV)

We continue to consider the fact that the divine Counsellor is at work within us, seeking to make us into the kind of person he sees that we can be. Emerson said, 'Could'st thou in vision see, Thyself the man God meant, Thou never more could'st be, The man thou art, content.' How does the Holy Spirit go about the task of enabling us to see the man or woman God meant? He can only do it when we get close to him or allow him to get close to us. No counsellor is effective unless he or she has the confidence and attention of the person being counselled. Charles Swindoll said, 'As theologians and teachers of the Word we study the Holy Spirit from a safe doctrinal distance; we are loath to enter into any of the realms of his super-natural workings or even to tolerate the possibility of such. Explaining the Holy Spirit is one thing; experiencing him another.'

I believe that the Holy Spirit yearns to transform us in the same way that Christ yearned to transform Simon Peter. But the cost is great. It means taking time to develop our relationship with him. Once we do that, however, he goes to work, inflaming, enlightening, prodding, enticing and moving us on until the difference in us is so marked that we need a new name. To you now, as to one long ago, the Spirit says, 'You are ... But you shall be ...'

✤ Loving heavenly Father, burn into me by your Holy Spirit the truth that unless we travel together I shall never be the person you see that I can be. Today I put my hand in yours. Lead me on dear Father. Amen.

No prayer – no power

FOR READING AND MEDITATION – LUKE 18:1–8

'… Jesus told his disciples a parable to show them that
they should always pray and not give up.' (v. 1: NIV)

We have seen something of the way in which our Lord counselled
Simon Peter. We noted also that the Holy Spirit constantly seeks to
set before us an image of the man or woman he sees us to be. We
look now at another counselling session which our Lord gave his
disciples – this time a group session.

The passage before us is just one of many in the Gospels in
which our Lord unfolded to his disciples the power and importance of prayer. He focuses on perseverance. We are to pray and not
faint. Often when people are overcome by troubles and trials, they
find it difficult to pray. Time and again I have asked people, 'What's
your prayer life like?' More often than not they have responded, 'I
find it very hard to pray.' It's not easy to pray when things all
around us are falling apart, although that is the time we ought to
pray the most.

One of the goals of a godly counsellor is to help a person get
back to a consistent prayer life, for without one there is little chance
of spiritual survival. If we do not pray, we faint.

✎ *O God, just as Jesus counselled his disciples to pray, may the Holy Spirit
counsel me along these lines, too. For I see that if I do not pray, then I faint.
Divine Counsellor, my heart is open and you have my total confidence. In
Jesus' Name. Amen.*

Running from the crowds!

FOR READING AND MEDITATION – LUKE 5:12–15

'But Jesus often withdrew to lonely places and prayed.' (v. 16: NIV)

Over and over in the Gospels our Lord counsels his disciples to pray. Like a watch, life has a tendency to run down. It needs re-winding. Prayer rewinds the springs of life by opening our spirits to the Holy Spirit. You don't have to tamper with the hands of a watch to make them go round if the mechanism is fully wound. Likewise, when we are in touch with God through prayer, the Holy Spirit supplies the energy we need to get through every day.

Our Lord is the perfect example of a Counsellor who practised what he preached. In today's passage we read that following the healing of the leper, the news about Christ's great ministry spread widely until the crowds flocked from far and near to hear his words and be healed of their diseases. On many occasions, we are told, he escaped from the crowds to pray. Christ ran away from the multi-tudes to get alone and pray. That shows how much of a priority our Lord gave to prayer. We run from praying toward the crowds; our Lord ran from the crowds to pray. Prayer helps us revise and renew our lives. Jesus needed to pray. So do we.

✎ Lord Jesus Christ, you are the greatest Man who has ever lived and yet you needed to pray. May the Holy Spirit work in me so that I, too, shall be primarily prayer-conscious and secondarily people-conscious. For your own dear Name's sake. Amen.

Pray! Pray! Pray!

FOR READING AND MEDITATION – THESSALONIANS 5:1–23

'… pray continually …' (v. 17: NIV)

Put quite simply, prayer is the heart of our faith. I know that many of our ideas about prayer are confused, and that many find it difficult to pray, even when no problems are crowding into their lives. A preacher tells of a woman who told him she was leaving the church. When he asked why, she said that her daughter had sat for a scholarship, and although she and her little girl had prayed hard, she had not passed. That proved, the mother claimed, there was nothing in prayer, and therefore she was not attending church any more. The preacher concluded: 'It struck me as I listened to her that I had not taught her much about prayer.' He knew the daughter well and realised she could not have passed a scholarship. She was a beautiful girl and would go on to fulfil some satisfying role in life, but did not have the ability to pass a scholarship.

Think of a mother losing faith in prayer because of that. Some see prayer as simply the means to get something from God. So they pray only when they want something. You may have heard of the little boy who told his vicar that he didn't pray every day because there were some days when he didn't want anything. What would you think of a friend who turned up only when he wanted something? Is that how we treat God?

O God, wean me from the idea that prayer is simply asking for things. Help me understand that when you say 'No' to my prayers it is because you know best. Teach me to pray, to really pray, dear Father. In Jesus' Name. Amen.

When disinclined to pray

FOR READING AND MEDITATION – EPHESIANS 6:10–20

'And pray in the Spirit on all occassions
with all kinds of prayers and requests.' (v. 18: NIV)

Prayer is much more than asking for things. Those who see it as such are in prayer's kindergarten. But even those who see prayer as more than that, often tell me they find it difficult to pray. The need for prayer is apparent, the command to pray is recognised, but the longing to pray is not in them. They have to push themselves to get down on their knees. What a tragedy. The very thing we most need, we desire the least. How can we escape from this impasse? Thankfully, the divine Counsellor is willing to come to our aid. Paul says (Rom. 8:26), 'The Spirit helps us in our weaknesses.' Some translations use the word *Helper* rather than *Counsellor*.

Once I went through a dark period when prayer lost all its appeal for me. I continued preaching and writing in a mechanical way. My words were carefully thought out, my sentences studiously crafted, but they were not soaked in prayer. Then the Spirit drew near and challenged me about my prayer life. 'But I don't feel like praying,' I complained. 'Then I will help you,' he seemed to say. He did, and by his grace lit the flame of prayer once again in my heart. Is the divine Counsellor talking to you now about this very problem? Then ask him to help you. And do it without any further delay – today.

❧ *O God, you put within me the desire to pray and can also help me overcome any disinclination I have to pray. Touch me today by your Holy Spirit and make my passion for prayer greater than ever before. In Jesus' Name. Amen.*

The Spirit is praying!

FOR READING AND MEDITATION – ROMANS 8:18–27

'... The Spirit himself intercedes for us with groans
that words cannot express.' (v. 26: NIV)

Today's passage tells us that on some occasions he will actually
pray in us and through us. These words spell out one of the most
astonishing truths about the Holy Spirit contained anywhere in the
Word of God. The Holy Spirit intercedes for us 'with groans that
words cannot express'. I think it means that the Holy Spirit does
not despise human frailties. Instead, he makes our weakness the
reason to plead our interests before God.

We all experience times when we lack clarity about what we
should pray, and then our prayers are very superficial. Thus the
needs we express are lesser needs, and not the things we really
ought to be praying about. But sometimes our divine Counsellor
takes up the task of intercession for us 'with groans that words
cannot express'. The relationship between God and the Holy Spirit
is so close that the prayers of the Spirit need not be audible. The
sighs of the Spirit are clearly interpreted by God, because it is for
God's own purpose for each one of us that the Spirit is pleading. It
is always an awesome moment when one senses that one is being
prayed through. All one can do, is to silence every other voice inside and say, 'Hush! The Holy Spirit is praying!'

✒ O God, how wondrous are your ways – especially the ways of your Spirit.
Help me understand that being prayed through is more occasional than gen-
eral, and I must not use it as an excuse for not initiating prayer. In Jesus'
Name. Amen.

The groan of God

FOR READING AND MEDITATION – JOHN 11:32–44

'… Jesus … was deeply moved in spirit and troubled.' (v. 33: NIV)

We see in our reading today that our Lord was deeply troubled in spirit. The *Authorised Version* translates this text: 'Jesus … groaned in the spirit and was troubled.' God was about to use Jesus to bring Lazarus back to life, yet immediately prior to this momentous event our Lord groaned deep within his soul. Why? Let us consider the words of Dr W.E. Sangster: 'All true progress in this world is by the echo of the groan of God in the hearts of his people.' What did he mean? In previous centuries Britain was engaged in the business of slave-trading. How did it eventually come to an end? One man woke up one morning and found the Spirit groaning in his soul. That man was William Wilberforce; he and his friends laboured until that most notable hour in our history when we paid a sum larger than our national debt to free the slaves.

Progress in spiritual things is not mechanical. It does not come from ourselves alone. Progress results from the groan of God in the hearts of his people. Was the groan that Jesus felt as he confronted death God groaning within him? Was it the spiritual precursor of something mighty and momentous? I think so. If what Sangster says is true, then ought we not to ask ourselves, 'When did we last feel the groan of God in our soul?'

⊰ O God, I feel somewhat saddened today to think that I might block some aspect of spiritual progress in this world because I am insensitive to your groan echoing in my soul. Tune me in more closely to your purposes, dear Lord. In Jesus' Name. Amen.

Three groans!

FOR READING AND MEDITATION – 2 CORINTHIANS 5:1–10

'For while we are in this tent, we groan and are burdened ...' (v. 4: NIV)

We spend one last day reflecting on the way in which the Holy Spirit encourages us, as did Jesus, to explore the depths and heights of intercessory prayer. The verse before us today takes our minds back to Romans 8, where the apostle Paul reminds us about three kinds of groans. He tells us there that the whole creation groans (8:22), we ourselves groan (8:23), and the Spirit makes intercession for us with groans that can't be expressed in words (8:26). First then, the whole creation groans. Who can doubt it? Everything that lives is subject to disease: human beings, animals, fish, birds, trees, plants. Second, we groan within ourselves. A.W. Tozer said, 'We have not progressed very far in the Christian life if we have not felt the groan that goes on in creation ... and felt also the groan in our own hearts – the longing to be released from bondage and be with Christ.' Third, and most astonishing of all, the Spirit groans within us. Is the groan of the Spirit the answer to the groan in creation? Is this God's way of ensuring spiritual progress in this world? Three groans! Hear the groan of creation. Hear the groan within yourself. Hear the Spirit making intercession for you with groans which cannot be uttered. But know this also: God's last word is not a groan. God's last word is joy, joy, joy!

❧ O Lord, while I am thankful for knowing about these three groans, I am thankful also for this reminder that your last word is joy. May I keep that thought always before me, too, so that I might live with a full understanding. In Christ's Name. Amen.

Face to face with reality

FOR READING AND MEDITATION – JOHN 4:1–26

'Jesus said to her, "You are right when you say you have no husband."' (v. 17: NIV)

So far we have examined just two aspects of our Lord's counselling approach. First, the way in which he holds out for us the vision of the person God sees us to be, and second, the importance of building a good and meaningful prayer life. These two aspects are regarded by all those who seek to counsel according to Scripture, as pivotal and fundamental.

Another aspect of good counselling is bringing important issues to a head through loving confrontation. This involves moving people away from symptoms on the surface to face the significant issues. Christ demonstrated this skill in his encounter with the woman at the well. How did Jesus get to the root problem in her heart without seeming to invade sanctities? Did he say bluntly, 'Woman, you are living an adulterous life'? No, he pinpointed her problem in a more delicate way: 'Go, call your husband' (v. 16). She replied weakly, 'I have no husband.' He acknowledged, recognising her honesty before touching the ugly areas of her life. It was just a step from there to confronting her with the real issues for which she needed help, and soon her heart was open. Christ always saw past the trivial issues to the major ones, and never hesitated, though always respectfully, to bring the hidden things to light.

✍ O God, perhaps I, too, need a lesson here, even though I may not be a counsellor. Help me to be concerned not about winning arguments, but winning people. Show me also how to respect a person even though I may disagree with their behaviour. In Jesus' Name. Amen.

Handle with care!

FOR READING AND MEDITATION – GALATIANS 6:1–10

'Brothers, if someone is caught in a sin,
you who are spiritual should restore him gently.' (v. 1)

'In almost every life,' said Dr E. Stanley Jones, 'there is an issue which needs confronting, which becomes the decision point from which we swing toward darkness or toward light – toward spiritual malformation or spiritual transformation. If that central issue is not faced, then the process of transformation is blocked. If faced courageously, then the process and power of redemption is at our disposal.' Powerful words. If this is true, what is to be done about it? It must be faced courageously. However, when confronting issues such as sin or moral failure, great care must be taken. Did you notice in yesterday's reading that Jesus said both at the beginning and end of his probing, 'You are right' (John 4:17–18)? He pointed out the good in her at the very moment he touched the terribly sore depths.

There is a form of Christian counselling known as nouthetic counselling, *noutheteo* being the Greek for to warn, admonish, confront. This type of counselling is strongly confrontational, and some of its practitioners appear to be more interested in exposing sin than restoring the sinner. Today's text reminds us that where there is moral failure, it is restoration, not exposure, that ought to be the overriding consideration. To confront does not mean to affront.

✎ *O Father, how much less pain there would be in all our relationships if we could follow the example of Jesus and hate sin but not hate the sinner. Help us learn that lesson and learn it quickly. In Christ's Name. Amen.*

The arguments of sin

FOR READING AND MEDITATION – JAMES 1:12–18
'… but each one is tempted when, by his own evil desire,
he is dragged away and enticed.' (v. 14: NIV)

One of the abilities of a good counsellor is to bring important issues to a head through loving confrontation. Note the word *loving*. Some people just love to confront. But if confrontation is to be successful, then it must be done in a way that shows a strong detestation of sin but respect for the person. Jesus models the way in which to do this. And so, too, of course, does the Holy Spirit.

An old hymn which describes the Holy Spirit as a Counsellor has some lines in it which go like this: 'Christ is our Advocate on high, thou art our Advocate within. O plead the truth and make reply, to every argument of sin.' The arguments of sin? What does that mean? Psychologists call it *the rationalisation of desire*. Let me explain. One day you find yourself being tempted by something that you have always resisted. But this time you begin to look at it differently. Perhaps you begin to talk to yourself like this: 'The pressures in my life at the moment are so strong that surely a little escape from them can be justified.' You see how it leads on? That is what the psychologist calls the rationalisation of desire, and that is what the hymn-writer had in mind when he spoke of the arguments of sin.

✑ *O God, how encouraging it is to know that when the arguments of sin are heard in my soul I have an Advocate who rises at once to rebut them. Thank you, my Father, for appointing the Holy Spirit as my Advocate. In Jesus' Name. Amen.*

David's great sin

FOR READING AND MEDITATION – 2 SAMUEL 11:1–27
'But the thing David had done displeased the Lord' (v. 27: NIV)

We spoke yesterday of the ease with which we can slip into what psychologists call 'the rationalisation of desire'. What makes temptation powerful, is the desire within us for the thing with which we are tempted. King David knew all about 'the rationalisation of desire'. He wanted the wife of Uriah, one of his officers, and while Uriah was on active service fighting the king's battles, David seduced the woman. Then, fearing the consequences, he 'arranged' the death of her husband and added murder to lust. The 'man after God's own heart' wallowed in sin. How did he ever get to that point? By 'the rationalisation of desire'. It would have started with a sinful thought. He dwelt on it when he should have blacked it out. He fed his imagination on it when he should have blasted it with prayer. He told himself later that Uriah had died in the discharge of his duty! And then he married the woman and convinced himself the problem was resolved. He was a victim of the arguments of sin. David was so self-deceived on this occasion that even the Holy Spirit was unable to get through to him, and so the Spirit used Nathan as one of his 'temporary assistants'. Nathan's barbed little parable did its work. Soon the wail of Psalm 51 arose: 'Have mercy on me, O God … wash me, and I shall be whiter than snow' (vv. 1, 7).

✎ *O God, help me never to get into the state where my conscience is drugged and I become self-deceived. I tremble lest my soul becomes so insensitive to sin that the Holy Spirit will be unable to get my attention. Save me from that, dear Father. Amen.*

He is always there!

FOR READING AND MEDITATION – EPHESIANS 1:1–14

'... you were marked by him with a seal, the promised Holy Spirit ...
guaranteeing our inheritance ...' (vv. 13–14: NIV)

Does the Spirit withdraw from our hearts if we ever fall into sin? I don't think so. He is hurt and grieved by our sin, but he remains with us and in us nevertheless. Some would like to believe that he does leave, for the thought of a grieved and hurting Spirit residing in the soul greatly increases their spiritual discomfort. Experiencing the sting of one's own conscience when one has sinned is bad enough, but the thought that the Holy Spirit is there in the soul also – hurting, grieved and pained – seems to make the sin more heinous still.

Many years ago the local Sheffield newspaper carried a report about a barrister who had to plead 'invisibility' in court because he was not wearing a wig and gown. In a British court, a barrister is obliged to wear a wig and a gown in court otherwise officially he is not present. 'I cannot see you,' said the judge as the barrister arose in court, 'you are invisible to me.' That, I believe, will never happen in the heart of one of God's children. The Spirit is always 'dressed' for the occasion. He will not desert you. You may grieve him and turn a deaf ear to him, and if you do not heed him it is possible that his voice may grow faint within you. But I don't believe he will leave. We are sealed by the Spirit until the day of redemption. He is always there for you.

O Father, how thrilling it is to know that your Spirit is unwilling to leave me. He knows the worst about me, but still will not desert me. My words cannot convey my gratitude. In Jesus' Name. Amen.

The purifying Spirit

FOR READING AND MEDITATION – ACTS 15:1–11

'[The Holy Spirit] purified their hearts by faith.' (v. 9: NIV)

The work of the divine Counsellor is perhaps needed more now than at any other time in history. I say this because looseness and moral permissiveness is so commonplace that we Christians are in danger of being brainwashed by the world into lowering our moral standards. Society tolerates things today that years ago would have brought an expression of horror to most people's faces. Take the area of entertainment. On stage and screen people used to worry about whether or not nudity was gratuitous. On TV we are treated to the most intimate and shameless sexual disclosures. In sport, brattish tennis players and footballers provide us with displays of loud-mouthed arrogance. Businessmen line up to boast about this or that takeover, and almost everyone in politics seems to be hard at work on self-aggrandising memoirs.

On a TV panel programme I recently watched, one person objected to the low standards being accepted everywhere today. A member of the panel retorted, 'But it's only human nature.' That sums up the spirit of the world: 'It's nature and therefore hardly sin.' This attitude must not be allowed to invade the church. We must not forget that the Spirit's greatest work is helping us to overcome and be cleansed from sin. He is the Holy Spirit.

My Father and my God, by your Spirit you are bringing things to the surface – not to shame us, but to save us. Give us grace as your church to follow through – from exposure to experience. In Jesus' Name we pray. Amen.

Sensitivity to sin

FOR READING AND MEDITATION – 1 JOHN 1:1–10
'If we claim to be without sin, we deceive ourselves …' (v. 8: NIV)

Today we ask ourselves: Is a sense of sin old-fashioned? Our fathers used to talk a lot about the way the Holy Spirit convicted of sin. It is true that earlier generations indulged in the most extravagant descriptions of their own sinful nature, and a glance through old hymn books certainly confirms that: 'Me, the vilest of the race, most unholy, most unclean. Me, the farthest from Thy face, full of misery and sin.' The Christians of a bygone age seemed to delight in their depravity. One Victorian commentator tells of a village shopkeeper who week by week used the same phrase in his prayers to describe his spiritual condition: 'My soul is a mass of putrefying sores.' Yet, he was by all accounts a perfectly honest and upright man.

Today we regard such attitudes as *old-fashioned*. Let us be on our guard, however, lest in our unwillingness to express ourselves in the self-depreciating language of our fathers, we grow smug in our attitude to sin. It is perilously possible that without realising we may have been affected by the tendency of this age to reduce the eternal distinction between right and wrong to a question of taste. Ask yourself now: Am I as sensitive to sin as God wants me to be?

✎ *O God, again by your Spirit you are bringing issues to the surface and confronting me with the reality of what may be going on within me. Help me not to indulge in my depravity, but help me not to overlook it either. In Jesus' Name. Amen.*

The scrutiny of God

FOR READING AND MEDITATION – PSALM 139:1–24
'Search me, O God, and know my heart.' (v. 23: NIV)

I want to instil a thought in your mind: the safest form of self-examination is that which is carried out in the presence and under the guidance of the Holy Spirit. Some Christians are always examining their hearts and become unhealthily introspective; others never examine their hearts and become spiritually lethargic. Spiritual examination ought to be a regular activity. I know many Christians who examine their hearts every Sunday. First invite the Holy Spirit to be present and to guide. The purpose of self-examination is to identify the things that should not be in our lives and to bring them to God. If the Holy Spirit is not invited to the moment of self-examination, we might end up in a state of self-pity. The Spirit never moves us to self-pity; the Spirit moves us to repentance. Self-pity is an enemy of repentance, because it is an attempt to remove the soul's pain by humanistic means rather than by entrusting oneself to God and his Holy Spirit.

The psalmist in today's passage prayed, 'Search me, O God ... See if there is any offensive way in me' (vv. 23–24). Begin with that prayer, and wait before him to see what he will make you conscious of. Then ask God for forgiveness and go out into the day – forgiven and cleansed.

O Father, help me to regularly open up the depths of my heart to your Spirit, the divine Counsellor. May he search me and see if there is any wicked way in me – anything that hinders the flow of your life through me. In Jesus' Name. Amen.

Whose voice was it?

FOR READING AND MEDITATION – ROMANS 8:1–11

'You … are controlled not by the sinful nature but by the Spirit,
if the Spirit of God lives in you.' (v. 9: NIV)

We've considered the truth that the Holy Spirit is at work within our hearts. He never hesitates to make us aware of important issues in our hearts, but he does so in the same way that Jesus did – tenderly, delicately and respectfully. Would that all Christian counsellors followed their example.

Do you know anything about what we have been calling *the arguments of sin*? Cast your mind back over your life for a moment. Can you recall times when temptation has come to you and you felt some sinful desire rise within you? In the courtroom of your soul, did you hear the plea of the arguments of sin? And did you hear another voice speaking to you of past victories, of the people who love you, of home, of your family, of the church? Who was that, pleading like a skilful advocate in front of a judge, calling to mind every good point from the past in order to help his case? Whose voice was it? It was your divine Counsellor. He was pleading the truth and making reply to every argument of sin. Where would you and I be today were it not for that blessed ministry of the Spirit? What if he had left us without a word? Jesus loved people enough to plead with them to give up their sin. The Holy Spirit does so, too.

✎ *Dear Father, I lay at your feet the tribute of gratitude that fills my soul today as I reflect on the many times your Holy Spirit has pleaded in my heart against every argument of sin. My gratitude is yours for ever. Amen.*

A piercing question

FOR READING AND MEDITATION – ROMANS 8:1–11

' "You do not want to leave too, do you?" Jesus asked the Twelve.' (v. 67: NIV)

We look now at a fourth characteristic of an effective counsellor – the ability to summarise a confused situation in such a way that the person being counselled sees clearly the direction in which they ought to go.

It was a critical moment in our Lord's career. The loud burst of applause was now over. The crowds were melting away, and he had deliberately wrecked his chance of success. Surely he was making things unnecessarily difficult, they must have thought; converts would soon find out for themselves the cost of discipleship. Why frighten them off early with a too-realistic recital of the facts? Discerning the unspoken thoughts of his followers and perceiving the mental and spiritual confusion they were in, Jesus brought the issue to a head: 'You do not want to leave too, do you?' Our Lord's question probably caused the disciples' minds to range far and wide. Who would replace Jesus? Where could one find a satisfactory alternative? Peter considered the possibilities. Would Hillel do? Or Shammai? Or Gamaliel? No. The Saviour's dramatic question had put the whole issue into clear perspective. Peter's reply was magnificent: 'Lord, to whom shall we go? You have the words of eternal life' (v. 68). No more perplexity, no more confusion. The Master's piercing question had left them in no doubt about the direction in which they should go.

Father, how reassuring it is to know that the ability to resolve confusion has been granted to the Holy Spirit. Help me draw on that gift. Amen.

Light for the way ahead

FOR READING AND MEDITATION – PSALM 73:1–28
'You guide me with your counsel ...'(v. 24: NIV)

One of the characteristics of a good counsellor is the ability to summarise a confused situation in such a way that the person being
counselled sees clearly the direction in which he or she ought to go.
Time and time again, when the disciples seemed unsure about
what they should do, Jesus would step in and say something that
illuminated the path ahead. This is the work of the Holy Spirit also.
God guides us with his counsel, but it is the specific ministry of the
Spirit to apply that guidance to our hearts. 'He,' said Jesus, speaking
of the Holy Spirit, 'will guide you into all truth' (John 16:13). It is the
Spirit who helps to clarify the issues that puzzle us and assists us in
seeing clearly the next step we must take.

All of us can remember moments in our life when we dropped
to our knees in confusion and cried out, 'Lord, what shall I do now?'
And all of us can remember moments when through the Holy
Spirit's ministry of guidance that prayer was answered. The divine
Counsellor remains at hand to bring clarity and illumination to our
minds whenever we need it. That guidance comes in different ways
– through Scripture, through circumstances, through sanctified
reasoning or through the Spirit speaking directly to our hearts.

✎ O God, you know how many times I can't think straight. At such times I
am so glad that your Holy Spirit is at hand to help me. All honour and glory
be to your precious Name. Amen.

A sense of being led

FOR READING AND MEDITATION – ROMANS 8:12–17

'... those who are led by the Spirit of God are sons of God.' (v. 14: NIV)

Why is it so necessary for Christians to receive divine guidance as they make their way through this world? Because we are carrying out purposes that are not our own. Thus every one of us must have a sense of instrumentation, of being guided by our God, of fulfilling a will that is ultimate. Without a sense of being led, life hangs at loose ends, lacks a goal, and lacks also the dynamic necessary to attain a goal.

'Anybody got a car that is going anywhere?' asked someone at the end of a weekend Christian conference. It sounded as if that person wanted to go somewhere but the destination didn't really matter. Much of our life may be like that – lacking direction or goals. If we lose the sense of being led by the Spirit we become victims of our circumstances. Guidance by the Holy Spirit, is the very essence of Christianity. In some Christian circles to talk of being guided by the Holy Spirit brings an adverse reaction. This reaction is most revealing. It shows how content we are to have a knowledge of God but not an acquaintance with God. If we are not being led by God, how can we claim to be his sons and daughters?

O God, forgive us for forgetting so often that we are carrying out purposes that are not our own. Help us walk through life with a sense of being divinely led at all times. In Christ's Name we ask it. Amen.

God where it counts

FOR READING AND MEDITATION – ACTS 2:1–21

'All of them were filled with the Holy Spirit ...' (v. 4: NIV)

We pause on this day to remind ourselves that the coming of the Holy Spirit has put the resources of the Trinity where they count – within. A little boy in Sunday school defines the Holy Spirit as 'God in action'. He is! The disciples were so fearful prior to Pentecost. They seemed to lack nerve, direction and a sense of reinforcement within ... until the Holy Spirit came. Then they were transformed and became invincible.

Theologians debate as to whether the last twelve verses of Mark's Gospel are part of his original text. Some say they were added by a later writer. If not, then Mark's Gospel ends with the words of chapter 16 verse 8: 'They said nothing to anyone, because they were afraid.' Suppose there had been no Pentecost. Then the gospel story would have ended at this point. The end of it all would have been that the disciples 'said nothing to anyone, because they were afraid'. The four Gospels without the Upper Room would have proclaimed a powerless gospel. But the Holy Spirit did come. Jesus said he would go away but that he would come again to them – in the power and presence of the Spirit. The coming of the Spirit has put God and Christ in the most vital place – within.

✎ O God, on this day when we your people celebrate the descent of the Spirit at Pentecost, come again and flood us out by a deluge of your Spirit. Enlarge our vision and set our hearts on fire. Give us more of your Spirit, dear Lord. In Jesus' Name. Amen.

Sub-Christian living

FOR READING AND MEDITATION – PSALM 48:1–14

'For this God … will be our guide even to the end.' (v. 14: NIV)

We return to focus again on the point we were considering – that the Holy Spirit is our Guide. 'If we are not conscious of being guided in our lives day by day,' said Dr Cyndyllan Jones, 'then we are living at a level that is sub-Christian.' Strong words. God wants to guide us not only in times of emergency, but at all times. One of the blessings of having the Holy Spirit within, is that we gain the sense of being led. And also the practical benefits that come from it. How aware are we of this?

I was struck by this statement made to a group of ministers in the United States by an evangelist with a reputation for 'telling it as it is': 'Some of the most active church leaders,' he said, 'well known for their executive efficiency, people we tend to admire, will have a shock in heaven when in the X-ray light of eternity they will be seen as agitated, half-committed, wistful, self-placating seekers to whom the power and serenity of the Everlasting had never come.' God being who he is – the Architect of fine detail – must have a purpose for every life. If we turn our backs on that idea, then, as Dr Jones put it, we are at a level that is sub-Christian.

✎ *Gracious Father, you have paid attention to the minute, fashioning the lowest cell with your hands. Help me to find the plan you have for my life, pay the price of working out that plan, and make it the adventure of my life. Amen.*

Continuous guidance

FOR READING AND MEDITATION – 2 CORINTHIANS 5:11–21
'We are therefore Christ's ambassadors …' (v. 20: NIV)

God has a plan and a purpose for every life. Each life has peculiar significance. If we find that plan of God for us and work within it, we cannot fail. Outside of that plan we cannot succeed. To be the instrument of the purposes of God is the highest thing in life.

On one occasion I heard a preacher say that whenever he stands up to preach, he reminds himself of this verse: 'You did not choose me, but I chose you and appointed you to go and bear fruit' (John 15:16). Repeating it gives me the sense of being sent with the backing of the Eternal One, and of speaking in a Name not my own. But it also lays on me a sense of obligation to surrender and be obedient to the working out of God's plan. It gives life a sense of mission and submission.

You may not have been called to preach, but you have been called to be an ambassador for Christ. An ambassador must weigh his words carefully. Everyone must feel that sense of being a representative. We are speaking, thinking, acting in a Name that is not our own. That is why guidance is a matter of the continuous.

❧ *O God, I begin to see that if I am to live, I must live in you. For you are the way to life and my way of life. When I find your plan, I find my person. Give me an understanding of what it means to be guided continuously. In Jesus' Name. Amen.*

Guidance demands surrender

FOR READING AND MEDITATION – PSALM 25:1–22

'He guides the humble in what is right and teaches them his way.' (v. 9: NIV)

We must note how important it is to be guided by the Holy Spirit not occasionally, but continuously. If we are Christians, we must walk through the world with a sense of mission. 'The significance of life,' I have read, 'is determined by the significance of what it is identified with and what it represents.' A sense of mission brings a sense of submission. Instead of making you proud, it makes you feel awed and humbled. You want to walk softly before God. You are on what has been called 'the adventure of humility'.

The whole thought of guidance strikes at the citadel of the personality and demands the surrender of self-sufficiency. If we are to be guided, then there must be a shifting from self-will to God's will. God's will becomes your constant frame of reference. Guidance should not be a spiritual luxury for a few souls, but the minimum necessity for every Christian. Remember the text of a few days ago: 'Those who are led by the Spirit of God are sons of God' (Rom 8:14)? Guidance is the very essence of Christianity. It gives mission to life – and demands submission.

Father, I see that I have been made in the very structure of my being for your ways. Your will is my peace. My will is my war. I am eager to know your mind, not only in moments of confusion, but always and in every area of my life. For Jesus' sake. Amen.

Healthy dependency

FOR READING AND MEDITATION – ISAIAH 8:11–22

'… should not a people enquire of their God?' (v. 19: NIV)

It's surprising how many Christians know little about his guidance. Hence their impact upon life is feeble. We have seen that God wants to guide us not just sometimes, but at all times. But the divine Counsellor's concern for us is the same as Christ's concern for his disciples – to guide and not to override.

Where I grew up, milk was supplied by two farmers who brought it daily to each home on a horse-drawn cart. I noticed that one farmer would lead his horse from one house to the next. The other had trained his horse to move at a command – stop or go. The first horse was helpless without the step-by-step guide. The other had more freedom. The Spirit guides us in a way that brings us to a point of healthy dependency. 'You Christians are so weak and lacking in courage,' a man once said to me, 'that you have to look to God before you make any move in life.' He had no idea of what he was saying, for if he had known how deeply entrenched in all of us is a spirit of independence, he would have realised that one of the biggest struggles we have is to bring our sinful and stubborn natures into submission to the divine will. Our need to be guided is often greater than our willingness.

Gracious Father, I bring my independent spirit to you for you to harness it and bring it under your control. I recognise there is still something in me that prefers my way to yours. But I want your way to be my way. Help me, dear Father. Amen.

Five forms of guidance

FOR READING AND MEDITATION – ACTS 8:26–40

'The Spirit told Philip, "Go to that chariot and stay near it" ' (v. 29: NIV)

The Holy Spirit must guide us, but also develop us as persons. 'Many parents are benevolent tyrants,' says a child psychologist, 'who snuff out all initiative and personality in their children. Guidance must be such that each person is guided into a free, self-conscious, choosing, creative personality.'

These are the general routes to guidance: First, guidance according to the *character of Christ*. We know God wants us to be like his Son. Second, guidance through *his Word*. He makes the Bible come alive to us, and throws a beam of light on the path ahead. Third, guidance through *circumstances* – putting us in situations where the circumstances indicate the direction in which we ought to go. Fourth, guidance through *the counsel of good and godly people*. Fifth, guidance through *the direct whispering of the Spirit within us*. This is a form of guidance that is clearly laid down in Scripture. Some call it 'the inner voice'. However, we must always be sure that the inner voice is the Spirit's voice, not our own.

𝒩 *Father, I am thankful for all the ways you guide me, and also for all the times you have guided me. But teach me more about how to distinguish your inner voice from the other voices that are heard in my soul. In Jesus' Name. Amen.*

Listen!

FOR READING AND MEDITATION – 1 SAMUEL 3:1–21
'Then Samuel said, "Speak, for your servant is listening." ' (v. 10: NIV)

If our divine Counsellor is willing to guide us, how do we recognise his voice when he speaks to us? 'My sheep know my voice,' Jesus told his disciples categorically (John 10:3–5). When I hear my mother's voice on the phone, I know it immediately. 'Ah,' you say, 'but a voice in your ear is a lot easier to discern than a voice in your soul.' Granted, but there is a way to tune in to the voice of the Spirit and learn to hear his accent in your soul. Train your spiritual ear to listen. When the king complained to Joan of Arc that he never heard the voice of God, she replied, 'You must listen, then you will hear.'

There are two main reasons why people fail to hear the Spirit's voice: their spiritual ears are untrained or they are unwilling. 'Your will be done' becomes 'Your will be borne'. When you commune with God, give as much time to listening as you do to talking. At first you will not be able to distinguish the voice of the subconscious from the voice of the Spirit, but in time the differentiation will be possible. Sometimes, of course, the Spirit booms so loudly in the soul that his voice is unmistakable. But it is more the exception. Usually he speaks quietly, and to a soul that is quiet before him.

✎ *O God, forgive me if I attempt to take short cuts in my spiritual life by being unwilling to go through the training. Help me to talk less and listen more in my daily communion with you. In Jesus' Name. Amen.*

The great Teacher

FOR READING AND MEDITATION – JOHN 3:1–15

' "You are Israel's teacher,"' said Jesus,
"and do you not understand these things?" ' (v. 10: NIV)

Yet another quality a counsellor should possess, is a basic ability to teach. There is a lot to be said for this approach, as it shows respect for a person's individuality and encourages them to develop their own decision-making processes. However, true Christian counselling is at times non-directive, and at other times directive. Individuals who are struggling with a problem, need clear direction on how to avail themselves of Christ's resources, and to provide a basic ability to teach. Note the word *basic*. A counsellor does not need to be an expert teacher, but he or she does need to be able to show a person how to take the steps that lead from where they are to where they should be.

Our Lord provides the supreme example of what and how to teach. No one can hold a candle to Christ's ministry – either in the Old Testament or in the New Testament. He is seen in the Gospels teaching huge crowds, then at other times small groups. Here we see him teaching an individual – Nicodemus – the principles of what we call *the new birth*. Around 19 such private conferences are recorded in the Gospels, when Jesus is seen closeted with a seeking soul and teaching him or her the steps to abundant living. Our Lord taught as no others have taught – before or since.

Loving heavenly Father, how can I ever thank you enough for your Son Jesus? What he has taught the world is wonderful, but what he did for us on the cross is even more wonderful. Amen.

Our Lord's authority

'… he taught as one who had authority,
and not as their teachers of the law.' (v. 29: NIV)

Let's look again at why our Lord's great teaching ministry was so powerful while he was here on earth. We see that the crowds were simply spellbound by the things he said. A verse similar to our text is found in Mark: 'They were all so amazed … saying: Whatever is this? It's new teaching with authority behind it' (1:27, MOFFATT). Obviously it was the 'authority' with which Jesus spoke that arrested people's attention. Other teachers quoted authorities, but Jesus spoke with authority. What was that authority? It was the authority of the facts. He was lifting up the meaning of life, the meaning of the laws and principles underlying life. He was uncovering reality.

Many people make the tragic mistake of regarding Jesus as a moralist imposing a moral code upon humanity which humanity was not made for. Jesus was not a moralist in that sense. He was the Revealer of the nature of reality. He revealed first the nature and character of God, and went on to show how the nature and character of God is the ground of God's conduct and ours. He then lifted up the laws of effective living and showed us that there is just no other way to live. It was not imposed idealism, but exposed realism. Reality itself was speaking. No wonder it was 'authoritative'.

✒ Lord Jesus Christ, when I look upon you, I know I am looking at Life. Your words take me to the heart of reality – the nature and character of a loving God. I am deeply thankful. Amen.

The Spirit – our Teacher

FOR READING AND MEDITATION – 1 JOHN 2:18–27

'… his anointing teaches you about all things …' (v. 27: NIV)

Our Lord's expert teaching ministry was not lost to the church when he returned to heaven. The Holy Spirit continues that ministry. What did our Lord mean when he said 'all' things (John 14:26)? Let me share with you the views of a prominent agnostic: 'The great difference between Christianity and science is that Christianity is fixed, but science isn't. Science is open and progressive because it is not fixed in terms of absolutes and non-optional dogmas.' While this is entirely true, it is not true entirely.

In the Person and teaching of Christ we have God's full and complete disclosure. The revelation which God has given us through Christ is final in the sense that nothing will be taught that is different from it, but we must see that it is also progressive and unfolding. The Holy Spirit brings out from the words and teaching of Christ new understanding, challenges and insights. These are all found in our Lord's words, in embryonic form at least, but the Spirit takes them and leads us to deeper comprehension. The divine Counsellor will teach us all Jesus taught, but not other than Jesus taught.

✎ *Father, I see that here is both conservatism and radicalism. The Spirit conserves all that Jesus taught, at the same time opening up from it radical new dimensions. Truth is fixed, yet unfolding. I am so grateful. Amen.*

Lopsided Christianity

FOR READING AND MEDITATION – JOHN 16:5–16

'But when he, the Spirit of truth, comes,
he will guide you into all truth.' (v. 13: NIV)

We linger on the words of our Lord in John 14:26: 'The Counsellor ... will teach you all things.' A similar affirmation is given in the verse before us now. We concluded yesterday that the Holy Spirit is at work in our hearts, unfolding all the words recorded for us in the Gospels, and thus leading us into all truth. There is another aspect of the word 'all'. When we are not under the Holy Spirit's guidance, we can soon become focused on one thing that Jesus taught and neglect the *all*.

Francis Schaeffer pointed out that the church in every age has made the mistake of taking some of Jesus' words, putting a fence around them, and claiming a particular emphasis as their own. This leads to a lopsided Christianity with an over-emphasis on some things and an under-emphasis on others. Sometimes whole denominations are in this way built around one truth. They live on a truth instead of on the Truth. Thus they have to be controversial to justify their lopsidedness. Christians who are truly open to the movement of the Holy Spirit in their lives will be creative rather than controversial.

❧ *O God my Father, move me from living on just one truth or even a cluster of truths. I want to live on all the truth. For I know I will become what I feed upon. Help me, my Father. In Jesus' Name I pray. Amen.*

Go the second mile

FOR READING AND MEDITATION – ROMANS 8:1–11

'When the Counsellor comes … he will testify about me.' (v. 67: NIV)

The Holy Spirit is not only our divine Teacher, but also our divine Remembrancer. He promises to bring back to our remembrance all that Jesus said. It doesn't mean that the Holy Spirit will magically bring into our minds the words of Jesus if we have not taken the time to read them and ponder them. Some time ago I met a man who told me he never read the Gospels because he believed the Holy Spirit's ministry was to bring home to him the things Jesus said. I pointed out that Jesus promised, '[He] will remind you of everything I have said …' (John 14:26). It implies that Jesus' words are already in our memory, and the Holy Spirit's work is to prompt us in ways that ensure we do not forget them. He was unconvinced. He suggested that I had lost my faith in the supernatural.

The fact that the divine Counsellor is ready to remind us of the words of Jesus is one of the greatest arguments for soaking our minds in Scripture where Jesus' words are recorded. The more we expose ourselves to his words, the more easily the Spirit can remind us of them. Recently a colleague and I were struggling to come to a decision about an important issue, when the Spirit reminded us of Jesus' instruction: 'Go the second mile.' We laughed for we knew that naturally it was not what we wanted to do. The divine Counsellor, however, thought differently.

✗ O God, I am especially thankful for the words of Jesus. They are my life, my energy, my spiritual substance. May I take every opportunity to expose my mind to them. For Jesus' sake. Amen.

Truth hurts

FOR READING AND MEDITATION – JOHN 16:5–16
'But when he, the Spirit of truth, comes,
he will guide you into all truth.' (v. 13: NIV)

Our text for today tells us that the Holy Spirit will guide us into all truth. What does this really mean? Sometimes a teacher is able to teach a certain truth but is unable to guide someone into it. When this happens in a church setting, it is a matter of concern, but when it happens in a counselling session, it is even more worrying. A counsellor should be able to teach the truth and guide a person into it. Councellors can ask: 'Do you understand what I have been saying? How do you respond to what I have just said?' Counsellors are taught never to present an insight to someone without checking that the person understands what is being said and making sure they are following them every step of the way. Counsellors know, too, that if they present to someone a truth that is challenging or demanding, the personality more often than not becomes adept at looking for ways of escape. It puts up defences or seeks to minimise the impact of a challenging truth through denial and rationalisation. Thus skill is needed not only to present the truth, but to outmanoeuvre the objections, overcome the difficulties, gently rebut the arguments, and thus guide people into possession of the truth.

The Holy Spirit is an expert not only in teaching truth, but in guiding us into it.

✣ *My Father and my God, I recognise the truth of this of the Holy Spirit's guidance and am deeply humbled by it. I can only wonder and cry: 'Thank you, my Father.' In Jesus' Name. Amen.*

The Spirit of truth

FOR READING AND MEDITATION –
1 CORINTHIANS 2:10B–16 AND GALATIANS 1:11–12

'... we speak, not in words taught us by human wisdom
but in words taught us by the Spirit ...' (1 Cor. 2:13)

We thank God for the wondrous ministry of the divine Counsellor who expertly guides us into the possession of the truths. I wonder sometimes whether we have too limited a view of the promise by Jesus that the Counsellor will guide us into all truth. Could it be that the Holy Spirit wants to lead us also into the truth about everything?

Think about times in your past when the Holy Spirit has guided you to put the truth about a matter into clear perspective. Can't that be understood as the Spirit guiding you into all truth? Have there been occasions in your life when you needed to understand the truth about a matter that was causing you confusion and then, in a relatively short time, everything seemed to open up? Could it have been the work of the Holy Spirit? That kind of situation has occurred thousands of times in my own life, but I have never thought of it in terms of the Spirit of truth. Can the promise of being guided into truth be seen also in the way the Spirit opens up a difficult scripture, or the truth regarding both options in a difficult decision? Why can't these be part of the truth which Jesus promised would be disclosed to you and me? Our Lord was an expert Teacher. And so is the Holy Spirit.

⁂ *Father, when I think of the insights I might have missed in the Bible, I realise more than ever that you are truly the Spirit of truth. I both revel and rejoice in it. In Jesus' Name. Amen.*

Being there

FOR READING AND MEDITATION – MATTHEW 16:21–28; 17:1–11

'After six days Jesus took with him Peter,
James and John the brother of James …' (v. 1: NIV)

The last qualification of a counsellor is the ability to come alongside someone who is hurt, and support them in their pain. It is
described as 'being there for someone'. One illustration is seen in
today's passage. It is suggested by the simple phrase 'after six days'
(17:1). It is linked to the preceding events. Dr G. Campbell Morgan
deduced that when the disciples discovered their Master was going
to a cross, they drew back in dismay. It will be seen that during this
period there was a sense of estrangement between the disciples
and the Master. Peter had gone so far as attempting to dissuade
Christ from even thinking about going to a cross. Christ's fore-
telling of his death seemed to make the idea of Messiahship impossible. The disciples wanted to reign with Jesus; he wanted to go
to a cross. The six days of confusion would be ended by the act of
Transfiguration, but what must it have been like for our Lord and
his disciples as they walked together? He was pained by their failure to understand; they were pained by the revelation that their
concept of Messiahship did not appear to match his. But did he
leave these misunderstanding disciples and go it alone? No, he
stayed with them. He was there for them even when they were not
there for him.

✎ *My Father and my God, the more I see of your Son, the more my heart
adores him. And I know that in adoring him I am adoring you. For you are
One. I cannot understand it, but yet I stand upon it. Amen.*

Non-verbal but empowering

FOR READING AND MEDITATION – JOB 16:1–22

'I have heard many things like these; miserable comforters are you all!' (v. 2: NIV)

We saw yesterday how our Lord was there for his disciples when none of them was fully following him. Being there is not giving advice; it is saying in non-verbal ways: 'This is not the time for talking, but, as far as I am able, I want to bear the pain with you.' I remember being faced with a distressing problem early in my life. Everyone I consulted suggested there must be some sin in my life, otherwise I would be problem-free. Finally, a man who was an incurable stutterer put his arm around me, and then, drawing back, placed his hands together in an expression of prayer as if to say, 'I can't help you on the verbal level, but I will be there for you in prayer.' That meant more to me than any words.

A little while ago I talked to a man whose wife had made his life almost impossible for a number of years. She humiliated him in front of friends, telephoned his boss and told lies about him, ran up debts that he was expected to pay, and ill-treated him. 'How are you handling it?' His reply moved me deeply: 'My only wish is that I might be able through a Christlike attitude to give her a taste of how much God loves her, and, above all else, my longing is to be there for her until she leaves this world for eternity.' I thought, 'Those words could be from the Holy Spirit.'

✎ O God, thank you for those in my life who have been there for me during a time of pain or sorrow. May I, in turn, be there for someone who needs me now or at any time in the future. I ask this through your Son's worthy and wonderful Name. Amen.

Counsellor and Comforter

FOR READING AND MEDITATION – ISAIAH 66:5–13

'As a mother comforts her child, so will I comfort you ...' (v. 13)

Let's face it, some of the problems we encounter will not go away, no matter how hard we pray. So what sort of help can we expect from our divine Counsellor? He will be there for us – empowering us sharing our pain and entering into all our sorrows. The translators of the NIV were all scholars. When deciding upon a name in English for the Holy Spirit, they therefore leaned toward a word that suggests the giving of advice or verbal direction.

But I have often noticed that the translators chose words with an intellectual ring – words which seem to be lacking in feeling. For instance, 2 Corinthians 5:14 is translated 'Christ's love compels us' in the NIV, whereas the NKJV translates it, 'The love of Christ constrains us.' See what I mean? The word *constrains* has a feel which the word *compels* does not have. The Greek term for the Holy Spirit is *parakletos*, derived from *para* (beside) and *kaleo* (call), and means 'one who comes alongside to help'. I wish the word could be translated 'Counsellor and Comforter' – a phrase which would convey the fuller idea that the Holy Spirit is not just someone who gives us advice, but someone who feels for us and with us.

✣ O Father, how is it possible that the Holy Spirit feels for me and with me in my problems and at the same time with all my brothers and sisters also? What strength he must have – what resources! And best of all, those resources are available to me. Thank you, my Father. Amen.

The ultimate Counsellor

FOR READING AND MEDITATION – 2 CORINTHIANS 7:1–16

'But God, who comforts the downcast,
comforted us by the coming of Titus ...' (v. 6)

The Holy Spirit is a Counsellor who does more than give us advice;
he enters into our hurts, empathises with our pain, and is there for
us in every difficult situation of life. *The Amplified Bible* translates
John 14:26: 'But the Comforter the Holy Spirit, whom the Father will
send in my Name ... he will teach you all things.' The Holy Spirit is
a Counsellor who has everything. The ability to give good advice?
Yes. The ability to empower with divine strength? Yes. The ability to
be our Advocate? Yes. The ability to pray through us when we don't
know what to ask in prayer for ourselves? Yes. The ability to stand by
us when we are overcome with worry? To comfort us? Yes! Yes! Yes!
There isn't a single thing we need in life that he isn't able to provide.

The word Comforter – *con* (with) and *fortis* (strength) – means
one who strengthens you by being with you. Prior to her death, my
wife spent many hours sleeping. At first I would steal away to my
study and work after she had gone to sleep, but she told me on one
occasion that even in her sleep she could sense whether or not I was
there. 'Just sensing you are at my side,' she said, 'is more of a comfort
to me than I can ever explain.' I have had the same thought at times
in relation to the Holy Spirit, haven't you?

✎ *Gracious Father, as I learn more of the resources of your Spirit my heart
becomes increasingly grateful. Your Spirit is a Counsellor who has everything. He specialises not in one thing, but in all things. Help me absorb all
this. In Jesus' Name. Amen.*

The Spirit's first work

FOR READING AND MEDITATION – ACTS 2:29–41

'… Repent and be baptised … and you will
receive the gift of the Holy Spirit.' (v. 38: NIV)

Some claim that the first task of the Holy Spirit is not really a work at all. Primarily, they say, he is there to be with us. If this is so, then we must see that our preoccupation with gifts rather than the Giver is entirely out of place. Many Christians seem to be more taken up with possessing the gifts of the Spirit than possessing the Holy Spirit himself. He is the gift, and although we are instructed by Paul in 1 Corinthians 14:1 to 'eagerly desire spiritual gifts', this does not mean that we are to think more highly of the gifts than the Giver.

In today's text Peter talks about the Holy Spirit being the gift. He is the gift of gifts, and when he is with us and in us, he supplies us with the gifts that enhance our spiritual effectiveness. Early in my Christian experience I made the mistake many make today. I was brought up in a church where great emphasis was placed on the gifts of the Spirit, but little on the Giver. Thus I went over all the gifts mentioned in the New Testament. I then laid out my shopping list before the Lord and said, 'Father, these are the gifts I want from you.' The Spirit whispered to my heart, 'Are the gifts more important than the Giver?' This gentle rebuke helped me to see that I was more interested in the gifts of the Spirit than the Spirit who gave the gifts.

O Father, forgive me if I have been making more of the gifts than the Giver. I don't want to do anything that will, grieve or quench the Holy Spirit. Steer me away from all dangers, dear Lord. In Jesus' Name. Amen.

Trust my love

FOR READING AND MEDITATION – JOB 42:1–17

'My ears had heard of you but now my eyes have seen you.' (v. 5: NIV)

There are occasions in life when problems don't go away, despite our most ardent praying. At such times the divine Counsellor ministers to us his comfort and supernatural strength. When I was a little boy, I was taken to hospital to have my tonsils removed. When I entered the place, I became very frightened. Looking up to my mother, I said, 'Do I have to go through with this? Will it hurt? Will I die under the anaesthetic?' My mother could have given me all the medical reasons why the operation should be performed, but I would not have understood. So she simply said, 'I can't save you from it, my dear. For your own good this has to be done, but some day you will understand. You must trust my love. I shan't leave you and I will be here waiting for you when you come out of the anaesthetic.' That boyhood experience has been a parable to me.

There have been many times in my life when the Holy Spirit has whispered in my soul, 'I cannot shield you from this. You will have to go through it, and you may feel some pain. But I will be with you all the way.' Job never got the answers he wanted to his questions, but he received something better: he came through his experiences with a richer sense of God's presence than he had ever felt before.

✎ O God my Father, your presence made real in my soul through the Holy Spirit is worth more to me than anything. I would far rather have a problem-filled life with you than a problem-free life without you. Thank you, Father. In Jesus' Name. Amen.

Supernatural comfort

FOR READING AND MEDITATION – ACTS 9:19B-31

'… the church … was strengthened; and encouraged by
the Holy Spirit, it grew in numbers …' (v. 31: NIV)

The comforting ministry of the Holy Spirit is not simply a theory; it is a glorious fact. Who has not felt the divine Counsellor's consoling presence during a time of personal difficulty? Early in my ministry I thought it was my task alone to bring comfort to people in distress. I remember on one occasion receiving a gentle rebuke from the Lord. As a young minister, every week seemed to bring its batch of difficulties. I confess there were times when my spirit rebelled. Constant contact with people drained me of energy. This drove me to prayer, but sometimes my prayers became complaints. I said to the Lord, 'I can't keep going into the homes of people who are repeatedly submerged in sorrow, give them sympathy and talk about a God of love.' Then God reminded me that beyond any comfort I could give, was that of the Holy Spirit. His work was to bestow not human but supernatural comfort. I must do my part and trust him to do his. When I realised that Another was ministering along with me to the sick, the suffering and the bereaved, I began to relax and turn over the major part of the task to him.

All who belong to Christ are expected to minister comfort to each other, but the biggest share belongs to the Holy Spirit. We comfort; he is the Comforter.

✎ *O Father, how reassuring it is to know that your Spirit is moving through your Body even now, using some to bring comfort to others, but also adding his own supernatural brand. Thank you, my Father. Amen.*

Grace – simply amazing

FOR READING AND MEDITATION – 2 CORINTHIANS 12:1–10

'Three times I pleaded with the Lord to take it away from me.' (v. 8: NIV)

How reassuring it is to know that the Holy Spirit is comfort. The passage before us is a classic example. Paul doesn't tell us what his problem was, but uses a metaphor – a thorn in the flesh – which is used elsewhere in Scripture to convey a troublesome issue. Many have speculated about that 'thorn', but no one knows for sure what it was. One preacher joked that Paul had a thorn in the flesh and no one knows what it was; if we have a thorn in the flesh, everyone knows what it is! Paul asked the Lord three times to take it away, but the answer was 'No'. The problem was to remain. But in the midst of his trouble God began to pour into Paul a special supply of his comforting grace; grace to accept the 'No', grace to endure the discomfort, and grace to handle the pain.

But how does grace work? Like this: you find yourself undergoing a period of testing and your heart becomes heavy. You lose your appetite, struggle with insomnia, and become increasingly irritated. Then you go to prayer. As you pray, the heaviness in your spirit continues, but then, suddenly, it is as if a weight is lifted from you. You breathe more easily and your spirit feels a little lighter. What has happened? Some might call it 'a spontaneous sense of relief'. Those who know, call it grace.

✎ O Father, I am seeing now something I always wanted to see but hardly dared believe – you never allow a problem to remain in my life without supplying me with the comfort and grace that sees me through. All honour and glory be unto you. Amen.

Brave if not blithe

FOR READING AND MEDITATION – ISAIAH 49:8–16
'Shout for joy, O heavens … For the Lord comforts his people
and will have compassion on his afflicted ones.' (v. 13: NIV)

In a fallen world we are confronted with issues which produce almost inconsolable pain. Sir Arthur Conan Doyle tells he constantly saw sights which he could not reconcile with the idea of a merciful God. He tells of going into a home where there was a small cot, and by a gesture from the mother he sensed the problem lay there. He picked up a candle, walked to the cot and stooped over it, expecting to find a young child. What he saw, was a pair of brown sullen eyes full of loathing and pain. He could not tell its age. Long, thin limbs were twisted, the face malignant. 'What is it?' he asked in dismay. 'It's a girl,' sobbed the mother. 'She's 19. Oh, if only God would take her.'

We have no adequate answers to explain such matters. It's easy to brush perplexing circumstances aside, but that still leaves huge issues unresolved. Why did God allow sin to strike the universe in such a way? Even if God gave us clear answers, I am not sure we would be able to understand them. We will understand everything one day, but meanwhile God simply says, 'Here's my comfort, you can get by with this.' In moments of bewilderment we need comfort. It may not keep us blithe, but it will keep us brave.

✤ *O God my Father, I see that no matter what happens to me and no matter how many problems I am called upon to face, you provide all the comfort and strength I need to carry on. Others may fail me, but you – never. Thank you, Lord. Amen.*

When the world goes grey

FOR READING AND MEDITATION – PSALM 86:1–17

'… you, O Lord, have helped me and comforted me.' (v. 17: NIV)

Sooner or later every one of us needs comfort. It does not matter how strong we may be, the time will come when we need to feel God's solace. The Holy Spirit is the Minister of grace. He is the One who brings into our hearts the resources of the Godhead. Let us never forget that.

Some, when needing comfort, turn to drink. But there is no real comfort to be found in the cup. Drink can no more cure our sorrows than an anaesthetic can cure a cancer. Robert Burns, Edgar Allan Poe and others have tried it and discovered that it only aggravates the trouble it was taken to heal. Others turn to literature. Relief can be found in a library. I love literature and have made it a habit to read several books a week. But in time of real sorrow there is no adequate comfort in books. You will not find your favourite author very comforting when the doctor diagnoses a serious medical problem. Novels will not be very effective on the day you come home from the cemetery. What about nature, or music, or art? They can be helpful supplements, but they can never be substitutes. They are not a fount of comfort in themselves. From a lifetime of facing trials, including bereavement, the only sure comfort when all the world has gone grey, is the comfort of God.

O Father, how reliable is your comfort. There are few things in life I can depend on, but I can depend on this. May the truth of this grip my soul and strengthen it today and every day. In Christ's Name I ask it. Amen.

Is optimism enough?

FOR READING AND MEDITATION – JEREMIAH 8:14–22

'Is there no balm in Gilead?' (v. 22: NIV)

There are those who advocate optimism as the way to approach life's problems. Sometimes posters are designed to catch people's attention with a cheerful word. Once I was on my way to a home that had been stunned by an awful bereavement, wondering what I would say to the distressed family. As I passed a church, I caught sight of a large poster that advised, 'Cheer up – it may never happen.' I remember shouting out in my car, 'But it has happened!' There is no lift in optimism in an hour like that. Like the nerveless needle of a broken barometer, it continues to point, even in a storm, to 'very fair'. No, the only reality we can depend upon in the hard and cruel world is the consolation of the Holy Spirit.

It saddens me about the day in which we live that few people read the biographies of the early missionaries any more. Many of them contain dramatic instances of the way in which the Holy Spirit comforts and consoles. Take Allan Francis Gardiner for example. He and his companions found themselves on Picton Island in the most difficult circumstances imaginable. It is hard to read the story without tears welling up. Yet, in his diary he wrote, 'Great and marvellous are the loving kindnesses of my gracious God to me.'

◆ Father, thank you for the balm that is available to every one of your wounded children through the gentle and comforting ministry of the Holy Spirit. I have known this solace, and so will millions more who need it this day. Blessed be your Name forever. Amen.

Wait till you get home

FOR READING AND MEDITATION – REVELATION 20:11–15; 21:1–5

'He will wipe every tear from their eyes.' (v. 4: NIV)

We have been emphasising that we are not always going to receive answers to the difficult questions that arise during our lifetime. Questions such as these: Why has God allowed this? What possible good can come from it? How can a loving God permit such a thing? A good deal of frustration can be avoided if we settle for the fact that God knows what he is doing.

I heard a minister tell how when he was a boy, he went to a youth camp for a month. Within a few days he had run out of money. The incident occurred earlier in the century when few people had telephones, so he sent a telegram to his father saying, 'SOS. More money please.' To his surprise no answer came. The first week ended and there was no answer. The second passed, again without an answer. His friends began to explain his father's silence in their own way. 'He has forgotten you are here,' said one. 'He is too busy to bother with you,' decided another. Then one of his companions asked him, 'What do you think?' He said, 'I don't know. I'll give him the benefit of the doubt. I'll wait until I get home and ask him myself.' Once home, his father explained, 'You needed to learn the value of money. Hard though it was for me, I saw this was the best way I could teach it to you.' The answers you don't get here, you'll get in eternity. Here, however, you are guaranteed the strength you need to carry on.

✎ *O Father, I have no guarantee that all my questions will be answered down here, but I am guaranteed strength, grace and comfort to carry on. Thank you, dear Lord. In Jesus' Name. Amen.*

What happens now?

FOR READING AND MEDITATION – ROMANS 8:1–11
'Come near to God and he will come near to you.' (v. 8: NIV)

We end our meditations on this note: as we make our way toward heaven, life may be hard and perplexing, but God has given us his Holy Spirit to be our Counsellor along the way. Let's revisit the characteristics of this matchless Counsellor. (1) He seeks to draw out of us all the potential which God has built into us, and is continually at work developing us into the kind of person God sees us to be. (2) He prods us to prayer, and when we don't know how to pray as we ought, he takes over and prays in us and through us. (3) He brings hidden things to light in our souls and seeks to rid us of all sin. (4) He shines the laser beam of knowledge and wisdom through the fog that sometimes surrounds us, and guides us in ways of which we are both conscious and unconscious along the path he wants us to take. (5) He teaches us as no other could teach us, and leads us into the thing our hearts were built for – truth. (6) He comforts us whenever we are in need of solace, and strengthens our hearts to go on even though we have no clear answers.

How sad that despite the resources of our divine Counsellor we prefer to muddle through on our own. When we refuse to open up to him, to depend on him and consult him, we deprive ourselves of the love, wisdom and spiritual sustenance we need to live effectively and dynamically. Open up to him.

✎ O God, you have shown me the resources that are available to me through your Holy Spirit. I open my heart to you fully now. Seal my commitment with an overwhelming sense of your presence. In Christ's Name. Amen.

Silence!

FOR READING AND MEDITATION – ECCLESIASTES 1:1–2

"'Meaningless! Meaningless!" says the Teacher.
"Utterly meaningless! Everything is meaningless." ' (v. 2: NIV)

Ecclesiastes has been described as 'the most dangerous book in the Bible'. Why? In it one comes face to face with the utter futility of trying to find happiness and meaning in the things of time, and this could lead some to opt out of life altogether.

An old Jewish tradition says that when the sages met to fix the canon of the Old Testament, they debated fiercely whether or not to include a book that was so full of cynicism and doubt. But prayer and wisdom prevailed, and the book was included. I myself am satisfied that Solomon is the author of Ecclesiastes, although there is much scholarly discussion about this.

The main message is: 'Everything is meaningless.' Seeing the utter futility of life is the first step to an encounter with God. Many are not ready to meet with the Lord until they have been silenced by the futility of the world in which they live. Someone once said that the first book of the Bible everyone ought to read is Ecclesiastes – because it silences you. When we see as clearly as Solomon that the world does not provide us with the life for which we were created, we are more likely to turn to the true source of happiness – the eternal God himself. Let Ecclesiastes silence you – and in the silence experience God.

O God, use your Word once more to silence my soul. Do whatever is necessary to bring me to the realisation that what my soul longs for can only be fully found in you. Amen.

Life without God

FOR READING AND MEDITATION – ECCLESIASTES 1:3–7
'Generations come and generations go, but the earth remains for ever.' (v. 4: NIV)

Ecclesiastes first seeks to silence us with the utter futility of life before pointing us to the one and only reality – God. Today the author begins to drag us through the pointlessness and the emptiness of life in order to force us to look elsewhere than the world around us for the water that our souls so deeply crave.

Three things are said about life without God – it is boring, fleeting, and repetitive. 'What does man gain from all his labour …?' asks Solomon. Some people enjoy working for a living, but most don't. They watch the clock, fantasise, just to fill the time until work is over. If we do not see our work as imitating the creativity of God, then it can become exceedingly boring. 'Generations come and generations go,' says Solomon. We're on earth for a short time. Life is so fleeting. How small and insignificant it makes us feel.

Every morning the sun rises, sets, then the next day the same thing happens … and the next … Life is repetitive. The same with the wind. Where does it come from and where does it go? Rivers, too, are no different. They keep flowing into the sea, but the sea is never full. Life on this planet is not all gloom, of course, but it is clear that there is something about earth that just does not satisfy.

✣ Gracious and loving heavenly Father, drive this truth deeply into my spirit that I am made by you, made for you, and my heart will never be content until it is filled with you. Indwell every empty space within me. In Jesus' Name. Amen.

Don't adjust your life

FOR READING AND MEDITATION – ECCLESIASTES 1:8–11
' … there is nothing new under the sun.' (v. 9: NIV)

It is surprising how many Christians have never read the book of Ecclesiastes. One woman told me that Ecclesiastes was the one book in the Bible she could not read. 'I am put off by all that pessimism and gloom,' she explained. There is, however, a purpose behind it.

Dr Cyndyllan Jones, a famous Welsh preacher who lived several generations ago, puts it like this: 'No Christian will be ready to open himself up to God until he has been gripped by the emptiness and pointlessness of life.'

An essential quality for a philosopher is a readiness to face reality, and then they come to the same conclusion as Solomon. Malcolm Muggeridge, for example, in the days before he found God, saw the world as 'an interminable opera'. Graffiti found on the walls of Bath University was even more to the point: 'Do not adjust your life, the fault lies in reality.' I believe Solomon uses such forceful language to break through our attempts to avoid reality. Life 'under the sun' can be boring, fleeting, repetitive and empty. Life will never be meaningful 'under the sun' until we make contact with the One who is above the sun. Those who try to find meaning apart from the Creator, inevitably see life as an 'interminable soap opera'. Is it any wonder?

✑ Gracious and loving Father, wean me off any ideas I may have that life can be found 'under the sun'. Grant that I might be gripped by the truth that life, real life, is found in you. Amen.

Education without God ...

FOR READING AND MEDITATION – ECCLESIASTES 1:12–18

'For with much wisdom comes much sorrow;
the more knowledge, the more grief.' (v. 18: NIV)

Solomon uses forceful language to break through our attempts to avoid reality. T.S. Eliot said, 'Humankind cannot bear too much reality.' Psychologists warn that stripping away people's defences could bring them face to face with reality too quickly and cause those who are fragile to slide into depression.

The author of Ecclesiastes seems unconcerned about this, however, and tells us with deep conviction that life 'under the sun' is futile. He tells us how his determination to find a purpose for living led him to serious study, but proved to be futile – a 'chasing after the wind' (v. 17). *Moffatt* translates our text for today: 'The more you understand, the more you ache.'

Real life cannot be found through education alone. 'Education – the great mumbo and fraud of the ages,' says the highly educated Muggeridge, 'purports to equip us to live and is prescribed as a universal remedy for everything from juvenile delinquency to premature senility. For the most part it serves to enlarge stupidity, inflate conceit, enhance credulity and puts those subjected to it at the mercy of brainwashing with printing presses, radio and television …' Lloyd George made this caustic remark: 'Education without God makes clever devils.'

O God, save me from the mistake of believing that life is to be found in profound thinking. Help me see that life is to be found in first knowing you; then Teach me to think as you think, dear Lord. In Jesus' Name. Amen.

Send in the clowns

FOR READING AND MEDITATION – ECCLESIASTES 2:1–11

"'Laughter,' I said, 'is foolish. And what does pleasure accomplish?'" (v. 2: NIV)

If education, intellectualism and philosophy are not the routes to making life work – then what is? Perhaps pleasure? Not so, says Solomon. Pleasure pleases, but it is powerless to still the ache that exists in the soul. A list of ways to derive pleasure is provided, but all of them are given the 'thumbs down' by Solomon.

The first is laughter. Send in the clowns. Bring on the jokers. But as almost everyone knows, those who bring laughter to thousands are themselves often desperately unhappy.

If not laughter, then perhaps drink will help. 'I tried cheering myself with wine,' Solomon tells us ... but clearly that did not satisfy either. He then threw himself into a round of activity – projects like building a house for himself, planting vineyards, filling his courtyards with slaves, buying up herds and flocks, amassing silver and gold, and finally equipping himself with a harem – what he describes as 'the delights of the heart of man' (v. 8). But did these things work? Here's his conclusion: 'Everything was meaningless, a chasing after the wind' (v. 11). His point is that these kinds of pleasures are ephemeral; they don't last.

My Father and my God, I see I am shut up to you. Earth's fountains are unable to quench the deep thirsts of my soul. To whom shall I go? Only you have the words of eternal life. I am so grateful. Thank you, my Father. Amen.

Where life ends

FOR READING AND MEDITATION – ECCLESIASTES 2:12–16

'Like the fool, the wise man too must die!' (v. 16: NIV)

Has the writer of Ecclesiastes had lost all objectivity when he wrote this book? His pessimistic mood certainly affected everything he looked at. As if anticipating that very argument, he says in verse 9, 'In all this my wisdom stayed with me.' Disillusioned though he was, his objectivity never left him.

In the section before us today he returns to re-examine wisdom, but this time to compare it with folly. We see his mind grappling with the idea, 'Shall I be a serious thinker, or just go the way of all fools?' His conclusion, initially anyway, is that wisdom has the advantage over folly: 'The wise man has eyes in his head, while the fool walks in the darkness' (v. 14). In other words, it is better to be wise than foolish, better to be learned than ignorant. But would wisdom in itself stop him from slipping toward meaninglessness?

He comes to the conclusion that if the wise man has eyes to see, what he sees is the limited usefulness of being wise. Both the wise and the foolish have to face death. He concludes, 'So what if I do have a fine education? What if I enjoy a good standard of living through the application of common sense? What's the point when it all ends in death?' The reality is that there is life in the hereafter, and the quality of life in the hereafter depends on what you are after here.

✎ O Father, let me be gripped by the fact that when I know you, life here on earth is too wonderful for words, and to die there is nothing but gain. All honour and glory be unto your matchless Name. Amen.

Life in the real world

FOR READING AND MEDITATION – ECCLESIASTES 2:17–23

'I hated all the things I had toiled for …
because I must leave them to the one who comes after me.' (v. 18: NIV)

Facing the realities of life can greatly provoke anxiety. The moment when we face the fact that there is nothing in this world – no person, place or thing – that can meet the deepest ache in our soul, is probably one of the most solemn moments of our existence. Many can't face that kind of reality, so they escape into such things as fantasies, endless rounds of activity, drink, sensual pleasures, and so on. It is this ability to face reality that endears Solomon to us.

What did he turn to next in his frustration with life? Work. Many try to find meaning in their work, and work, especially creative work, can be very satisfying. But Solomon says that work is not where life is to be found. Clearly, Solomon had considered throwing himself into activity partly to leave something to his children. But then he concludes, when you die, you have to leave it all to someone else (v. 18); you cannot be sure if he or she will look after it or ruin it (v. 19); you have no choice but to give it away as a gift to someone who has not worked for it (v. 21); and finally, what benefit does the one who has worked derive from it? (v. 22).

Don't dismiss this as just despairing pessimism. Keep in mind the whole purpose of the book – to show us that true meaning is not found in the temporal but in the eternal.

✎ O God, the conviction is quietly being borne in upon me – only in you am I equipped to face the realities of life. I am so grateful that I know the one true reality – Jesus. Amen.

It's tough out there!

FOR READING AND MEDITATION – ECCLESIASTES 2:24–26
'To the man who pleases him, God gives wisdom,
knowledge and happiness …' (v. 26: NIV)

Oswald Chambers said, 'No Christian makes much progress in the Christian life until he realises that life is more chaotic and tragic than orderly.' Life in a fallen world can be tough! The sooner we face that fact and allow it to silence us, the fewer expectations we will have of the world, and the more eagerly we will turn to God. In today's section Solomon moves out of the godless corner into which he has been driven by life's disappointments. Suddenly we see a chink of light shining through his pessimism and gloom.

The passage begins with what might appear to be a contradiction: 'A man can do nothing better than to eat and drink and find satisfaction in his work. This too, I see, is from the hand of God' (v. 24). If life's ultimate meaning can't be found in such activities, it is not to be found in rejecting them either. Things in themselves are not bad; the wrong values we attach to them make them bad.

Enjoyment, he says, is God's personal gift (v. 25). Satisfaction in things is found only when they are seen as being behind God. When God is not first, then everything around which we wrap our affections is an idol. We have two choices: one is to find life in God and enjoy the provision of his hands; the other is to find life in things, and turn our back on God. The latter is 'meaningless', says Solomon.

Father, when you step into my world, I step out into a new world. Help me to put nothing in front of you – not even my closest relationships. Amen.

The time tunnel

FOR READING AND MEDITATION – ECCLESIASTES 3:1
'There is a time for everything, and a season for
every activity under heaven.' (v. 1: NIV)

We concluded that no one is able to make life work apart from God. Now consider time. Longfellow asked, 'What is time?', and then went on to say that although time could be measured, it could not be clearly defined. One of the best definitions of discipleship I have heard is this: 'Discipleship is what a person does with his time.'

Imagine someone who loves you puts into your personal bank account every day the sum of R1 440, with the stipulation that you have to use it all every day, and anything left over will be cancelled by the bank. Sounds too good to be true, doesn't it? However, someone who loves you puts into your life every day 1 440 minutes – the gift of time. You have to use it all, and anything left over is forfeited.

So ask yourself now: how do I manage my time? Do I squander it, or see it as a sacred trust? Solomon is showing us how life on this earth breaks down into measurable spans, and that there is a controlling schedule behind all things. Does not this in itself suggest that a loving God presides over the circumstances of life? Kierkegaard said, 'Life has to be lived forwards, but it can only be understood backwards.' Reflect for a moment on the things you worried about a year ago. Aren't you aware that an eternal God has been marshalling your progress in this tunnel of time?

✎ O Father, help me to see the issue of time not as a burden, but as a blessing. I want to use my time wisely. Keep me sanely balanced in all this. Amen.

You will laugh again

FOR READING AND MEDITATION – ECCLESIASTES 3:2–4

'... a time to weep and a time to laugh,
a time to mourn and a time to dance.' (v. 4: NIV)

Perhaps no better cross-section of life can be found anywhere than in these poetic verses. Solomon unfolds for us the variety of life, all of which takes place under the providential hand of God.

There are, in fact, fourteen contrasts, and every one of them is familiar to us all. (1) There is a time to be born and a time to die. No one can negotiate his or her arrival into this world, nor the natural time of departure. (2) A time to plant and a time to uproot. Mess around with Mother Nature by planting when it is time to reap, and you won't get anywhere; follow the order, and you get results. (3) A time to kill and a time to heal. This is an approval of killing, but a simple statement of fact – wars, killing, and then healing are part of human life. As Charles Swindoll puts it, 'Life seems strangely fixed between a battlefield and a first-aid station, between murder and medicine.' (4) A time to tear down and a time to build. Demolition is followed by construction, then after a while more demolition and more construction – a pattern with which every generation is familiar. (5) A time to weep and a time to laugh. Are you shedding tears over some great difficulty at the moment? I promise you in God's Name, sometime in the not too distant future your heart will laugh again.

Help me see, dear Father, that though I pass through times of sorrow and difficulty, nothing can shake the rock of existence on which I stand. In sorrow or in laughter, may I never lose sight of you. In Jesus' Name I ask it. Amen.

The end of searching

FOR READING AND MEDITATION – ECCLESIASTES 3:4B-6A

'… a time to scatter stones and a time to gather them …' (v. 5: NIV)

We continue looking at Solomon's fourteen contrasts of life. (6) A time to mourn and a time to dance. We lose a loved one, and then, a year or so later, a family member gets married. Mourning is turned to dancing. Isn't this true of almost every family on earth? (7) A time to scatter stones and a time to gather them. Some commentators believe this refers to the act of scattering stones over a difficult neighbour's field in order to hinder him from ploughing; to then go and retrieve those stones implies an act of sorrow or repentance. We have all made things difficult for others and then felt remorse and try to make it right. (8) A time to embrace and a time to refrain. Some times we need the quiet embrace of a friend to comfort and console us. But there are times when what we need is not so much consolation, but confrontation. We need to be faced with some hard truths. For life to be balanced, both must be part of our experience. (9) A time to search and a time to give up. How much easier life would be if we would give up searching for something we inwardly sense will never be found. It's good to have hope, but hope must be based on something that is realistic. As someone once put it, 'It's better to be a sane pessimist than a silly optimist.' I agree.

༄ O Father, how can I sufficiently thank you for helping me to give up searching for satisfaction down paths that were all dead ends. I need no longer search, for I have found. All honour and glory be to your peerless and precious Name. Amen.

One foot in eternity

FOR READING AND MEDITATION – ECCLESIASTES 3:6B–8

'... a time to be silent and a time to speak ...' (v. 7: NIV)

We look now at the last of the list of Solomon's fourteen contrasts. (10) A time to keep and a time to throw (or give) away. Isn't it better to give all the stuff you might have crammed in your home that you will never use to someone who could make good use of it? (11) A time to tear and a time to mend. This is the idea of not getting anything new but instead patching it up, although some things must never be given up – truth, for example. However, we ought to try out new ways of doing things, too. (12) A time to be silent and a time to speak. It's not often you hear someone confess, 'I feel sorry for the things I did not say,' but you will hear many admit, 'I wish I knew how to keep my mouth shut.' Learn when to talk and when to listen. (13) A time to love and a time to hate. Love that does not have another person's interests at heart is not love, but mere sentimentality. To love means you must also be willing to hate. Not people, but the thing that may be hindering them from fulfilling their spiritual potential. (14) A time for war and a time for peace. Wars start, it is said, 'when someone has something somebody else wants'. As I write, there are over sixty wars going on in the world. Solomon's words, therefore, rise to almost cosmic proportions: there must be a time also for peace.

⇔ *My Father and my God, this focus on the events that take place in time drives home to me my need to have one foot also in eternity. I am grateful that, although a creature of time, because I am in you I am bound for eternity. Amen.*

All things beautiful

FOR READING AND MEDITATION – ECCLESIASTES 3:9–11

'He has made everything beautiful in its time.' (v. 11: NIV)

Reflect on the pairs of opposites we have looked at over the past three days. Wouldn't it be wonderful if we knew how to react properly to all of life's events? Sometimes we know what we ought to do, but our timing is not right. To do the right thing at the wrong time is almost as bad as not doing right.

Solomon asks, 'What benefit do we get from time?' It might seem a blessing, but actually it is a burden. As he looks at the interesting cycles of time, he concludes that without God all is boring and futile. But here's a sentence that brushes aside futility: 'He has made everything beautiful in its time.' To look at time through mere human eyes alone, is to see it as interesting but futile; to look at it through the lens of faith, is to see a beautiful picture coming together under the hands of the Divine Artist. He takes our sorrows and turns them into symphonies; he takes our tears and turns them into telescopes; he takes our calamities and turns them into opportunities.

If you could see through your troubles at his purposes, you would never again shake your fist in his face and tell him your life is a mess. The timing of things may not be as you would like them to be, but remember he is making everything beautiful – in its time.

✎ O God, save me from the demandingness that wants to change things simply because I see no point or purpose in them. Help me understand that you are working out all things beautifully. But in your time, not mine. Amen.

What time is it?

FOR READING AND MEDITATION – ECCLESIASTES 3:11
'He has also set eternity in the hearts of men …' (v. 11: NIV)

The text before us today reads like a conundrum. God has set eternity in our hearts, yet we cannot understand what he has done. God has not only established a timetable by which everything is ordered, but he has also placed within our spirits a deep longing for eternity. Because of this, there is something in every one of us that earth cannot satisfy. We live on earth, but we do not belong to it. We belong to eternity.

Wordsworth, in his well-known *Intimations of Immortality*, speaks of this secret reminiscence of the soul when he says, 'But trailing clouds of glory do we come, from God who is our home.' This nostalgia we have for heaven is built into every human being, and although with many it is denied, ignored, or overlaid with other things, indisputably it is there. And it is a wonderful moment when a man or woman realises it is there.

Most of humanity go about their daily tasks largely unaware that there are deep thirsts and deep longings in them which temporal things can never meet. Why is it, they say, that when I have everything I have ever wanted, it still does not satisfy? If only they would stop to consider and ask in relation to spiritual things, 'What time is it?', they would then be ready to hear the answer, 'It is time to come to terms with eternity.'

✣ *O God, it seems too good to be true – that the thing most of humanity is searching for, I have found. You are the homeland of my soul. In you I am safe, steady, and growing. I shall be eternally grateful. Amen.*

God-given abilities

FOR READING & MEDITATION – ECCLESIASTES 3:12–13

'That everyone may eat and drink, and find satisfaction in
all his toil – this is the gift of God.' (v. 13: NIV)

Solomon's main point gets clearer every moment – without God
life on this earth can be pretty boring and empty. But when God is
in our lives, his presence makes a world of difference. God gives us
four things so that we might enjoy our life here on earth.

(1) The ability to be happy (v. 12). Happiness is not something
we earn; it is a gift. Only God can give us the perspective on life that
enables us to remain happy even when things don't go our way. A
new Christian put it like this: 'I am happier now when I am sad than
before when I was happy.' (2) The ability to do good (v. 12). Any one
of us can be good to those who are good to us, but it takes God to
help us be good to those who are not good to us. We don't have that
kind of hearts. That ability flows from God's heart of love into ours.
(3) The ability to eat and drink (v. 13). If you consider before you
eat and drink that your appetite is something that comes from
God, it will help you enjoy your food much better. (4) The ability to
see good in our labour (v. 13). The whole workplace could be
transformed overnight if men and women saw it from God's perspective. Instead of asking, 'What is the least I can do for a day's
wages?', we'd ask, 'What is the most I can do for a day's wages?'
Hard to take? That's because it is an 'above the sun' perspective.

*O God, when I see how much of my life depends on you, I feel ashamed
at how slow I am to appreciate that fact. Forgive me, Father, and evoke within me a growing consciousness of your own continued goodness. Amen.*

A thorough God

God is thorough. However ragged life may seem in a fallen world, the Creator knows no such imperfections. The Almighty builds things to last. And what he does, is not only permanent, but complete: 'Nothing can be added to it and nothing taken from it' (v. 14). Ever sent for something and found that when it comes a part is missing? That's not the way it is with God. His quality control is 100 percent. Why? '… so that men will revere him.'

'Religion,' it has been said, 'begins with a sense of awe, the recognition of God's greatness and our limitations.' When do we feel awe? Not when we stand in front of something manmade, such as a plane, or a towering glass building. We feel fascination then, but not awe. Awe fills us when we look at the works of God – a majestic mountain or a glorious sunset. You don't say as you stand before the Niagara Falls, 'Isn't that cute?' You simply stand in silent awe.

But what does Solomon mean when he tells us that whatever is, has already been, and that 'God will call the past to account' (v. 15)? *Moffatt* translates this statement, 'God is ever bringing back what disappears.' It means that God repeats situations in our lives until we learn the lessons they are meant to teach us. Think of the heartache we would be saved if we could just get hold of this.

O God, when will I learn? I go through the same situations time and time again simply because I have not heeded your voice. Make me alert to each passing moment, and show me how to draw from it the lessons permanently. Amen.

The patience of God

FOR READING AND MEDITATION – ECCLESIASTES 3:16–17

'God will bring to judgment both the righteous and the wicked ...' (v. 17: NIV)

Ever found yourself feeling frustrated because of the way in which wickedness seems to win over justice? Then you know something of how Solomon feels in the verses before us today. James Russell Lowell put it this way: 'Truth forever on the scaffold, wrong for-ever on the throne.' Solomon struggles with the fact that in the very place where you would expect to see justice, you find wickedness and corruption prevailing.

As a pastor, I often went to court with people who had a gen-uine case to be heard, only to see it broken down by tactics that were dishonest and unjust. This was not always so, of course, and is more the exception than the rule, but I have seen enough injust-ice in my time to share something of Solomon's cynicism. Are you a victim of judicial injustice? Then don't allow yourself to become too cynical, for, as Solomon said, 'God will bring to judgment both the righteous and the wicked ...' The day is coming when all cor-ruption and injustice will be called to judgment before the throne of God's truth. But of course, being human, we wish the injustices we have received could be put right – now.

God is much more patient than we are – we need to ask for grace to be patient with the patience of God.

୬ *O God, give me the divine perspective on things so that present injustices may be swallowed up in the long-term purposes. Help me see that I will have my day in court – your court. Amen.*

How error occurs

FOR READING AND MEDITATION – ECCLESIASTES 3:18–22

'Man's fate is like that of the animals … As one dies, so dies the other.' (v. 19)

Have you noticed that when Solomon looks 'above the sun' he gets the right perspective, but when he looks 'beneath the sun' his cynicism rises? We saw yesterday that when he looked away from the injustice he observed on earth to the day when all wrongs would be righted, he appeared to be in a better frame of mind. In today's verses he has descended into deep cynicism again. This is what happens when we don't keep our eyes on God – we come to the same exasperating and heretical conclusions as Solomon. He says that we are like animals, and will end up like animals – in oblivion.

We are bound for a different destiny. But Solomon is not talking truth here; he is talking cynicism. When we take our eyes off God and the truths he unfolds in his Word – we can slip into making the same kind of rash and heretical statements. His words represent what he felt at the time, but they are not to be taken as true, for they are contradicted in other parts of Scripture.

We ought never to forget as Christians that unless we have a full Biblical perspective on issues, we too can descend into making rash and heretical statements. Cynicism numbs us spiritually and leaves us feeling downcast and disillusioned. Always have a full view of Scripture and God's perspectives.

✎ *O Father, how thankful I am that you have given me a Book which enables me to have the right perspective on all things. Teach me how to compare one Scripture with another. To say not merely, 'It is written,' but 'It is written again.' In Jesus' Name. Amen.*

It's lonely at the top

FOR READING AND MEDITATION – ECCLESIASTES 4:1–6
'Better one handful with tranquillity than two handfuls with
toil and chasing after the wind.' (v. 6: NIV)

As we said yesterday, Solomon seems fine when his gaze is focused
'above the sun', but he becomes filled with cynicism when he looks
around at what is 'under the sun'. Today his gaze is once again hori-
zontally focused. He 'looks around', as he puts it, sees people caught
in the grip of oppression, and his heart is filled with despair. His
cynicism reaches new depths when he concludes that, in the circumstances, those who had died were fortunate, and those who had
not lived and died – the unborn – were in an even better position.

Some commentators see these sentiments as marking the lowest point in the book. The savage rivalry and competitiveness that
he sees all around causes him to say again that life is meaningless.
Those who get to the top by riding roughshod over people's feelings, find when they get there they have everything they thought
they wanted – except friends, who were pushed aside on the way
up. It is lonely at the top.

One handful of contentment is better than two handfuls of
that kind of competitiveness that leaves you feeling lonely at the
top. *Moffatt* puts it beautifully, 'A handful of contentment is better
than two handsfull of toil, and futile effort.' It is.

◁ *Gracious Father, I come to you again to ask that you will touch my heart
and deliver me from anything that might deter me from being the person
you want me to be. Make me a truly contented Christian. In Jesus' Name I
ask it. Amen.*

A threefold cord

FOR READING AND MEDITATION – ECCLESIASTES 4:7–12
'A cord of three strands is not quickly broken.' (v. 12: NIV)

People are lonely because of the oppression of others or because their own competitiveness separates them from friends or, like in today's passage, family connections. It is easy to throw oneself into an endless round of activity and get buried in work. But money and possessions are not much good when you have no one to share them with.

Life at this level is also meaningless. Solomon makes a statement which is often misunderstood, 'Two are better than one ... If one falls down, his friend can help him up ... if two lie down together, they will keep warm' (vv. 9–11). Note the emphasis on two people. But at the end of the passage Solomon says something very strange: 'A cord of three strands is not quickly broken.' The point being made that when you are in a close relationship with someone you love and who loves you, you not only have what the other person gives you, but you have a third quality – a strength and power which unfolds from out of the relationship, and which you could never have experienced if you had stayed apart.

In the fusion of friendship you discover something you could never discover – except in a relationship. It is your strength, plus your friend's strength, producing an even greater strength. This is the secret is friendship.

Father, I see that I am built for relationships, not only with you, but with others, too. And in a relationship lies a power that is greater than the sum of its two parts. May I discover more of this. Amen.

The best friend ...

FOR READING AND MEDITATION – ECCLESIASTES 4:13–16

'Better a poor but wise youth than an old but
foolish king who no longer knows how to take warning.' (v. 13)

There is no comfort quite like a true friend when one finds oneself
on 'the ragged edge of time'. Yet, it is possible to have many friends
and still be lonely. That's the point Solomon is making in today's
verses. The picture he presents verse 13 is one of two people: one a
poor but wise youth, the other an old but foolish king. Who would
you think has the advantage? The king? Not so, says Solomon. He
may have more experience of life, but more than experience is
needed if we are to walk effectively through the world.

What we need is – wisdom. The whole of chapter 4 has been
taken up with the issue of loneliness, and Solomon ends by under-
lining the fact that it is not our circumstances that make us lonely,
but our inability to apply wisdom to our situation.

Take two people who are in the same circumstances, surrounded by helpful companions. One enjoys the company of
friends, but the other complains that he is lonely. Where lies the
problem with the one who feels lonely? Not in the outer circumstances, but in the 'innerstances' – his attitudes. He lacks the wisdom to see that no human being can provide him with the comfort
the soul so deeply craves. The wise are those who understand that
while human friends are important, the best friend to have is God.

*My Father and my God, grant me the wisdom to understand that whilst
the making and keeping of earthly friendships are important, the making and
keeping of your friendship are even more important. In Jesus' Name. Amen.*

Watch your step

FOR READING AND MEDITATION – ECCLESIASTES 5:1–3
'Guard your steps when you go to the house of God.' (v. 1: NIV)

How spiritually uplifting, after a week of having one's focus on a horizontal perspective on life, to enter the house of God and have one's gaze turned toward heaven. In this chapter we catch Solomon in one of those rare moments when he breaks free of his cynical frame of mind.

He begins with a strong and positive declaration: 'Guard your steps when you go to the house of God. Go near to listen …' *The Living Bible* says, 'As you enter the Temple, keep your ears open and your mouth shut!' God's people, Solomon is saying, are far too casual in their approach to worship. If familiarity doesn't breed contempt, it certainly can breed insensitivity. Our approach to God's house will determine what we receive at God's house. 'Bad preaching,' said one famous Bible expositor, 'is God's curse on an unexpectant and not spiritually alert congregation.'

Generally, there is too much talking and not enough listening in church services. Our minds are bent on getting God to see things from our perspective instead of desiring to see things from his. We fill every silence with words. If you are not hearing God in church, the problem is not that God is not speaking; it is more likely that you are not listening. Next time you go to the house of God, say to your restless, talkative spirit, 'Shh! Listen!'

✎ *Gracious God, forgive me that so often both in church and in my daily devotions I am more interested in letting you know what I want to say than in listening to what you have to say. 'Speak, Lord, Thy servant heareth.' Amen.*

Stand in awe

FOR READING AND MEDITATION – ECCLESIASTES 5:4–7

'… do not protest to the [temple] messenger, "My vow was a mistake." ' (v. 6: NIV)

Talking instead of listening is one of the great dangers we can fall into when going into the house of God. Did you know the more talkative you are, the more likely you are to fall into sin? If you have any doubt about that, read Proverbs 10:19.

There is another danger – making promises to God which we fail to deliver. How many of us in the emotion of a church service have made promises to God that we have conveniently forgotten? The promises we make in haste, we repent of at leisure. Perhaps we rationalise the issues and say such things as, 'I didn't really mean it,' or 'I was carried away by the emotion of the moment.' A vow made to God ought to be treated seriously. It is the seed plot of action. We ought not to vow impulsively, but only after careful and prayerful consideration. Solomon's advice on the subject of vows is: first, don't delay in delivering it (v. 5), and second, don't deny you said it (v. 6). Have you made a vow to God and never followed through on it? Ask God's forgiveness and the grace, if the vow is still capable of being undertaken, to do what you promised.

We live in an age when vows and commitments do not seem as important as they once did. God keeps his vows; so should we.

🖊 O God, help me to see what tension I set up inside myself when I make vows to you that I do not keep. You keep your word to me; may I also keep my word to you. Help me, where possible, to catch up on any unfulfilled promises. In Christ's Name. Amen.

Money! Money! Money!

FOR READING AND MEDITATION – ECCLESIASTES 5:8–12

'Whoever loves money never has money enough ...' (v. 10: NIV)

Solomon is now being cynical again. The rich tend to be the leaders and most influential, he says, and the poor the followers.

Solomon is not the only one who is cynical about bureaucracy; sometimes I feel the same way, too. His main point, however, is to show us that wealth is not everything. As Derek Tidball puts it, 'Money ... increases your appetite but not your satisfaction.' There is nothing wrong with possessing money; it is when money is allowed to possess you that trouble comes. My father wrote on the flyleaf of my Bible the day after I was converted, 'Money is a universal provider for everything but happiness and a passport everywhere but to heaven.' Wise words I have never forgotten. 'Wealthy people,' says Solomon, 'find it difficult to sleep, because they are worried about their investments.' The more money you have, the more you have to worry over.

All this, of course, refers to those who have no sense of stewardship, for when money is surrendered to God, it becomes a 'trust' – a 'trust' which is owned by God. We are not meant to be proprietors, but trustees of the Lord's money. God is the owner of everything on the face of the earth, and we are the 'owers'.

Father, help me in relation to material things to see that I am a steward, not a proprietor; a servant, not a master; an ower, not an owner. Change my perspectives so that I look at everything from your point of view. In Christ's Name. Amen.

Gold – or God?

FOR READING AND MEDITATION – ECCLESIASTES 5:13–17

'Naked a man comes from his mother's womb,
and as he comes, so he departs.' (v. 15: NIV)

Solomon is still harping on about money. Isn't he putting his finger on the very pulse of our problems? We try to find in gold what we ought to be finding in God. Solomon forces us to consider how foolish it is to try and find security in something that is so uncertain.

Consider this, says Solomon, 'Savings are put into risky investments that turn sour, and soon there is nothing left to pass on to one's son. The man who speculates is soon back to where he began – with nothing … all his hard work has been for nothing; he has been working for the wind. It is all swept away. All the rest of his life he is under a cloud – gloomy, discouraged, frustrated, and angry' (vv. 14–17, TLB). Clearly, the soul's security cannot be found in money. When will we learn this?

Some of the ancients used to have their wealth put into their tombs alongside their bodies when they died, to keep it with them in the afterlife. We are more enlightened – we know that we can't take the treasures of time into eternity; that's why you never see a trailer behind a hearse. Either we transform the material into the image of the spiritual, or the material will transform us into its own image. The light dies out in the eyes of those who allow the material to get the upper hand.

O God, save me from being transformed into the image of the material. Help me to keep my gaze constantly on you so that I become more and more transformed into the image of your Son. Amen.

Occupied with gladness

FOR READING AND MEDITATION – ECCLESIASTES 5:18–20

'… God keeps him occupied with gladness of heart.' (v. 20: NIV)

You are likely aware by now that Solomon does not stay too long in the darkness of his cynicism without seeking to throw some light across the road. He sets out in today's verses a three-point sermon.

First, he says, set your face against the idea that happiness lies in the possession of material things, and refuse to put a priority on making money just for the sake of it. Take life as it comes, laugh a little bit more, and try to find pleasure in the simple things. Second, enjoy your work. It will not meet the deep needs of your soul, but it is good to be engaged in a task, however menial. Third, see everything God has given you as a gift rather than as something you have earned. Those who say, 'I made so much money this year,' forget that if God had not given them the health and strength to achieve, they would never have made it. A grateful spirit ought not to be far from any one of us.

This is not a bad outline for a modern-day sermon. If you ever pass it on, remember to give the credit to Solomon! And can you think of anything more wonderful than to have a heart that is 'occupied with gladness'? All the riches in the world, all the honours, all the accolades, all the applause, all the achievements, are as nothing compared to the joy of a heart occupied by the King of kings.

✒ *O God my Father, help me put a sign on my heart that says, 'Occupied by the King of kings.' Then, when lesser things seek to invade my soul, they will see that there is no more room. Amen.*

Source of contentment

FOR READING AND MEDITATION – ECCLESIASTES 6:1–2

'God gives a man wealth, possessions and honour …
but God does not enable him to enjoy them …' (v. 2: NIV)

In this chapter Solomon continues to focus on those whom we generally refer to as 'well-heeled'. But he draws our attention to an issue which he has not covered before, namely the plight of those who have everything life can offer, yet are prevented from enjoying it, not by circumstances, but by God himself.

At first it seems almost unbelievable. Why would God do this? Is the Almighty an ogre who looks out for people who are enjoying themselves and then sadistically denies them any feelings of pleasure? Those who know God are aware that his purposes are always beneficent. Nothing he does is done out of peevishness or caprice. When God acts to deny people enjoyment, it is because he wants to show that he is the One who enables us to experience pleasure in things; things themselves do not give pleasure.

It might look like exploitation to us because we are short-sighted and cannot see the end from the beginning. But if people were able to find contentment in money, then they would become spiritually myopic and look no further – money would become their idol and they will never find contentment. Any god that usurps the place of the true God puts the soul 'out of joint'. The power to give contentment belongs to God alone.

✎ *Gracious Father, I acknowledge with gratitude that you and you alone have the power to give contentment. I want no other god to reign in my heart except you. Rule always, dear Father. Amen.*

Shut up to God

FOR READING AND MEDITATION – ECCLESIASTES 6:3–6

'… [a man] cannot enjoy his prosperity …
a stillborn child is better off than he.' (v. 3: NIV)

Obviously there are some advantages in having plenty of money here on earth. A wealthy man could afford to have a hundred children, says Solomon. Those who love lots of children and could afford to look after a hundred might think that this is the solution to the deep inner frustration that exists in their souls. Wealth can sustain a big family, but there comes a moment when those who live only for the family realise this is not where real life is to be found.

There is nothing wrong in enjoying one's family (indeed Scripture encourages it). However, even the most loving family is powerless to quench the ache that resides deep in the human psyche. As Solomon reflects on this, he becomes cynical again, and says that it is better to be a stillborn child than to be caught up in the meaninglessness of trying to find life outside of God. Even a longer life is powerless to quench the ache that throbs at the core of our being. In my experience, those honest enough to admit to this deep inner emptiness yearn for a shorter life rather than a longer one. In the end, to those who do not know God, whether they have been rich or poor will make no difference.

O God, I see now why this book is designed to silence me. For nothing can satisfy my soul except you. I need to take this lesson on board, for I tend to rely more on the visible than the Invisible. Help me, dear Father. Amen.

Where is your identity?

FOR READING AND MEDITATION – ECCLESIASTES 6:7–9

'All man's efforts are for his mouth, yet his appetite is never satisfied.' (v. 7: NIV)

If having a large family or living another thousand years does not meet the needs of the soul – then what does? Hard work perhaps? No, says cynical Solomon, not even that. *Moffatt* translates our text for today, 'A man toils on to satisfy his hunger but his wants are never met.'

Nothing brings satisfaction to a life where God is absent, not even hard work. Psychologists talk nowadays about A-type personalities, people who are obsessed with work and see their whole identity in terms of what they do rather than who they are. It's interesting that the word *appetite* in our reading today is the Hebrew word *nephesh*, or 'soul'. The soul can never be satisfied with anything less than God. Not even a bright mind and a good education can do so either. Both the fools and the wise end up in the same place if they do not know God.

If you could put a stethoscope on the soul, you would hear a rumbling which, if translated into words, would sound something like this, 'I'm so hungry … so thirsty … why won't you give me what I really long for?' And what does the soul long for? God. Far too many Christians try to make their souls work with things. When we get more satisfaction out of the things we do for God, rather than from God himself, then we are in serious spiritual danger.

O God, forgive me if I seek my identity in the things I do rather than finding it in who I am. Show me even more clearly that your estimation of me is not based on my performance, but on the fact that I belong to you. Amen.

Stop arguing!

FOR READING AND MEDITATION – ECCLESIASTES 6:10–11

'… no man can contend with one who is stronger than he.' (v. 10: NIV)

Solomon is 'above the sun' now, putting the focus once again on God. What do we make of him? How does he fit into our lives? Is he in charge, or not? Have you not found that whenever you make sure God is in his place, everything around you falls into place, too? You see things from a different perspective. God is sovereign and the sooner we recognise that, the better.

A purpose was written into the universe long before we arrived, and though at times it may look as if God is not in control, this is not so. And, he adds, because God is bigger than we are, it is useless to put ourselves in conflict with him (v. 10). C.S. Lewis put it well in *The Problem of Pain*: 'To argue with God is to argue with the very power that makes it possible to argue at all.' God is the Potter; we are the clay. God is omnipotent; we are impotent – relatively speaking, anyway. God is consistent; we are inconsistent. God has a crystal-clear perspective on everything; we more often than not are confused.

What is this saying to us? Human beings may have a lot going for them, and a lot of things to their credit. Might and omnipotence, however, are not among those things. Arguing against the divine purpose is a waste of time. Better trust the Almighty; he always knows what he is doing.

O God, help me to have confidence in your confidence. When I don't know what to do, help me see that is a dilemma you never experience. I draw new strength and encouragement from your sovereignty and power. Blessed Lord, I love you. Amen.

Accept your destiny

FOR READING AND MEDITATION – ECCLESIASTES 6:12

'For who knows what is good for a man in life … ?' (v. 12: NIV)

It doesn't do us any harm to see ourselves set over against the might and omnipotence of God, Solomon has been telling us. We, who sometimes feel so important and full of ourselves, need to be reminded of how puny and weak we really are. We are just a heart-beat away from eternity, and if God were to cause our hearts to stop at this very moment – we would die. We are very vulnerable people, and to try to go against the all-powerful Creator is futile. Life functions best when we accept the destiny God has for us and close in with it.

This picture of God as all-powerful is not being presented in order to bring us to our knees in weak and helpless submission. It is simply a matter of fact, a matter of truth. God is stronger than we are and stronger than anything we might want to put our trust in – wealth and money in particular. He and he alone deserves the adoration of our hearts, and the obedience of our wills.

We do not know the future. If we are wise, we will get to know the One who knows the future. Contentment does not lie in a large bank balance, status, ambition, material possessions, or earthly success. It comes only when we are in a close relationship with God. Only he can give us the power to enjoy life. Be wise: build on God, not on gold.

✎ O God, help me to stand before you with an open heart, mind and being. For I want to be changed not into the image of things, but into the image of you. I will have no idols in my life. You are my only Lord. Amen.

Better than Chanel No 5

FOR READING AND MEDITATION – ECCLESIASTES 7:1

'A good name is better than fine perfume …' (v. 1: NIV)

At the halfway mark of Ecclesiastes one notices a change of perspective. Solomon's cynicism does not altogether disappear, but a new note is being struck which rings out most clearly in this chapter and continues to the end of the book. That new note is – wisdom. As wisdom begins to break through, Solomon changes from a narrative style to a proverbial style, and its effect is as dramatic as the sun breaking through the clouds on a dark and stormy day.

He begins with seven comparative proverbs. Let's focus on them one by one. First, 'A good name is better than fine perfume.' A modern translation might read, 'A good name is better than Chanel No 5.' When we say a person has a good name, we mean that he has a good character. On earth nothing is more important than character. It has been said that reputation is what others think of us, character is what we are deep down inside. Second, 'The day of death [is] better than the day of birth' (v. 1). If this it so, then ought we to be mourning people's birth and celebrating their death? Solomon seems to be turning life on its head. Why? Because the days that follow our death (for those who have accepted Jesus as their Saviour) are more joyous than the days that follow our earthly birth.

It's good to feel 'at home' with those who love us in this life, but much better, as the old hymn puts it, to be 'at home with the Lord'.

✑ *O God, you are the centre of my life. Can this life die within me? It cannot die any more than you can die. Death is the end of one life and the beginning of a new one. I rest in glad assurance. Thank you, my Father. Amen.*

Wise advice!

FOR READING AND MEDITATION – ECCLESIASTES 7:2–10

'Do not be quickly provoked in your spirit,
for anger resides in the lap of fools.' (v. 9: NIV)

The third proverb states, 'It is better to go to a house of mourning than to go to a house of feasting' (v. 2). Solomon means you are more likely to face reality in a funeral parlour than a restaurant. Being unwilling to face reality is to be ill-prepared for dealing with life. Fourth, 'Sorrow is better than laughter' (v. 3). After a quick laugh, it's amazing how what we laughed about is so easily forgotten. Not so with sorrow. Any preacher will tell you that the best audience to address is a funeral audience. They listen with rapt attention.

Fifth, 'It is better to heed a wise man's rebuke than to listen to the song of fools' (v. 5). We much prefer to listen to a song that's making its way up the charts than to listen to a rebuke, but in the long run the rebuke will be better. I thank God for the rebukes I have had in my time. They have helped shape me and my character.

Sixth, 'The end of a matter is better than its beginning' (v. 8). The way things end is reality. Fantasies are over, truth is all that can be seen. Seventh, 'Patience is better than pride' (v. 8). Are you one of those who pray, 'Lord, give me patience … and give it to me right now!'? Beneath a patient spirit is a ground swell of wisdom. Pride shuns wisdom, and then it is easy to play the role of a fool.

My Father, I have gathered some wisdom in my lifetime, but now I pray for the wisdom that is greater than all earthly wisdom – your wisdom. In Jesus' Name. Amen.

People of destiny

FOR READING AND MEDITATION – ECCLESIASTES 7:11–14

'... the advantage of knowledge is this:
that wisdom preserves the life of its possessor.' (v. 12: NIV)

After pointing to the dangers and disadvantages of folly, Solomon now invites us to look at the benefits and advantages of wisdom. 'Wisdom is a shelter,' he says (v. 12). It protects us from pitfalls or from entering into foolish schemes and ideas. Wisdom protects us from being overtaken by an unexpected financial crisis, for example, by showing us the importance of 'saving for a rainy day'.

Wisdom tells us that we should make sure our liabilities never exceed our assets; if possible, to avoid temptation rather than confront it; that to harbour resentment is like harbouring a snake in your bosom, etc. If you possess wisdom, you won't fall apart under pressure. Wisdom won't stop you experiencing problems, but it will protect you from unnecessary ones. Secondly, it gives us a clearer perspective on life. He asks, 'Who can straighten what he has made crooked?' (v. 13). Wisdom will help us focus on the things that can be changed, and not to spend time and energy trying to change the unchangeable. A divine thread of sovereignty runs through our lives, so whether times are good or bad – be happy.

Wisdom enables us to see that everything is under God's control – the up and the down times. We are not victims of fate or chance. God is in control of all things. We are people of destiny.

✎ O Father, help me trace your hand in all of my life, not just the 'good' bits. May I see that the setbacks as well as the successes are part of your purpose for me, and thus praise you in everything. Thank you, dear Father. Amen.

Keep your balance!

FOR READING AND MEDITATION – ECCLESIASTES 7:15–18

'The man who fears God will avoid all [extremes].' (v. 18: NIV)

One situation for which wisdom and a divine perspective is needed, says Solomon, is when we see the righteous suffer and the wicked prosper. The psalmist struggled with it (particularly in Psalm 73), and so have millions since.

Idi Amin, the tyrant who once ruled Uganda, lives on, while a missionary family on their way to bring help and medical care to others are lost in a plane crash. You can't make sense of that unless you have an unshakable trust in God, and believe that one day he will answer all our questions.

The second issue needing wisdom is that of spiritual balance. 'Do not be over-righteous,' is his advice (v. 16). He is thinking here, I believe, of those who are too heavenly-minded to be of any earthly good. I know people who think they are head over heels in love with the Lord, but who have no love for others. The apostle John call these people 'liars' (1 John 4:20).

Super-spirituality is out, says Solomon; it's an extreme. But lest we go to the other extreme, he speaks out against this also: 'Do not be overwicked' (v. 17). All of us, because of the Fall, have a wicked streak within us, and we should watch that we do not indulge it. He is not saying you can get away with a little wickedness, he is saying don't give way to it. Solomon is pleading for moderation. Extremes and excesses are destructive. Keep your balance.

O God, teach me how to avoid all excesses and extremes so that I might be a truly balanced Christian. Help me, my Father. In Jesus' Name. Amen.

Wisdom – only from God

FOR READING AND MEDITATION – ECCLESIASTES 7:19–24
'Whatever wisdom may be, it is far off and most profound –
who can discover it?' (v. 24: NIV)

Wisdom provides us with an inner strength. That is the emphasis in this passage. One who operates with wisdom possesses more strength than ten city officials. And most of us know that that is some strength! When we have wisdom, we have the inner strength to cope with whatever comes – tensions, stresses and problems that are not easily resolved. However, possession of wisdom does not mean we become popular. You will still get criticised, he tells us, but don't let that throw you. 'You may hear your servant cursing you … how many times have you cursed others?' (vv. 21–22).

A friend once shared with me his formula for handling criticism. 'When people criticise me,' he said, 'I am thankful they don't know how bad I really am, or they would have much worse to say.' I have found that very helpful. Solomon's next statement about wisdom is one we must not overlook: 'I [was] determined to be wise, but this was beyond me' (v. 23). Why is that? Because whilst we have an innate ability to gather knowledge, we cannot be wise without the help of God.

In James we read, 'If any of you lacks wisdom, he should ask God, who gives generously to all without finding fault' (1:5). You can find knowledge in the world, but wisdom – true wisdom comes only from God.

✎ *O God, I acknowledge that I just haven't got the wisdom I need to handle life. Give me your heavenly wisdom, dear Father. In Jesus' Name. Amen.*

What's scarce?

FOR READING AND MEDITATION – ECCLESIASTES 7:25–29

'... I found one [upright] man among a thousand ...' (v. 28: NIV)

Wisdom was very important to Solomon. It was what he asked for as a young man when God said to him, 'Ask for whatever you want me to give you' (1 Kings 3:5–9). In spite of God's promise to grant his request, Solomon had set out to discover all he could about earthly wisdom. He talked to knowledgeable people, dialogued with scholars, but when he put all his findings together, he concluded human wisdom was not all it was cracked up to be.

Here he makes the point that whilst wisdom was elusive, so also was righteousness, and although he had found one righteous man in a thousand, he had not found one righteous woman at all. Does this mean that men are better than women? Of course not. Solomon is just making a comparison which in his culture would not have the connotation it has today. He is using what we call hyperbole – an exaggerated statement made for emphasis. The real point he is making is seen in the last verse of the chapter – righteousness is scarce. And why? Well, it's not God's fault, because in the beginning he made humankind pure and upright. But through the wilful disobedience of Adam and Eve, sin tragically invaded our human nature. Clearly, then, our problems are not God's fault, but ours. They are not around us, but within us.

We can only blame ourselves for our lack of righteousness. The reason we are not righteous is because we don't want to be.

✎ *Father, I am so thankful that although I cannot find righteousness in myself, I can find it in you. I am eternally grateful. Amen.*

A self-portrait

FOR READING AND MEDITATION – ECCLESIASTES 8:1

'Who knows the explanation of things?
Wisdom brightens a man's face …' (v. 1: NIV)

A centuries-old saying states: 'Wise men are rarely academics, and academics are rarely wise men.' From reading Solomon's writings, one gathers that wisdom is not something academic; it is designed to have a practical outworking in our lives.

Many commentators believe that Solomon is giving us a self-portrait using himself as an illustration of how wisdom works in the lives of those in a position of authority. Look at the text before us again. Two things are said about a wise man in authority: first, he has an understanding of the big picture, and second, he has a cheerful disposition. Take the first – seeing the big picture. Those who are not leaders, concentrate on how to bring their skills to bear on the task in front of them – the 'how'; those who are leaders, however, concentrate on the wider perspective – the 'why'. That is the reason why, as someone put it, 'the person who knows how will usually have a job, but will usually work for the one who knows why'. Followers need to know how, leaders need to know why.

The second qualification of those who are called to lead, is a cheerful disposition. Leaders are often scared people – scared they might not lead well. Their faces become stern, hard, unsmiling and intense. Wisdom from God, lights up the face.

Father, give me a face that reflects your wisdom. I know I am not responsible for the face I started life with, but I am responsible for the face I finish up with. May my face reflect your face. In Jesus' Name. Amen.

More leadership qualities

FOR READING AND MEDITATION – ECCLESIASTES 8:2–8

'As no one is discharged in time of war,
so wickedness will not release those who practice it.' (v. 8: NIV)

Whatever position of authority you hold in life, you will do well to heed Solomon's thoughts on the qualities of a wise leader. We have looked at two, now we look at the other three.

The third quality is this – a high regard for authority. 'Obey the king's command,' (v. 2) says Solomon; respect those in authority over you. Those who have no respect for those higher than them, will never get the respect of those under them. For those under them will sense they are not loyal to the ones above them, and the whole chain of command will be negatively affected.

A fourth quality is to be willing to ride out the tough times without withdrawing your support (vv. 3–4). Unless clearly sinful practices are involved, Solomon is telling us that you can't change authority unless you are higher than it, so the thing to do is to work effectively from beneath. Not by subversive or rebellious attempts, but by applying the fifth quality of leadership – knowing when and how to appeal (vv. 5–6). Many have ruined situations because they did the right thing but at the wrong time. 'The wise heart will know the proper time and procedure' (v. 5). The final words of this passage (vv. 7–8) remind us of man's limitations. Leaders need to recognise that all of us must die one day.

✣ O Father, I see that no matter what position I have in life, I can do nothing to change the fact that one day I will die. May this understanding evoke in me a continuous attitude of deep humility. In Jesus' Name. Amen.

How to handle mystery

FOR READING AND MEDITATION – ECCLESIASTES 8:9–15

'... joy will accompany him in his work all the days of [his] life ...' (v. 15: NIV)

This section begins with a warning for those in positions of authority that if they lord it over others in an unfair way, they will hurt themselves more than they hurt others. From here Solomon focuses on several mysteries, things for which we have no really clear answers. The first is this – wicked people being praised at their funeral (v. 10). Ever witnessed such a situation? It bothered Solomon so, he called it 'meaningless'.

A second thing that mystified Solomon is why a sentence for a crime is not quickly carried out (v. 11). If Solomon lived in our day when rapists and psychopaths on remand are let out to re-enact their crimes, he would say more than that it is meaningless. A third thing that mystified the wise king is something he has mentioned once before – how Providence seems to treat the good as though they were wicked and the wicked as though they were good. There is no clear or adequate explanation. It still remains a mystery even when you have said all you have to say.

Solomon's way of dealing with mystery is quite simple: eat, drink, and put your trust in God (v. 15). In other words, continue the routines of life and keep going even though the mysteries remain unsolved. With God we can cope with anything that comes, even though we can't explain it.

◁ *Father, help me to still serve you and love you even in the absence of explanations. This I ask in Jesus' Name. Amen.*

It's better to trust

FOR READING AND MEDITATION – ECCLESIASTES 8:16–17

'Even if a wise man claims he knows,
he cannot really comprehend [what goes on under the sun].' (v. 17: NIV)

The sooner we come to terms with the fact that there are things in this life which defy explanation, the better we shall be. I have seen people almost drive themselves insane by insisting that God was honour-bound to give them a clear explanation for some dark or difficult situation into which they were plunged. Not that it is wrong to desire answers from God, but when it escalates into a demand, we head for trouble. We must accept that and live with it.

Life 'under the sun' will always be a puzzle. Once we stop trying to find the missing pieces to the puzzles of life, we will we be able to get on with living and channelling our energies in the right direction. Just remember that the missing pieces of every puzzle in your life are in the hands of the One who put this universe together in the first place.

Derek Tidball tells the story of a small boy who was bullied by other boys because they said his father was a Frankenstein who put people to sleep, cut them open, took out parts and put in others. The boy's father, of course, was a surgeon. The little boy, however, was untroubled because he knew and trusted his father and was aware that even though he could not understand why his father did the things he did, he would not be involved in anything that was evil or bad. It is the same with God.

✎ Father, help me to grab hold of this revelation that there is a good reason for everything you do. May I trust you even when I cannot trace you. Amen.

Turning the corner

FOR READING AND MEDITATION – ECCLESIASTES 9:1–6

'For the living know that they will die, but the dead know nothing ...' (v. 5: NIV)

In this chapter Solomon focuses our gaze more clearly on 'above the sun' issues. Four facts are laid out that every believer should know and understand. The first – everything is in God's hands (v. 1). When I think of myself as being in 'God's hands', I feel greatly reassured. Nothing can get out of control. Matters may seem out of control to me, but not to him. It is true, as Solomon says, that 'no man knows whether love or hate awaits him' (v. 1). But when we have God, nothing will ever confront us that we can't handle together.

The second – the certainty of death (vv. 2–3). Death is a common debt all of us must pay. But how blessed are those whose goals reach beyond death, and who have an assured eternal future with God. Anyone who lives only for time is a fool. I hope, by the way, you have settled the question in your own heart about where you are going to spend eternity.

The third – madness resides in the human spirit (v. 3). Don't expect too much of humanity and you won't be disappointed. One of the best descriptions of sin I know is insanity. It is sheer insanity to think we can run our lives successfully without recourse to God. Yet, most of humanity try to do it every day. Utter madness! Now the last fact – where there's life, there's hope (vv. 4–6). 'Better a live dog than a dead lion,' says Solomon (v. 4). As long as there's life, there's hope that one's eternal destiny can be settled.

✣ *Father, help me now, while I am alive, to know for certain that I will spend eternity with you. I yield myself to you today. In Jesus' Name. Amen.*

Go ... with gladness

FOR READING AND MEDITATION – ECCLESIASTES 9:7–10

'Always be clothed in white, and always anoint your head with oil.' (v.8: NIV)

We continue with the thought that where there's life, there's hope. 'Go, eat your food with gladness,' Solomon says, 'and drink your wine with a joyous heart' (v. 7). Hedonists reading these words might think, 'Just what I want ... freedom to go out and indulge myself.' But hold on, read the next line: 'Always be clothed in white, and always anoint your head with oil' (v. 8). That isn't to be taken literally, of course. It simply means – keep yourself clean.

Solomon is not giving us permission to gorge ourselves, but to enjoy every day as it comes. A helpful paraphrase might be, 'The arguments for the meaninglessness of life are powerful – injustice, suffering, criminals getting away with murder while the good die in penury and shame. My mind tells me to give up the search for meaning because there isn't any. But as I reflect on God, I find my heart beating again with the hope that I shall spend eternity with him. Because of that I can go on, eating my food with gladness and drinking my wine with a joyful heart.' Solomon's counsel continues: husbands, enjoy your wives (v. 9). Enjoy, not put up with. You have a wife? Love her. Have fun in your marriage. Don't wait until you retire to enjoy married life.

Solomon adds, 'Whatever your hand finds to do, do it with all your might' (v. 10). Some people don't enjoy life; they simply endure it. You enjoy God, enjoy living, too.

Gracious Father, save me from thinking that I must wait until I die before I live. Help me to throw myself fully into life in the here and now. Amen.

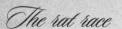

The rat race

FOR READING AND MEDITATION – ECCLESIASTES 9:11–12

'… time and chance happen to them all.' (v. 11: NIV)

An explanation is necessary for Solomon's reference to death in yesterday's verses: 'In the grave, where you are going, there is neither working nor planning nor knowledge nor wisdom' (v. 10). Death, to the Old Testament saints, was a mystery. They believed in life after death, but they were not sure of the quality of that life. Thus death is often spoken of in negative terms. Only since Christ came and defeated death, have we been able to see it in its true perspective.

This has to be kept in mind when reading v. 10. In the previous verses of this chapter Solomon gave us one side of the coin; in today's section he gives us the other side. He is concerned that his instruction to enjoy ourselves is not taken too far, and we get caught up, as so many do, in what is often described as 'the rat race'. 'The race is not to the swift,' he says, 'or the battle to the strong …' (v. 11). The philosophy that drives most people, is this: if you want to get ahead, run faster than anyone else. People who love God and want to honour him, will resist that pressure. You can build a good business and be competitive without spending your life in the fast lane. True success is walking with God.

Keep in mind the fact that everything is in God's hands, and things happen when you least expect them. Nothing is certain. God alone knows the end from the beginning.

⊗ Father, I realise the truth that the strong are not always the strongest, the clever are not always the cleverest. I am challenged to discover a new place of trust in my life. All my trust is in you. Amen.

A tale of one city

FOR READING AND MEDITATION – ECCLESIASTES 9:13–18

'The quiet words of the wise are more
to be heeded than the shouts of a ruler of fools.' (v. 17: NIV)

Solomon addresses the issue of avoiding getting caught in the rat race – by putting it in the form of a story. Imagine, he says, a small city with only a few people in it. Suddenly an invading army surrounds the city and puts it under siege. In the city is a wise but poor man who comes up with an idea that saves the city. We are not told what the idea was, but we are told that when the city was saved, the poor man was forgotten. The punch line is, 'Wisdom is better than strength' (v. 16).

Strength is more impressive than wisdom, but in the long run wisdom is more effective. But people easily overlook the importance of wisdom, and Solomon reminds us so that we won't be surprised when it happens. The way of the world is this – be strong, be smart, be clever, be competitive. But when trouble strikes and people are under threat, they are ready to listen to wise words that get them out of trouble. Then, when the crisis is over, they forget what they heard and go back to being strong again.

Enemy forces surround our world. Marriages are crumbling, and the moral ropes that once held us firm are now frayed. We have the Bible which contains the wisdom the world needs. We must draw more attention to it. People may listen, or they may not – that is not our responsibility. We must speak so that God can work.

✎ Father, may my mind be soaked in the wisdom of Scripture so that when I speak my words become your words. In Christ's Name. Amen.

The anatomy of a fool

FOR READING AND MEDITATION – ECCLESIASTES 10:1–3

'Even as he walks along the road, the fool lacks sense ...' (v. 3: NIV)

If you want to know the anatomy of a fool, you'll discover it in this chapter. You might even begin to think you are surrounded by fools. Then remember that when you point a finger at someone, three are pointing back at you. Didn't our Lord warn us in Matthew 5:22 that we should not call anyone a 'fool'? When Jesus used the word, he was using a term which meant a 'worthless' person. A person may do silly things, but no one who has been made in God's image should be called worthless.

The Old Testament use of the word *fool* refers to someone who ignores the principles on which life was designed to be built. He prefers going against the universe to going with it. Folly, points out Solomon in the opening verse of this chapter, is like dead flies in a costly perfume. A lot of extremely precious liquid is ruined by a very small thing. How many people do you know whose lives and reputations have been torn apart by one foolish act of indiscretion?

Then hear this, says Solomon – the wise go to the right, the foolish go to the left (v. 2). Politicians, especially those on the right, often quote this verse. This text, however, has nothing to do with politics; it refers to walking in the right direction. You can spot a fool, Solomon says, as he walks down the street. Fools have no sense. And everyone can see it.

✎ *Father, pour into my heart the wisdom that overcomes all folly, and enable me, I pray, to avoid the carelessness and senselessness that characterises a fool. This I ask in Christ's Name. Amen.*

Don't take the huff

FOR READING AND MEDITATION – ECCLESIASTES 10:4–7

'Fools are put in many high positions, while the rich occupy the low ones.' (v. 6: NIV)

We continue to look at Solomon's 'anatomy of a fool'. A further characteristic of a fool is that he cannot control his anger. If a boss is hot-headed, then don't react in the same way (v. 4). A fool quits his job in a fit of temper, but a wise man remains calm. How many people reading these lines look back to difficulties that could have been avoided if only they had learned not to take the huff.

Solomon identifies the problem caused by putting a foolish and incompetent person in authority, who then, in turn, lords it over the ones who really ought to be in charge. 'I've seen this evil,' admits Solomon, and so, I am sure, have you. You see it in governments, in the civil service, and in businesses. Sadly I say it, but it is to be seen also in some parts of the Christian church.

We must be careful that we don't focus our criticisms only on government. Dr Kenneth Gangel says in his book *Thus Spake Qoheleth* (a pseudonym for Solomon), '… certainly we see things every day in our own country and around the world which make us wonder whether there is a great deal more of foolishness than wisdom in every human government. Maybe God just wants us to see how foolish we are and how useless it is to trust in the vanities of mankind "under the sun".' Unfortunately fools cannot always be kept at a level where it is impossible for them to do much harm.

O God, perhaps it is true that we get the government we deserve. Can it be that we are more party-political than prayerful over matters, and because of this we sometimes elect the wrong people? Forgive us. In Jesus' Name. Amen.

Poetic justice

FOR READING AND MEDITATION – ECCLESIASTES 10:8–11
'… skill will bring success.' (v. 10: NIV)

Solomon uses this graphic language to drive home the point that fools can't see further than their noses. They go blindly on and see only what they want to see – thus they come to grievous harm. Fools don't see danger, and it is these words of Solomon, I understand, which gave rise to the saying, 'Fools rush in where angels fear to tread.'

A 'fool' digs a pit for someone to fall into, and falls into it himself. A 'fool' breaks through a wall, and gets bitten by a serpent. A 'fool' quarries stones without taking proper precautions, so he gets hurt by loose ones falling on him. A 'fool' splits logs without taking enough care, and an accident occurs. A 'fool' wields an axe without a sharpened edge, and ends up using more strength than he needed to. A 'fool' handles a snake before it is charmed and it bites people, so he makes no profit because people avoid him.

Such mishaps need not happen in any of these activities, Solomon is saying, if people operated from wisdom rather than foolishness. A phrase that is often used to describe the situations Solomon has listed above, is 'poetic justice'. Fools, of course, do not understand this. They continue doing foolish things, using and abusing people, and end up losers. When will they learn?

✎ O Father, day by day it has become clearer and clearer that we cannot get through this life successfully without wisdom. And the best wisdom is your wisdom. Again I pray, fill my heart and mind with the wisdom that comes from above. In Jesus' Name I ask it. Amen.

Put out your tongue!

FOR READING AND MEDITATION – ECCLESIASTES 10:12–15

'At the beginning his words are folly;
at the end they are wicked madness …' (v. 13: NIV)

Question: What has stirred up more strife than any other thing in the history of the world? Answer: The tongue!

Our tongue, Solomon suggests, the little thing we use to frame words, needs examination. Whereas the words of a wise man are gracious, Solomon tells us, the words of a fool consume him. The one who suffers the most consequences in life is the fool, not those he offends. The fool is 'consumed' (v. 12). Strong word. It really means to be 'swallowed up'. The fool is the one who finishes up in difficulty, in police court, or even in prison. He speaks words that lead to his own undoing.

Early in my ministry I learned to differentiate between people who are naive or silly and those who are just plain 'fools'. I learned also not to spend time trying to counsel a fool, but I would give all the time I could to help those who really wanted to be helped. Listen to this: 'No one knows what is coming – who can tell him what will happen after him?' (v. 14). Then, continues Solomon, fools exhaust themselves by their inefficiency (v. 15). They can't even find their way to town or get from here to there. And it's not a matter of IQ. It is just plain stupidity. Fools are ever learning but never arriving.

✎ *O Father, save me, I pray, from having the tongue of a fool. May my words be your words, coming from thoughts that are your thoughts. And help me not simply to learn, but to arrive. In Jesus' Name I ask it. Amen.*

A little bird told me

FOR READING AND MEDITATION – ECCLESIASTES 10:16–20

'Do not revile the king … because a bird of
the air may carry your words …' (v. 20: NIV)

Solomon makes us look at a land governed by an immature king. The NIV says 'servant' (v. 16), but the real thought here is of immaturity. MOFFATT translates verse 16: 'Woe betide you, O land, when your king is a mere boy.' Thus, '… when you have a fool on the throne.'

In Isaiah 3:1–5 God predicted that if Israel did not listen to his word, then boys would become their officials, and mere children would govern them. In due course, that is what happened, and with foolishness on the throne of life, chaos and disorder reigned throughout the land. In v. 18 he returns to the characteristics of a fool. Fools are senseless people. Above them are sagging rafters and a leaky roof, brought about by idleness and procrastination. Fools talk a lot, and say things such as, 'Money is the answer,' but wise people know that responsible living is the real answer. Just talking will not make things improve. In fact, it could make matters worse (v. 20).

The saying 'A little bird told me' comes from this very scripture. Be careful how you talk about a fool, Solomon warns, because the fool will surely find out what you have been saying. Then watch out, because he will come at you! So when dealing with a fool, learn to keep things to yourself.

✎ O Father, help me discern the difference between a 'fool' and a person who is simply naive or immature in order to relate to people in the way that honours and glorifies you. Amen.

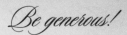

Be generous!

FOR READING AND MEDITATION – ECCLESIASTES 11:1–2

'Give portions to seven, yes to eight …' (v. 1: NIV)

Solomon begins this chapter with a saying that is often repeated and well known: 'Cast your bread upon the waters, for after many days you will find it again' (v. 1). What Solomon is conveying, is this: 'Be generous, share yourself with others.'

I like Charles Swindoll's paraphrase of this verse, which reads thus: 'Don't put the bread in the deep-freeze – it'll dry out. Release it.' The main thought underlying this statement is not simply to give, but to give boldly, energetically and enthusiastically. Are you bold in generosity? Do you cling to the creek when you ought to be out on the broad, wide ocean? It is not the giving of money that is being emphasised here, but the giving of oneself. When we give of ourselves generously, we do not lose, for in this universe things have a way of coming back to us – both good and evil.

Suppose the little boy had refused to let Jesus have the five loaves and two fishes, saying they were his and he would not let them go? He would have missed becoming the most famous little boy in history. The phrase 'give portions to seven, yes to eight' is similar to our modern saying, 'Give to the nth degree.' Give without measure. You never know when disaster is going to strike, so do your giving while you have the chance. God has opened himself to us – generously. Ought we not to do the same to others?

✎ O God, help me to give of myself boldly, energetically and enthusiastically. From now on I shall be the channel and not the stopping place of all your generosity to me. In Jesus' Name I promise it. Amen.

Choose life!

'Whoever watches the wind will not plant;
whoever looks at the clouds will not reap.' (v. 4: NIV)

We are powerless to change certain things. Like the weather. When clouds are full of rain, they drench the earth. And where the stick falls, it lies. Do not allow your thoughts to become preoccupied with things that are unchangeable. Rather get on with living, and work at changing the things that can be changed.

A sign on a rough unmade road somewhere in northern Canada reads, 'Choose your rut carefully. You'll be in it for the next 200 miles.' Solomon's advice is that we should do all we can to stay out of ruts. How many of you are stuck in ruts when you could be using your God-given creativity to explore new horizons? Don't just drift through life – pursue it. Instead of focusing on the predictable things of life, turn your gaze to new activities. If you have retired, come out of retirement. I don't mean go back to doing what you used to do, but take up new interests. Study for a degree, start helping a group of some sort, join a keep-fit class … You won't have the same energy that you had when you were forty, but don't stop being creative.

Don't get into a rut. Don't just stand around and just watch the wind. Don't drift like a lazy cloud. Pursue something new and beautiful for God.

O God, forgive me that I spend so much time worrying about such things as whether it's going to rain or shine, instead of pursuing new things and new purposes. In Jesus' Name. Amen.

Do Not Disturb!

FOR READING AND MEDITATION – ECCLESIASTES 11:5–6

'… you cannot understand the work of God, the Maker of all things.' (v. 5: NIV)

Some things in life we will never fully understand. We don't know which course the wind will take, or how bones are formed in a tiny foetus, but it happens anyway. Why? Because God is at work in everything, and the best thing we can do is trust him.

Modern-day science has cleared up many mysteries but we are still faced with a good deal of unexplained phenomena nevertheless. I am not against scientific research, providing it stays within ethical guidelines. However, whether mysteries can be explained or not – we must carry on living. 'Sow in the morning and don't be idle in the evening,' is Solomon's next word. He is not saying that we ought to work all day or that it is wrong to have a time of leisure. He is pointing out the benefits of having other interests besides work.

There is something wrong in the lives of those who, having finished their day's work, hang a sign on the door of their lives that says, 'Do Not Disturb.' If, after your day's work, you are too tired to focus on something else, then perhaps you ought to re-evaluate your whole lifestyle. I can tell you that because I've just done it myself. Solomon's advice came to me at a crucial moment in my life. Perhaps today is a crucial and challenging moment for you, too?

✑ O God, help me today to take a prayerful and careful look at my lifestyle. Am I really living – or just going through one dreary day after another? Teach me how to pursue life, not have it pursuing me. In Jesus' Name. Amen.

It's great to be alive!

FOR READING AND MEDITATION – ECCLESIASTES 11:7–9

'However many years a man may live, let him enjoy them all.' (v. 8: NIV)

Do you need permission to enjoy life? Then Solomon gives it to you in these verses. I love the MOFFATT translation of verse 7, 'Sweet is the light of life and pleasant is it for the eyes to see the sun.' He is clearly talking about natural light, but these words are also symbolic. God is often spoken of in terms of light and warmth. The light of God's love is ever present, and it is good for us to focus on it as often as we can. The joy of living, he goes on to say, ought to permeate every period of our lives, right up to old age. 'If a man lives many years, let him have joy throughout them all' (v. 7, MOFFATT).

Of course many have had some pretty rough experiences in life – evils such as sexual and physical abuse, abandonment, and so on – but with good Christian counselling these experiences can be overcome. Indeed, Solomon recommends remembering the days of darkness, for when you experience the light and love of God, you can look back at painful events without the loss of your soul. You are pained by the memories, but not overwhelmed. Dark days throw into even greater relief the brightness of joy that from God.

The main theme of these two verses is this – enjoy life now, not later. Many young people say, 'I'll study now, work hard and enjoy life later.' That is good, but don't miss enjoying life with God today. Whatever your age, remember to enjoy just being alive.

✎ O Father, thank you that you lift the gloom and take the pain of depression out of life. Help me focus more on the warmth and light of your love than on the darkness of circumstances. In Jesus' Name. Amen.

Have a great childhood

FOR READING AND MEDITATION – ECCLESIASTES 11:9–10

'… let your heart give you joy in the days of your youth.' (v. 9: NIV)

Solomon's final comments are aimed at the young. Enjoy your days one by one, because before you know it, you will be an adult.

The words that come next have sent some Christians into apoplexy: 'Follow the ways of your heart and whatever your eyes see …' (v. 9). A youth leader in a church I pastored was teaching the book of Ecclesiastes to the young people. He deliberately missed out these words. He said, 'That's bad advice for young people. They are inclined that way already, so I thought it best not to draw attention to it.' I pointed out that he was being unfaithful to Scripture by dodging issues, and drew his attention to the words that follow: '… but know that for all these things God will bring you to judgment.'

This is Solomon's message: 'There will be many things that appeal to your eyes. Follow them, but keep in mind there will be a day of accountability. So don't let your impulses go wild, and don't let the things that appeal to your eyes lead you into illegitimate areas of living.' Some believe that warning takes the joy out of living, but if we ignore the God to whom we must all answer, we leave ourselves open to experiencing not life but unrestricted liberty. That kind of freedom is bad for us. So banish all worries and avoid those things that bring pain to your body – things such as alcohol, drugs, overeating, and so on. Stay close to God and you'll get the most out of it.

✣ *Thank you, Father, for reminding me that there is no freedom without limitations. Help me see the wisdom behind your restrictions that enables me to trust and follow you all the days of my life. In Jesus' Name. Amen.*

No greater joy

FOR READING AND MEDITATION – ECCLESIASTES 12:1
'Remember your Creator in the days of your youth,
before the days of trouble come ...' (v. 1: NIV).

At long last we are introduced to the only One who can give life meaning – God. I suspect Solomon has been wanting to say this from the start, but like a good preacher, he keeps the best to the last. Also, some people need to feel the utter futility of trying to quench the thirsts of their souls in any other way but in God.

An Hassadic story tells of a man who went for a walk in a forest and got lost. He wandered around for hours attempting to find his way back home, trying one path after another. Suddenly he came across another traveller who was also lost. They sat down to discuss what they could do. 'I know', said one, 'let's tell each other what paths we have tried and then it will be that much easier to find our way out.' They did, and within a few hours both emerged safely from the forest. This is how many people find God – they try one meaningless path after another until they find the Way.

Solomon says here that the best time to know God is when one is young. It is possible that if the opportunity to open one's heart to God is not taken in youth, procrastination can build strong resistance into the soul that makes it difficult to respond in later life. I gave my life to God when I was in my teens. I have had the privilege of knowing him, of serving him also. Believe me, there can be no greater joy.

Father, there is indeed no greater joy than knowing you and serving you. May the wonder of these privileges increase. In Jesus' Name. Amen.

The plus of the Spirit

FOR READING AND MEDITATION – ECCLESIASTES 12:2–4

'... those looking through the windows grow dim ...' (v. 3: NIV)

We are now drawn into a picture of very old age that might be a little too vivid for our liking. Solomon's purpose is to point out the advantages of serving God while young. We can serve God in old age, but the reality is that very old age slows us down and we can't give as much energy to the work of God as once we did.

Verse 2 talks about mental ageing. The sun and the light – symbols of clarity and sharpness – recede, and darkness begins to descend on the mind. Verse 3 focuses on physical deterioration when 'the keepers of the house tremble'. This term refers to our limbs which begin to tremble and become weak. We are left, also, with few teeth of our own, which lies behind the expression 'when the grinders cease because they are few'. Verse 3 speaks of the eyes growing dim, and v. 4 speaks of enforced inactivity: 'the doors to the streets are closed and the sound of grinding fades.' The latter part of the verse reminds us that even sleep becomes difficult for the elderly, as they usually wake up at dawn. Some are not even able to hear the singing of the birds any longer. Thus they suffer a double denial – sleeplessness and deafness.

Young people find it difficult to believe that they will be like this one day. Therefore give God your best – while you can.

✎ Father, I know I have to face reality, but I know, too, that the touch of your Spirit can be upon me when I grow old. Sustain me through all the years of my life so that I might know the plus of your Spirit as well as the plus of the years. Amen.

Knowing how to die

FOR READING AND MEDITATION – ECCLESIASTES 12:5–8

'Remember him – before the silver cord is severed ...' (v. 6: NIV)

Can you handle another day focusing on the characteristics of old age? Well, remember the ability to face reality is one of the most clear evidences of mental health! Solomon is saying we don't have to dwell on the facts of old age, but we do have to face them. Four more characteristics are given in v. 5.

First, fear of heights and being out in busy streets. Second, the appearance of grey hair. Clearly, the phrase 'the almond tree blossoms' is a reference to a head of silver hair. Third, the difficulty of walking – 'the grasshopper drags himself along.' One has a picture here of walking-frames or walking-sticks. As you know, it takes old people a little longer to get where they want to go! Fourth, the waning of the sex drive. In v. 6 Solomon returns to a point he made in the opening verse of the chapter – remember God, before 'the silver cord is severed or the golden bowl is broken'. These graphic word pictures (and the ones that follow) all point to death.

To stop just there would be gloomy indeed, but Solomon gives us something to lift our hearts: 'the spirit returns to God who gave it' (v. 7). Death, to those who love God, is not the end, but the beginning of union with God. To those who do not know God, however, death is a transition from emptiness to even greater emptiness (v. 8). Those who know how to live, know also how to die.

❧ O God, thank you for Christ's victory over the grave. Help me to live in that victory from one day to another. In Jesus' Name I ask it. Amen.

The marks of a preacher

FOR READING AND MEDITATION – ECCLESIASTES 12:9–10
'The Teacher searched to find just the right words ...' (v. 10: NIV)

In these last few verses Solomon moves into a brief autobiographical section. These are a wise man's studied reflections and conclusions. The Preacher opens up his heart and tells us what a preacher should be like. There are five characteristics.

First and foremost, a preacher should be wise. He gets this wisdom not from his years, but from his communication with God. Second, he should be able to impart knowledge to others – help them understand the principles for a godly life. Third, he must ponder things, reflect on them, and search them out; wrestle with them as a dog wrestles with a bone. Fourth, he must then set those things in a logical order and sequence. In doing this he must pay particular attention to the use of proverbs, says Solomon – something we seem to miss out on in this day and generation. A sad comment, don't you think?

Fifth, a preacher should be able to search out and use the right words. A preacher depends on the Holy Spirit, of course, but he needs words to make his meaning clear. And not just words, but the right words. 'The difference between the right word and the almost right word,' said Mark Twain, 'is the difference between a lightning flash and a firefly.' The words of a good preacher are like windows through which the light of truth shines.

✎ My Father, give us more preachers who know you and who know their craft. Work by your Spirit in the hearts of those you have called to preach, so that the next generation might not be failed. In Jesus' Name. Amen.

Improving our adjectives

FOR READING AND MEDITATION – ECCLESIASTES 12:11

'The words of the wise are like goads, their collected sayings,
like firmly embedded nails …' (v. 11: NIV)

Living as he did in an agricultural community, it is easy to see why Solomon likens words to goads – a long stick with an iron point that is jabbed against the tough hindquarters of an animal to make it increase its speed. Words motivate and urge us to action.

J.B. Phillips used a different picture: 'If words are to enter men's hearts and bear fruit, they must be the right words, shaped cunningly to pass men's defences and explode silently and effectually within their minds.' Isn't this how Solomon used words? Words and wise sayings are also like firmly embedded nails, says Solomon. Sir Winston Churchill once said about one of his generals, 'He reminds me of an iron peg hammered into the frozen ground – firm, solid, immovable.'

We must use the best and the most precise words we can when talking about Christ, remembering all the time, as C.S. Lewis said, that we are just adjectives striving to point others to the Noun. 'And for people to believe that Noun,' he added, 'we must improve our adjectives.'

✍ O Father, help me understand that it is not increasing my vocabulary that you are after, but doing the best with what I already have. You deserve nothing but the best. May I therefore be the best I can be. In Jesus' Name. Amen.

A person of the Book

FOR READING AND MEDITATION – ECCLESIASTES 12:12

'Be warned, my son, of anything in addition to them.' (v. 12: NIV)

Solomon's counselling to his son will go down well with those of you who are students. First, he counsels his son not to put too much trust in words or books that go beyond the Scriptures. MOF-FATT'S translation reads, 'My son, avoid anything beyond the scriptures of wisdom; there is no end to the buying of books, and to study books closely is wearisome to the flesh.'

The trouble with books is that you have to read a lot to get a little. That is not the same, however, with the Scriptures. 'All scripture,' said Paul to Timothy, 'is inspired by God and is profitable ...' (2 Tim. 3:16, RSV). If we were to spend as much time in the Bible as we do in books about the Bible, we might be better off spiritually.

In my time I have studied many subjects – psychology, sociology, communication, and so on. Many of these subjects I found tiresome. The same cannot be said of Scripture, however. When I open the Bible, I come to it with an enthusiasm, eagerness and expectancy that is not there with any other book. *Every Day with Jesus* may help you with your daily devotions, but don't let it take the place of Scripture in your life. Believe me, I would be heartbroken if I thought it did.

✎ *O God my Father, whilst I am thankful for all the books that help me learn of you and know about you, help me never to put these ahead of your Word, the Bible, but always behind it. Make me a person of the Book. In Jesus' Name. Amen.*

The end of the search

FOR READING AND MEDITATION – ECCLESIASTES 12:13–14

'For God will bring every deed into judgment …
whether it is good or evil.' (v. 14: NIV)

Our exploration of Ecclesiastes ends today. We have travelled with Solomon over many roads, and have listened to a wide range of reflections. The world does not have the resources to meet the needs of the soul, he has been saying, and any attempt to find meaning in life apart from God is utterly futile.

Meaning comes only when we attach ourselves to God. It all boils down to this: 'Fear God and keep his commandments' (v. 13). To 'fear God' means we must revere him and put him first. To 'keep his commandments' means we obey him whether we feel like it or not. Winning souls does not mean forcing the gospel down people's throats, but quietly going with them down one road after another and showing them that this is not where life is found, then bringing them back without fuss or fanfare to the inescapable conclusion that the one true reality is God.

Solomon's last statement is simple yet staggering: 'God will bring every deed into judgment … whether it is good or evil.' We can't live irresponsibly and get away with it. God always has the last word. The message of Ecclesiastes: fear and serve God because one day you are going to stand before him. I'm ready. Are you?

✎ *My Father and my God, if I am not ready, then let your Spirit be in my heart, and help me make the decision to turn my life over to you today. I do so now in humble repentance and simple trust. Take me, cleanse me, and make me your child. In Jesus' Name I ask it. Amen.*

The ultimate phrase

FOR READING AND MEDITATION – EPHESIANS 1:1–12

'Praise be to the God and Father of our Lord Jesus Christ, who has blessed us ...
with every spiritual blessing in Christ.' (v. 3: NIV)

Over the next eight weeks we will focus on some of the passages in the New Testament which contain the endearing phrase 'in Christ' – equivalent to 'in the Lord' or 'in him' – found no fewer than 172 times in the New Testament. The words 'in Christ' occur over 124 times in Paul's epistles.

Think about it. There are thirteen letters of Paul in the New Testament, some of which are very short, and yet in this little bundle of letters the great apostle uses the phrase more than one hundred times. Dr W.E. Sangster said, 'The phrase "in Christ" is the thread which Paul used to sew all his letters together. What a great deal these two words appeared to mean to him.'

Students once asked Dr William Barclay, the famous Bible commentator, 'What do you think is the one concept which reduces the Christian life to the utmost simplicity?' He thought for a few moments and answered, ' "In Christ". These two words locates us in a Person – Christ. To be in him is to find the answer to our deepest longings and our deepest needs.' Whenever he was asked where he lived, an old Welsh preacher used to reply, 'In Christ.' He then explained that he resided at a certain address, but he lived – in Christ.

✎ Blessed Lord Jesus, show me even more clearly in the weeks that lie ahead that when I belong to you, life is reduced to its utmost simplicity. Help me see that the home in which I dwell is just my residence. I live in you. Amen.

You're dead!

FOR READING AND MEDITATION – ROMANS 6:1–14

'In the same way, count yourselves dead
to sin but alive to God in Christ Jesus.' (v. 11: NIV)

'In the same way, count yourselves dead to sin …' (Rom. 16:11) Is this all we have to do to overcome sin – count ourselves dead to it? Some would see in these words a reference to 'positive thinking' – if you think positively, you will get positive results.

A woman I knew described herself as 'a positive thinker'. For years she would repeat to herself the sentence, 'I can deal with every problem that comes my way; nothing can defeat me or overcome me.' Then her mother died and, as she put it, 'Reality closed in and I went to pieces.' Why did positive thinking not work then? Because she was saying to herself, 'I can do it … nothing can defeat me.' *She* was the centre of her life, and when self is at the centre, then the personality is off-centre.

God made us to function effectively with him at the centre. When he is not there, we have little or no hope of overcoming anything – let alone sin. Today's passage does teach the power of positive thinking, but it is positive thinking *in Christ*. When we are in Christ, we are alive to God and thus have a right to consider ourselves dead to sin, because we just fill our minds with the privileges of being in Christ and sin is expelled; it has nothing to thrive on.

✎ O Father, help me lay hold on this thrilling truth that when I am alive to you, I am dead to sin. The more clearly I see you, the more clearly I see the emptiness and unattractiveness of sin. Amen.

Death now – life now

FOR READING AND MEDITATION – ROMANS 6:15–23

'… but the gift of God is eternal life in Christ Jesus our Lord.' (v. 23: NIV)

In the second of Paul's 'in Christ' passages is a vivid portrayal of what happens to us when we decide to commit ourselves to Jesus Christ. 'For the wages of sin is death …' It is not God who gives death, it is sin which does that. Death is not part of God's perfect purposes – he purposes life. The young man who said he had better become a Christian, otherwise God would punish him, missed the point. It was not so much God who would punish him (although in an ultimate sense that would be true) as that he would punish himself.

To refuse to trust Christ would begin within him the inevitable process of decay. Note the tense that Paul uses: 'the wages of sin *is* death'. Death is not just something that happens in the future – it reigns now, in the lives of those who do not know our Lord. Someone said, 'We do not break the laws of God – we rather break ourselves upon them.' The other side of this text shines with a light that is pure and undimmed: '… but the gift of God is eternal life in Christ Jesus our Lord.' Note, again, the use of the word *is*.

Eternal life is not something we receive after we leave this world; it is something we receive now. We are not worthy of it – it is a free gift from God that is ours only as we are in Christ – in life.

✒ *Gracious and loving heavenly Father, how can I sufficiently thank you for depositing in my heart the gift of eternal life? Help me never to take it for granted but with gratitude. Amen.*

No condemnation now I dread

FOR READING AND MEDITATION – ROMANS 7:14–8:1
'Therefore, there is now no condemnation for those
who are in Christ Jesus.' (v. 1: NIV)

When we are in Christ, we are set free from condemnation. The most important thing that can happen to the human personality is the lifting of the sense of condemnation. Here Christianity and psychiatry meet – both concerned with removing the damaging effects of condemnation and guilt, but approaching the issue very differently.

Psychiatry (if secular psychiatry) seeks to lift the condemnation by denying the reality of sin and removing the standards by which God judges the affairs of men. It attempts to take away the feeling of condemnation in the personality by saying that there is nothing for which we ought to be condemned. The Christian approach is to show that man is a sinner and therefore under condemnation – hence he will feel guilty. 'Guilt,' says American Bible teacher Bill Gothard, 'is God's way of saying, "You have broken one of my principles." But when someone repents of sin, God moves into the centre of that person's spirit and removes the guilt and condemnation, thus setting him or her completely free.'

Nothing can set the human spirit free from the heavy load of condemnation except entering into the redemption available 'in Christ'. Christ's door is always open – walk in today.

O Father, through your Word I see your face. And on your face I see a willingness and a readiness to forgive and cleanse me from all my guilt and condemnation. I repent of sin and receive your full and free forgiveness. Thank you, Father. Amen.

Free from the law

FOR READING AND MEDITATION – ROMANS 8:2–16

'... through Christ Jesus the law of the Spirit of life
set me free from the law of sin and death.' (v. 2: NIV)

When we are in Christ, we are set free from the awful feeling of condemnation. How does God achieve this, puts it like this: 'For the law of the Spirit of life which is in Christ Jesus, the law of our new being, has freed me from the law of sin and death' (AMPLIFIED). In Romans 7 Paul has been talking about the 'law of sin and death'. Now, in Romans 8, he introduces us to a new law – 'the law of the Spirit of life in Christ Jesus' (8:2, NKJ).

This higher law sets us free from the lower 'law of sin and death'. Just as the law of flight and motion makes it possible for a bird to overcome the law of gravity, so when we put ourselves at the disposal of 'the law of the Spirit of life in Christ Jesus' we are lifted above the downward pull of the 'law of sin and death'. But if we do not take advantage of the higher law, the lower law will take advantage of us.

In a plane people do not struggle or flap their arms up and down in an attempt to fly; they simply surrender to the power of the plane and it takes them to their destination. We find release from 'the law of sin and death' by surrendering to 'the law of the Spirit of life in Christ Jesus'. The 'law' is really a Person – Christ Jesus the Lord. And what a Person! He is God become available.

✎ Father, help me to understand that just as sin and death have met their match in Jesus, so, now I am in him, they have also met their match in me. I am in him – he is in me. Amen.

Quietism which is dynamism

FOR READING AND MEDITATION – ROMANS 8:28–39

'... neither death nor life ... nor anything else in all creation,
will be able to separate us from the love of God
that is in Christ Jesus our Lord.' (vv. 38–39: NIV)

This must be one of the most marvellous passages in the whole of the New Testament. Paul sweeps away any possibility of anything ever separating us from the love of God. He presents four pairs of opposites that could be barriers – death and life, angels and demons, the present and the future, height and depth – and then scatters them in all directions. If we stay in the love of Christ by surrender, faith and obedience, nothing can separate us from Christ.

Rufus Mosely, a Christian writer, says that when he was reading this passage, God spoke to him in these words: 'See – you have nothing to do in life except to live in union with Me.' Mosely claims that this was the greatest revelation he had ever received. Inside Christ, we live effortlessly; outside Christ, we tear around in ceaseless activity and wear ourselves out.

Some object to this and call it 'quietism' – a passive type of existence which fails to get to grips with reality. I say, 'Yes, it is quietism, but it is quietism which is dynamism.' Like a plug fits into a socket and remains there, receptive and passive, you do not have to succeed or fail – you simply live in union with Christ.

❧ Father, I am so thankful that 'in Christ' I have found the one and only way to live. I am rich beyond all riches, free beyond all freedoms. Nothing in all creation can separate me from you, for I am in the Creator and he is in me. Hallelujah! Amen.

A true conscience

FOR READING AND MEDITATION – ROMANS 9:1–16

'I speak the truth in Christ … my conscience
confirms it in the Holy Spirit.' (v. 1: NIV)

Here is an extremely practical passage – speaking the truth in Christ. There are two ways of speaking the truth: you simply speak the truth – the bare, harsh truth or speak the truth in Christ motivated by love, truth that honours Christ's character and Name. The things you say may be true – verbally correct – and yet your so-called 'truth' could still be a lie in an attempt to deceive. The phrase, 'I am speaking the truth in Christ,' must not be separated from the phrase that follows it, 'my conscience bears me witness in the Holy Spirit' (RSV).

Conscience by itself is not a safe guide. It is the moral sense inside us which approves or disapproves, excuses or accuses our thoughts and our actions. Each of us puts into our conscience (or our parents do) the standards by which it operates. A missionary once stopped a woman throwing her baby into the river Ganges and when he asked her why she wanted to do it, she said, 'My conscience tells me to do it.' He answered, 'My conscience tells me to stop you.'

A true conscience is one trained 'in Christ'. Do not accept the standards of the world. Submit to the tutelage of the Holy Spirit who sensitises our consciences 'in Christ'.

✎ *Holy Spirit, take my conscience today and cleanse it of all false standards so that it becomes a truly Christian conscience, trained in the school of Christ. Amen.*

Many but not one

'So in Christ we who are many form one body …' (v. 5: NIV)

'So we, numerous as we are, are one body in Christ, the Messiah, and individually we are parts of one another – mutually dependent on one another' (AMPLIFIED). There is no such thing as a Christian in isolation. Everybody who belongs to Christ, belongs to everybody else who belongs to Christ. We may betray this relationship, but we can never deny it.

Note the force of Paul's language in this passage, 'We … are one body' (NKJ). Not 'ought to be' or 'called to be' or 'let us consider ourselves as such', but 'we are one body'. As long as we are 'in Christ', we are in the body. This one body is made up of many different individuals, diverse but a unity. The whole of the New-Testament pattern for the church can be summed up in these words – 'many', yet 'one body'. Unfortunately we fail to follow that pattern. Some of the many look upon themselves as the one body. 'Join us,' they say, 'and then we will be one.'

A woman once indicated in her will that she did not want to be buried alongside her husband. Her husband belonged to a different denomination. She thought that when Jesus comes, she will be raised and he will be left behind. How very sad. Denominations may have a useful purpose, but not denominationalism. It divides God's people – in life and death.

✎ *Father, thank you for reminding me that the cords which bind me to Christ are the cords which also bind me to my brothers and sisters. Help me to banish all bigotry out of my life. Amen.*

A place for pride

FOR READING AND MEDITATION – ROMANS 15:14–22

'Therefore I glory in Christ Jesus in my service to God.' (v. 17: NIV)

The Living Bible words today's text as follows: 'So it is right for me to be a little proud of all Christ Jesus has done through me.' Is there a place for pride in the Christian life? Yes, there is. When pride is rooted in an unsurrendered ego, it is sinful pride and self-centred – flee from it. Pride rightly rooted, however, can be an incentive that nerves us forward and helps us be at our best.

When pride is rooted in egotism, it is an ugly weed; when it is rooted 'in Christ', it is a beautiful flower. Pride that glorifies God must draw its sustenance from the Person of Christ. When it boasts, it does so 'in Christ,' and then our boasting is legitimate and proper. What we accomplish is achieved by the grace of God and not by our own strength. This kind of pride is immediately converted into gratitude and follows the line which Paul followed when he said, 'I will not venture to speak of anything except what Christ has accomplished through me …' (v. 18, NIV).

Paul realised that he was not a source, but a channel. The grace and power that flowed in his life came not from him, but through him. This understanding saved him from false humility (a veiled form of pride) and gave him instead self-respect and self-acceptance that was spiritual and legitimate. Pride is only acceptable when it is pride in what God is doing in us and through us.

✎ *Father, help me to understand the difference between righteous pride and unrighteous pride. Amen.*

How to be full of confidence

FOR READING AND MEDITATION – ROMANS 15:23–33
'I know that when I come to you, I will come in
the full measure of the blessing of Christ.' (v. 29: NIV)

This is another important 'in Christ' passage found in Romans: 'I shall come in … Christ.' What amazing confidence Paul demonstrates here as he says, 'I shall come …' – not with a blessing from Christ, but – '… in the fullness of the blessing of the gospel of Christ' (NKJ). Paul had an amazing confidence in Christ because he had an amazing submission to Christ. The reason why many do not have self-confidence is because they do not have Christ-confidence.

The unsubmitted will is always hesitant because, without complete surrender to him, it cannot take complete boldness from him. Full confidence follows full surrender. Fully surrendered, we can fully take. Martin Luther described this principle as 'the divine exchange'. He said, 'We can only fully receive from Christ when we fully give ourselves to Christ.'

The great apostle Paul had discovered the secret which millions of Christians still fail to grasp: that full surrender to the Person of Christ means full supply of the power and resources of Christ. Someone who is fully committed to Christ, is fully capable of doing everything God wants him or her to do. MOFFATT translates Philippians 4:13 like this: 'In him who strengthens me, I am able for anything.' Everything depends on how securely we rest in him.

❧ Father, I see that it is only when my hands are empty that I can fully take from you the power and resources I need. Today my hands are empty – and outstretched. Fill them, please. Amen.

Family connections

FOR READING AND MEDITATION – ROMANS 16:1–16

'… my fellow-workers in Christ Jesus.' (v. 3: NIV)

In this last chapter of Romans Paul sends greetings to his Christian friends and fellow-workers in Rome. 'Greet Priscilla and Aquila, my fellow-workers in Christ Jesus'; 'Greet Andronicus and Junias … they were in Christ before I was'; 'Greet Ampliatus, whom I love in the Lord'; 'Greet Urbanus, our fellow-worker in Christ'; 'Greet Apelles, tested and approved in Christ'; 'Greet those in the household of Narcissus who are in the Lord'; 'Greet Rufus, chosen in the Lord' (vv. 3, 7–13).

These astounding passages lead us to pose the question: is this idea of being 'in Christ' simply a theoretical concept, or is it a fact of life? If it is a theoretical concept, then we approach it as we do any other verbal proposition – intellectually and academically. If it is a fact of life, then we come to it to see how it can be utilised and woven into our daily experience. Personally, I view the phrase 'in Christ' as a fact of life – and so, I believe, did the apostle Paul.

When the great apostle links the phrase to the simple matter of a written greeting, it suggests that he sees his fellow-Christians as closer than any of his blood-relatives. Being in Christ is not just a concept, it is a condition; it is not just a proposition, it is a position. In the family of God no one is an only child.

✎ *Thank you, dear Father, that being in you is not just a concept; it is something that totally affects the whole of my life and the whole of my living. Help me to love as I am loved. Amen.*

Sanctification or crankification

FOR READING AND MEDITATION – 1 CORINTHIANS 1:1–9

'... to those sanctified in Christ Jesus and called to be holy ...' (v. 2: NIV)

We turn now to Paul's use of 'in Christ' in his two epistles to the Corinthians. The first passage is: '... to those sanctified in Christ Jesus'. This tells us where sanctification – personal holiness – lies: not in ourselves, but in Christ. It is often misunderstood. It comes through submission and surrender to Christ and remains as long as we stay submitted and surrendered to Christ. Justification is a completely different subject.

Justification refers to our standing, that is, our position, in Christ; sanctification refers to our state, that is, our progress, in Christ. Sanctification should not be a doctrine, but a dynamic. When we take a scriptural truth, separate it from Christ and its context, and subordinate it to a denomination, a group or even to ourselves, we misuse it.

If I say, 'I am sanctified,' instead of saying, 'I am sanctified in Christ Jesus,' then I am in danger of calling attention to my experience rather than to the One who brings about that experience. When I am self-conscious, the experience fades; when I am Christ-conscious, the experience grows. As someone put it, 'When sanctification remains "in Christ", it is sanctification; out of him, it is "crankification".'

✣ Gracious Father, help us never to forget that we ought to be living a different kind of life from the men and women of the world. And help us never to forget that this different life can never be lived apart from you. Amen.

Total enrichment

FOR READING AND MEDITATION – 1 CORINTHIANS 1:4–17

'For in him you have been enriched in every way …' (v. 5: NIV)

The next 'in Christ' passage in Corinthians tells us that 'in him' we 'have been enriched in every way'. Some argue that when a person becomes a Christian, he or she is impoverished by the experience and loses their spontaneity. I do not believe that.

Our text today tells us that 'in Christ' we are enriched, not in one or two ways, but 'in every way'. He enriches the mind by cleansing away alien thinking, giving it sharpness and direction and driving it to great ends. He enriches the soul by cleansing it from contradictions and conflicts, and filling it with a single loyalty and love. He enriches the body, too, for many of our physical problems are passed on to our bodies from the mind and the emotions.

A Christian doctor said, 'I have often imagined a convention of bodies talking about the people who inhabit them. One body stands up and says, "The person who lives in me doesn't know how to live. He ties me up in knots by his fears and worries and resentments. Then he blames me for getting out of sorts and doses me with all kinds of medicines that have nothing to do with my ailments." Another body stands up and says, "The person who lives in me is wonderful. He is a Christian and hence knows how to live. He is happy and harmonious. We get along fine. I would do anything for him – and I do."' The enrichment we receive 'in Christ' is a total enrichment – of spirit, mind and body.

Father, thank you that you did not come to demean me but to develop me, not to take away from my stature but to add to it. Amen.

Four things found only in Christ

FOR READING AND MEDITATION – 1 CORINTHIANS 1:18–31

'... you are in Christ Jesus, who has become for us wisdom from God –
that is, our righteousness, holiness and redemption.' (v. 30: NIV)

Our next 'in Christ' passage tells us that because we are in Christ Jesus, we receive wisdom, righteousness, holiness and redemption. Wisdom and righteousness were the respective goals of the Greek and Jewish cultures. Paul tells us that 'in Christ' we inherit both.

The Greeks, despite their intensive search, found only a degree of wisdom, but it was not linked to Christ and turned out to be mere foolishness. The Jews sought for righteousness, but tried to find it outside Christ, and found only self-righteousness. The Pharisee was the end product. It became legalistic and destroyed itself.

Some cultures have tried to produce the third quality – holiness. Many religions of the Far East focus on ceremonial and outer cleanness, yet know nothing of that inner change which comes only through a personal encounter with Jesus Christ. It is the same with redemption. Many attempt self-atonement. They pay penance, endure hardships, experience punishments, and involve themselves in acts of great self-denial in the vain hope of alleviating their sense of guilt. But all four things Paul mentions here are not attainable in our own strength. They come to us 'in Christ' or they do not come to us at all.

◁ Father, thank you for reminding me that only in you do I find the Real; all the rest is unreal. You alone are my wisdom, my righteousness, my holiness and my redemption. Amen.

Spiritual babies

FOR READING AND MEDITATION – 1 CORINTHIANS 3:1–9, 21–23
'And I, brethren, could not speak to you as
to spiritual people but as to carnal, as to babes in Christ.' (v.1: NKJ)

The phrase 'babes in Christ' is usually applied to those who have recently come into the Christian faith, but Paul described the Corinthians in this way because they had centred their allegiance around religious teachers instead of around the Lord himself. The Corinthian Christians were in Christ, but they were just babies. How sad. How many of us in today's church fall into this category? Far too many. Every emphasis detached from the living Christ soon becomes sterile and exhausted of meaning. We must respect Christian leaders and honour them for their work, but we must not elevate them or their words to a position alongside Jesus Christ. Christianity that is not centred on Christ is an immature Christianity. According to the Scriptures, the sign that someone is a spiritual baby is that he or she still clings to a spiritual leader rather than to Christ. Yet millions do it.

Some people hang on to every word I say as if I were infallible. But I have no desire to build up a following around the world. I have a desire to draw people to Christ – and nothing more. To be centred in Jesus – and in him alone – makes for external expansion and growth.

✎ *Father, I see that I cannot be mature until I am yours and yours alone. Help me evaluate whether my spiritual life has grown up around another person other than you. And, if so, show me how to shift my basis from that person to you. In Jesus' Name. Amen.*

Free to give: with both hands

FOR READING AND MEDITATION – 1 CORINTHIANS 6:1–11

'... But you were washed, you were sanctified, you were justified in the name
of the Lord Jesus Christ and by the Spirit of our God.' (v. 11: NIV)

Today we come to one of the most amazing 'in Christ' passages in the New Testament. Amongst the Christians in Corinth were men and women who had once been involved in the grossest sins. Some had been idol worshippers, prostitutes, practising homosexuals, adulterers, drunkards, thieves and swindlers. However, their lives had been totally transformed. How did this come about? Was it by a strong and determined effort of the will? No, it came about as a result of their being washed in the cleansing power that flows from Jesus Christ.

Could it have come directly from God without coming through the Name of Jesus Christ and the Spirit of our God? No. If it were claimed that washing, sanctification and justification could come through any other name, that would be a lie. 'There is no other name under heaven given among men by which we must be saved' (Acts 4:12, NKJ).

God can manifest his grace to them only in and through Christ. God is a Christlike God. Only in Christ can God give with both hands.

❧ Gracious and loving heavenly Father, thank you for reminding me that in Christ you are free to give with both hands. This enables me to come to you with confidence. You are free to give and I am free to take. Thank you, my Father. Amen.

A change in vocabulary

FOR READING AND MEDITATION – 1 CORINTHIANS 15:12–28

'Then those also who have fallen asleep in Christ are lost.' (v. 18: NIV)

Today we look at how the condition of being 'in Christ' produces in Paul a new perspective on the subject of death. A contemporary of mine maintains that after the death and resurrection of Jesus no one who was 'in Christ' was ever described in the New Testament as having died. He points out that Luke, commenting on the death of Stephen, refrains from using the word 'death' or 'died' and simply states, 'When he had said this, he fell asleep' (Acts 7:60; John 11:11, RSV).

And when Paul was referring to his own death, he refrained from using the word and said, 'I desire to depart and be with Christ, which is better by far' (Phil. 1:23). Later, when his execution was actually impending, he said, 'The time of my departure is at hand' (2 Tim. 4:6, NKJ). The word *death* is used many times in the New Testament, but whenever the writers refer to the death of an individual, they seem to refrain from it.

Why should this be so? Because they came to see that 'in Christ' there really was no such thing as death. In him, everything lives. When we are 'in Christ', death is simply unthinkable. The glorious fact of being 'in him' is that we are incapable of dying. In Jesus we cannot die, for life can do naught but live.

O Jesus, Lord and Master of both life and death, thank you for reminding me that in you everything is alive – alive for ever more. I am destined to live for ever. When I merge with life, I surge with life. Glory! Amen.

Everything safe and secure

FOR READING AND MEDITATION – 1 CORINTHIANS 15:42–58

'... Always give yourselves fully to the work of the Lord,
because you know that your labour in the Lord is not in vain.' (v. 58: NIV)

How different are the above words from these in a newspaper report: 'I have worked long and hard for my country. I have given the people of my constituency the best years of my life. Somehow it seems that my years have all been spent in vain.' Why this sad lament? Because his labour was not 'in the Lord'.

As a citizen of the same country, I feel quite differently. I have no regrets over my own service to the community, for it has been 'in the Lord'. Outwardly I am not as 'successful' as he. But then, I have been working for and in the Lord. Outside the Lord, the politician felt a failure; 'in the Lord' there can be no failure. Remember that as a Christian you have one business in life – to live and work 'in the Lord'. Results must be his concern.

A missionary returning to India, after being in this country on furlough, said, 'The romance of missions is over. I know exactly what I am going back to, much of it drab and dreary. But if my heavenly Father told me that I would see no successes, only failure, for the balance of my days, I would reply – my business is to be true to the vision I was given. That makes everything safe and secure.' Wonderful words. When everything we do is in him, it is lifted above the vagaries of success and failure. It is safe and secure – in him.

✎ *Father, I see that when I have a holy concern about whether or not what I am doing is in you, then I shall be wholly indifferent to success or failure. Only then is everything wholly safe. Help me live in that frame of mind. Amen.*

The expression of a great love

FOR READING AND MEDITATION – 1 CORINTHIANS 16:13–24

'The grace of the Lord Jesus be with you.
My love to you all in Christ Jesus. Amen.' (vv. 23–24: NIV)

Paul ends his first epistle to the Corinthians with the touching words, 'My love to you all in Christ Jesus.' Why didn't Paul just say, 'My love to all of you'? Why did he add 'in Christ Jesus'? The answer must be that the love which is found 'in Christ Jesus' is the highest type of love that can be found anywhere in the universe, and Paul wanted to convey this love to his brothers and sisters in Corinth.

Someone has said, 'There is no expression of greatness except the expression of a great love.' What is a 'great' love? In English the word *love* has a medley of meanings ranging from the highest to the lowest. So we cannot understand the phrase *expression of a great love* until we have fixed the content of love. In the Greek language there are four words for love, the highest being *agape*, which means a love that is everlasting and unconditional. Unredeemed human nature can demonstrate love, but it can never reach the heights of *agape* love. It does not come up from the heart of man, but down from the heart of God. Outside Jesus Christ it is impossible to love with *agape* love. The highest love human nature can reach is *philia* love, which means a close and deep friendship. Paul loved the Corinthians with a love that came down from above – the love with which he himself was loved.

✎ *Dear Father, there is no expression of greatness except the expression of a great love, then help me share with others the love with which I myself am loved. Amen.*

He is the Yes!

FOR READING AND MEDITATION – 2 CORINTHIANS 1:12–24

'For no matter how many promises God has made,
they are "Yes" in Christ ...' (v. 20: NIV)

We move on now to examine the first of Paul's 'in Christ' passages in his second epistle to the Corinthians. For years I could never understand the text. It only became clear to me when I read it in the *Moffatt* translation: 'The divine "yes" has at last sounded in him ...'

There are some who regard the Christian faith as a denial of the will to live. They say, 'When you become a Christian, you can't do this and you can't do that.' In fact, one critic of Christianity, Solomon Richter, said, 'The Christian faith is a set of scruples imposed on the ordinary framework of humanity to keep it from functioning normally; it is a "No" to human living.' This verse says the opposite – in him it has always been 'Yes' to human living. Everything outside him is 'No'. God meant us to live out our lives on this earth more by affirmation than by negation. Negation is needed in saying 'No' to sin.

Take any thought, attitude or deed that is not of Christ. The result will be sadness, defeat and despair. Take a thought, attitude or deed that is in harmony with the character of Jesus Christ, build on it, and the result will be stupendous success. When Judas went away from Jesus, he finished up by hanging himself. Jesus is the 'Yes'; the 'Yes' to joy, the 'Yes' to growth, the 'Yes' to creativity, the 'Yes' to life itself.

✎ *Gracious Father, I am so grateful for this wonderful 'Yesness' that I find in Christ. I affirm his lordship and so I myself am affirmed. Help me to take Christ's thoughts and attitude into everything I do and say. Amen.*

Solid rocks and sham-rocks

FOR READING AND MEDITATION – 2 CORINTHIANS 1:21–2:4

'Now it is God who makes both us and you stand firm in Christ ...' (v. 21: NIV)

Yesterday we examined the 'in Christ' passage which said that our Lord is the divine 'Yes'. Today we are bidden to stand firm – in him.

If we allow ourselves to be centred on a particular doctrine, we will be swayed and 'tossed to and fro and carried about with every wind of doctrine' (Eph. 4:14, NKJ). I heard of a denomination of over a hundred thousand members which was rocked to its depths over a controversy concerning the way in which the service of holy communion should be conducted. In doctrine they were one (all saw the need for regular communion), but in practice they were divided. If we allow ourselves to be centred on a religious ceremony, or even a popular and powerful preacher, we will find ourselves going up and down according to our likes and dislikes. Only in Christ can we stand firm.

A famous old hymn puts it like this: 'On Christ the solid rock I stand, all other ground is sinking sand.' An Irish preacher I knew used to change the words of the second line to read, 'On Christ the solid rock I stand. All other rocks are sham-rocks.' I only add – they are!

⊰ O Father, how can I thank you enough for establishing my feet on the solid rock which is Christ. Help me stand firm in you – and only in you. In Jesus' Name I ask it. Amen.

He always leads us in triumph

FOR READING AND MEDITATION – 2 CORINTHIANS 2:5–14
'But thanks be to God, who always leads us in
triumphal procession in Christ …' (v. 14: NIV)

What a word to begin a day: 'But thanks be to God, who in Christ always leads us in triumph as trophies of Christ's victory …' (v. 14, AMPLIFIED). If this is so, then why is it that so many of us are defeated and discouraged? Because we do not know how to stay 'in Christ'. When we stay in him, we manifest a spirit which cannot be defeated.

This does not mean that God will intervene to stop unpleasant things from happening to us. What it does mean, is that as we stay in Christ, we will draw from him the spiritual power and energy to be able to wrest something good out of every bad thing that happens. Jesus went to the cross in seeming defeat, but at that very moment of what looked like his greatest failure, he manifested his greatest victory. When a Roman persecutor said to a first-century Christian, 'What can your Master do for you now?', he was given the answer, 'He can help me to forgive you.' Who was the victor in that situation? The Christian's spirit of forgiveness was the victory. This kind of victory is not just inside us, it spreads outside us, too: '… and through us spreads and makes evident the fragrance of the knowledge of God everywhere' (v. 14, AMPLIFIED). The victory is positive, expansive and compelling. It is power – converting power.

✎ *Father, I see that when I manifest the spirit of Christ amid seeming defeat, I am 'being led in triumph'. For it is the spirit which is the victory – the victory that overcomes the world. I am so thankful. Amen.*

Peddlers of God's Word

FOR READING AND MEDITATION – 2 CORINTHIANS 2:12–17

'… we do not peddle the word of God for profit. On the contrary,
in Christ we speak before God with sincerity …' (v. 17: NIV)

What an arresting phrase we find in today's 'in Christ' passage.
Peddlers peddle their wares in order to make a living. It seems in
Paul's day (as in ours) there were those who peddled God's Word
for their own ends – to make a living. How many preachers and
teachers peddle God's Word to gain attention, to put themselves in
the limelight, to satisfy the craving of their own ego? When we
preach, teach or write for our own glorification, and do and say
things that bring us attention, we are peddlers of God's Word. A
critic of Christianity said to a group of ministers, 'Jesus died on a
cross, but you are making a living by it.' He sensed that some men
in the group were more interested in themselves than in Christ.
One of the men said, 'I think he was wrong, but there was enough
truth in his remarks to make them sting.'

A missionary tells how he saw a bird sitting on top of a cross.
When an insect came near, the bird would dart out, gobble it up
and return to the cross. We do the same when we use the cross for
our own self-centred purposes. Paul continues, 'On the contrary, in
Christ we speak before God with sincerity, like men sent from God.'
When we speak in Christ, we proclaim good news; we speak in and
from ourselves, we are peddlers of ecclesiastical wares.

*Jesus, help me to sense whether I am speaking in and from myself or in and
from you. For I see that it is only as I speak in you that I shall stand as an illustration and proclaimer of the good news. For your Name's sake. Amen.*

I am a new creation

FOR READING AND MEDITATION – 2 CORINTHIANS 5:11–17

'Therefore, if anyone is in Christ, he is a new creation …' (v. 17: NIV)

This passage is one of the clearest statements in the New Testament on what happens when a person becomes a Christian. Paul tells us that when someone steps into Christ, he is a completely new creation. In the first account of creation, in Genesis, we read: 'The earth was without form, and void; and darkness was on the face of the deep' (Gen. 1:2, NKJ). Those words picture for us the condition of the heart of a sinner prior to conversion: 'without form' – no purpose running through it, no goal before it, complete and utter chaos; 'and darkness was on the face of the deep' – hopelessness and despair. Then the miracle takes place. The Holy Spirit moves upon the face of this dark, empty, purposeless waste, and out of the chaos comes cosmos.

The moment someone surrenders to Christ, the Holy Spirit moves upon the face of his or her dark, purposeless existence and out of the darkness a new and transformed personality emerges – one with purpose, meaning and a new identity: 'The old has passed away, behold, the new has come' (v. 17, RSV).

The new creation is a miracle. It cannot be accounted for by psychological factors. It can happen to anyone, providing they are willing to recognise that their desire to run their lives on their own terms is a violation of the laws of the universe.

Heavenly Father, move across the face of this formless void that is in the hearts of multitudes this day, and bring them, as you have brought me, to a knowledge of what it means to be in Christ. In Jesus' Name I ask it. Amen.

The heart of redemption

FOR READING AND MEDITATION – 2 CORINTHIANS 5:18–21

'… God was reconciling the world to himself in Christ …' (v. 19: NIV)

Today's 'in Christ' passage is a window through which we look into the heart of redemption. I can't begin to count the number of times over the years I've heard people say, 'I don't like God very much, but I greatly admire Jesus.' A little girl in Sunday school put it like this: 'God wanted to destroy the world, but Jesus wouldn't let him.' She had picked that up from Christian teaching. A Christian woman whose husband was killed in an accident, said, 'If he had been brought home still alive I would have fought with God to save his life.' Her idea of God was of someone with whom you fight in order to get what you want. That is not the picture of God we see in the face of Jesus Christ. God and Christ are one – one in purpose, one in compassion, one in sacrifice. When the first man, Adam, fell into sin, God immediately began to suffer.

Back there in the dim and distant ages of the past, God had an answer to the problem of sin, as we read in Rev. 13:8 '… the Lamb slain from the foundation of the world'(NKJ). The cross lifted up at Calvary is a reflection of the inner cross that was lying upon the heart of God from all eternity. God did not delegate to Jesus the task of loving the human race; God was in Christ, loving and reconciling the world to himself.

✒ O Father, thank you for the truth that you and Jesus are one – one in purpose and in essence. Just as you, dear Father, were in Christ reconciling all things to yourself, so may I be in Christ to reconcile everything I touch. In Jesus' Name. Amen.

His emphasis and his spirit

FOR READING AND MEDITATION – 2 CORINTHIANS 12:14–21

'… We have been speaking in the sight of God as those in Christ …' (v. 19: NIV)

Ending his second epistle to the Corinthians, Paul emphasises that whether he has been condemning or commending, he has been 'speaking in the sight of God as those in Christ'. The *AMPLIFIED* puts it like this: 'It is … in Christ, the Messiah, that we have been speaking, dearly beloved, and all in order to build you up spiritually.' To be in Christ is to speak in Christ. One commentator says, 'To speak in Christ is to speak with his emphasis and with his spirit.'

There are two things we need to do if we are to speak with his emphasis and his spirit. First, we must saturate ourselves in the Gospels, for this is where we find the clearest exposition of his emphasis. A preacher says, 'I was in a plane that was being tossed about by a strong wind. The lady next to me was reading a book about overcoming tension, but despite that, she got sick. I turned to my New Testament, read how Jesus walked on the waves, and rode out the storm as he did – with joy.' Second, we must absorb his spirit through times of prayer and devotion in which we quietly wait before him for his spirit and power to be passed into us. We must have more than his words; we must have his spirit. I have heard people say, 'Now I'm telling you this in love.' Remember to speak in Christ is to speak with his emphasis *and* his spirit.

◁ *Gracious and loving Father, help me always to speak in Christ – openly, honestly and lovingly. And may my words and my tone of voice convey the same message – the message of love. In Jesus' Name. Amen.*

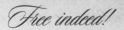
Free indeed!

FOR READING AND MEDITATION – GALATIANS 2:1–10

'Some false brothers had infiltrated our ranks to spy on
the freedom we have in Christ Jesus and to make us slaves.' (v. 4: NIV)

We turn now to consider Paul's first 'in Christ' passage in the epistle to the Galatians: 'our freedom which we have in Christ Jesus'
(RSV). Some in the Galatian church felt that Christ was not enough.
They were quite willing to receive Christ as their Saviour, but they
wanted him *and* the rite of circumcision.

Before we criticise or condemn the Galatians, let's examine our
own spiritual behaviour. Whenever we attempt to add anything to
Christ – Christ *and* our interpretation of him; Christ *and* our doctrinal slogan; Christ *and* our special emphasis; Christ *and* our particular ritual – we are really saying Christ is not enough. Paul set his
face against any 'and' being added to Christ, for he knew that when
we do that, we step out of freedom into bondage. The great apostle
passionately presented a freedom from these endless 'ands', affirming that Christ alone is necessary for salvation. The freedom Paul
enjoyed was the freedom to walk among these laws keeping only
two: 'Love the Lord your God with all your heart and love your
neighbour as yourself.' Paul was free to love Christ and Christ alone,
and in loving him he was freed from complexity to simplicity, from
the marginal to the central. In fighting the Judaisers he was fighting
for freedom – for himself and us.

✍ *Father, I am so thankful for this freedom. In Christ I'm free from a thousand inner and outer bondages. Bound to you, I walk the earth free – free to
live and free to love. Thank you. Amen.*

Salvation: merit or mercy?

FOR READING AND MEDITATION – GALATIANS 2:11–21

'… a man is not justified by observing the law, but by faith in Jesus Christ.
So we, too, have put our faith in Christ Jesus …' (v. 16: NIV)

Today's 'in Christ' passage goes straight to the heart of the problem – are we saved by what we do or by what God has done for us in Christ Jesus? Do we climb up the ladder of self-righteousness to heaven, or does God come down to meet us where we are? This is the question separating Christians from people of all other religions. They all attempt to climb the ladder of salvation and endeavour to earn their entrance into heaven by human merit. But it can't be done. Those who try to climb into God's presence by and through their own efforts, are always on the way – they never arrive. They are wistful, but can never become witnesses. Salvation is just beyond their fingertips. But those who are humble enough to empty their hands of self-righteousness and human striving, receive the gift of eternal life and have the positive assurance that they belong to God and are citizens of heaven.

We are justified not by faith in what we are, but faith in what he's done. Paul puts it like this: 'By grace you have been saved through faith, and that not of yourselves; it is the gift of God' (Eph. 2:8, NKJ). The central truth of the Christian faith is that we do not have to climb a ladder to get to God: God has come down the ladder to get to us.

✏ *O God, what a wondrous thing – we could not get to you, so you came down to us. Nothing on earth or in heaven could be more wonderful than this. I shall be eternally grateful. Amen.*

Jesus – immediately available

FOR READING AND MEDITATION – GALATIANS 3:15–29

'You are all sons of God through faith in Christ Jesus.' (v.26: NIV)

The verses just before today's 'in Christ' passage say, 'The law was our custodian until Christ came, that we might be justified by faith' (v. 24, RSV). Note the transition in these verses from being in custody to being sons of God. When, in Christ, we became sons of God and there was immediate contact with the Father – go-betweens were needed no more. It is often said that the great discovery of the Reformation was the truth that 'the just shall live by faith'. I think there was another great discovery – the immediate availability of Christ. For centuries Christ had been imprisoned in a system. You could not get to him without going through an intermediary. Then came the illuminating truth that no custodians are needed – he is immediately available to all who seek him.

One of the great philosophers of India was one day approached by a brilliant student who said, 'Make me one of your disciples. Be my guru.' The philosopher replied, 'I am not worthy to be your guru.' The student asked, 'Well, who is?' The philosopher said, 'There is only one – Jesus Christ.' 'But I thought he was a dead Jew?' 'No, his followers believe him to be alive.' 'How can I get to know him?' 'Buy a New Testament and you will find him.' The student did just that – and became a Christian. Can you think of anything more wonderful than the immediate availability of Jesus?

No, dear Father – nothing could be more wonderful. Help me to absorb into my spirit all that is involved in this most amazing truth. Amen.

No distinctions – in Christ

FOR READING AND MEDITATION – GALATIANS 3:15–29

'There is neither Jew or Greek, slave nor free, male or female,
for you are all one in Christ Jesus.' (v. 28: NIV)

Today we focus on yesterday's passage by concentrating on verse 28. It tells us that in Christ all distinctions are eliminated. In Christ there is neither Jew nor Greek – so all racial distinctions are eliminated. There is neither slave nor free – so all social distinctions are eliminated. There is neither male nor female – so all sexual distinctions are eliminated. In Christ a new society has emerged – a society without discrimination.

I am always intrigued by a verse in Acts which reads, 'Now in the local church at Antioch there were prophets and teachers, Barnabas, Symeon (called Niger) and Lucius the Cyrenian, besides Manaen (a foster-brother of Herod the tetrarch) and Saul' (Acts 13:1, MOFFATT). In this passage Barnabas is given top billing and Saul is last. But look also at this phrase: 'Manaen, a foster-brother of Herod'. To have a foster-brother of the king in a local church was quite a catch. If it happened today, Christian magazines would vie with each other to get an interview. The inspired record, however, tucks Manaen in the middle of the list, with a Negro above him. Evidently, in that first community of Christians all class distinctions were wiped out. Where Christ is, distinctions are not.

O Lord Jesus, you whose love has an all-embracing character and quality, set me free from every distinction that disrupts and divides. Make me less class-conscious and more Christ-conscious. In Jesus' Name I pray. Amen.

Try preaching the truth!

FOR READING AND MEDITATION – GALATIANS 5:1–9

'In Christ Jesus … the only thing that counts is
faith expressing itself through love.' (v. 6: NIV)

Paul penned three important passages in relation to the Jewish rite of circumcision. The first is found in 1 Cor. 7:19, the second in Gal. 6:15 and the third in today's passage. This is how they read: 'Circumcision is nothing and uncircumcision is nothing. Keeping God's commands is what counts'; 'Neither circumcision nor uncircumcision means anything; what counts is a new creation'; 'For in Christ Jesus neither circumcision nor uncircumcision has any value. The only thing that counts is faith expressing itself through love'. In all these passages Paul shows that circumcision – the dividing sign between Jew and Gentile – is no longer of any importance, for in Christ Jesus there are just three things that matter: keeping the commandments of God; a new creation; and faith expressing itself through love.

Some Christians act as if their faith must be expressed through combat, through argument, through criticism or by exposing others and proving them wrong. This kind of 'faith' is not Christian faith. Faith that does not work by love is one of the most unattractive things in the world. Our faith must work by love, or else it will not work at all.

✎ *Gracious and loving Father, give me, I pray, a faith that works by love and by nothing but love. For I see that if it works by anything else, it is not the Christian faith. Help me, dear Father. In Jesus' Name. Amen.*

His views – my views

FOR READING AND MEDITATION – GALATIANS 5:10–16

'I am confident in the Lord that you will take no other view ...' (v. 10: NIV)

This passage contains both an invitation and a warning. We're invited to be so identified with the Lord that our views become his views. We're warned that we should not take it for granted that our views are necessarily 'in the Lord'. Paul is convinced that making the rite of circumcision part of the Christian commitment would be a grave error. If it had been retained, it would have crippled the Christian faith throughout the ages.

Views often reflect customs and conditioning – or even egoism turned religious. They may be left-over prejudices from the past – not so much 'in the Lord' as in our class-consciousness, in our upbringing, in our tradition ... We can project our subconscious desires into our personal opinions and then believe we are 'in the Lord'. Paul was conscious as he wrote that he was speaking 'in the Lord' and that those who really knew the divine Shepherd would recognise the Master's voice. Listen: 'I have confidence in the Lord that you will take no contrary view of the matter but will come to think with me' (AMPLIFIED).

When we stay close to the Scripture, our words have an author-ity which they lack when we simply share our own opinions. May we dwell so deeply 'in the Lord' that day by day our views will be more and more his views.

✎ *O Father, grant that the Spirit will constantly be at work to correct all wrong judgments and bring my views more in line with yours. Help me be humble enough to heed those corrections. In Jesus' Name. Amen.*

Saints – in Ephesus!

FOR READING AND MEDITATION – EPHESIANS 1:1–6
'Paul, an apostle of Christ Jesus by the will of God,
to the saints in Ephesus, the faithful in Christ Jesus.' (v. 1: NIV)

We now look at some 'in Christ' passages in Paul's epistle to the Ephesians. In the very first verse, Paul presents two striking and contrasting phrases: 'in Ephesus' and 'in Christ Jesus'. The RSV marginal reading of this verse puts it like this: 'The saints who are at Ephesus and faithful'. Put this way, Paul seems to express wonder and admiration that the saints could live in Ephesus *and* be faithful. Ephesus at the time of Paul was a heathen hell-hole, a cesspool of iniquity, a veritable hive of debauchery and sin; Ephesus was hard on saintliness. But there were saints in Ephesus, nevertheless.

How could people live a saintly life in Ephesus? They could when they were 'in Christ'. Being 'in Ephesus' meant sinfulness, but being 'in Christ' in Ephesus meant saintliness. Being 'in Ephesus' for you and me might mean an office, a household, a factory, a schoolroom, a hospital ward, a shop, a university or college campus where Christ's Name is constantly blasphemed and where sin and corruption abound. Lay hold of the truth that you are not just 'in Ephesus,' but 'in Christ in Ephesus'. It can help turn the irritations into irradiations and make an outer hell into an inner heaven. You may be environed by Ephesus, but you are also environed by the kingdom of God.

My Father, thank you for reminding me that Ephesus does not have the final word in my life – you do. That in Christ I am in a greater environment than my daily physical environment. Thank you, dear Father. Amen.

Everything we need – in him

FOR READING AND MEDITATION – EPHESIANS 1:3–8

'For He chose us in him before the creation of the world ... in love he predestined us to be adopted as his sons through Jesus Christ ...' (vv. 4–5: NIV)

Today's verses present us with a glorious constellation of 'in Christ' passages. We are 'blessed' in Christ, 'chosen' and 'predestined' in Christ and 'adopted' through Christ. What does it mean to be 'blessed' in Christ? It means that we have everything we need for our moral and spiritual development – in him. In other words, everything that is good for us in the realm of the moral and the spiritual is found in the Person of our Lord Jesus Christ.

What does it mean to be 'chosen' and 'predestined' in Christ? Literally it means 'to be marked out beforehand'. The Almighty saw our entrance into the world and, even though we did not yet exist, determined to make us his own children through the redeeming work of Christ. John Stott says about verse 5, 'God put us and Christ together in his thinking.' When I first came into the Christian life, I used to think that I had chosen God. Then I saw that God had chosen me.

We have one more truth to look at – we are 'adopted' through Christ. What a wondrous truth this is, too. I am reminded of the little girl who, taunted by her school friends because she was an adopted child, replied, 'Anyway, your parents had to have you – my parents chose me from amongst everyone else.'

Loving Father, how can I ever sufficiently thank you for the endless blessings you have given to me 'in Christ'? You have given everything to me – help me now to give everything to you. In Jesus' Name. Amen.

No other way

FOR READING AND MEDITATION – EPHESIANS 1:7–10

'In him we have redemption through his blood,
the forgiveness of sins …' (v. 7: NIV)

This must surely be the greatest blessing we have 'in Christ' – 'In him we have redemption, deliverance and salvation, through his blood, the remission and forgiveness of our offenses, shortcomings and trespasses, in accordance with the riches and generosity of his gracious favour' (AMPLIFIED). Can we not have redemption some other way? The answer is 'No!' When we have offended someone on a human level, we can redeem ourselves in their sight by making our own atonement for our transgression. We can beg their forgiveness, promise to make amends, even humiliate ourselves, and by so doing atone for our misdemeanor. We cannot do that in relation to God. All our begging of forgiveness, all our good intentions, all our humiliation, can in no way bring about our redemption in his sight. The broken relationship between us and God could only be mended by God himself taking the initiative. God did this on Calvary when 'he himself bore our sins in his body on a tree' (1 Peter 2:24).

Now when we come to God and ask for his forgiveness, he is able to forgive us, on the basis of his giving. Our asking for forgiveness is important – but it is not the basis for our redemption; Christ's death procures that.

✎ Father, the fact that you can be so loving to the unlovely, so gracious to the ungracious, so kind to the unkind, completely overwhelms me. In the light of this I shall own no other allegiance. You are my rightful Lord. Amen.

Christ – the centre of our unity

FOR READING AND MEDITATION – EPHESIANS 1:9–14

'And he made known to us the mystery of his will according to
his good pleasure, which he purposed in Christ.' (v. 9: NIV)

Today's passage shows us that God has done more than choose us in Christ and give us sonship now, as a present possession. It reveals that he has also given us 'complete insight and understanding of the open secret of his will, showing us how it was the purpose of his design … that all things in heaven and earth alike should be gathered up in Christ' (vv. 9–10, MOFFATT). God has a supreme purpose – the gathering up of all things in Christ. This means that history is moving toward a predetermined goal. The 'mystery' referred to here is the inclusion of the Gentiles on equal terms with Jews in God's new society. This ethnic unity is a symbol or foretaste of the marvellous unity which we shall see in hea-ven. We need to keep in mind that God's plan is to unite all things 'in Christ'. It is God's purpose and pattern right here and now – as well as in heaven. Any plan for Christian unity that is not based on the fact that we are 'all one in Christ Jesus', will just not work.

Some Christians seem to mistake 'unity' for 'uniformity', or even 'unanimity'. They only feel united with those who share their particular view on doctrine. We can differ in our view of doctrine and still enjoy unity in Christ, as long as we agree on the essentials.

Gracious Father, help us to hold on to the fact that your plan is to unite all things 'in Christ' – here, as well as in eternity. Help us to make Christ the centre of our faith and nothing but him. Amen.

Awaiting collection

FOR READING AND MEDITATION – EPHESIANS 1:13–23

'… Having believed, you were marked in him with a seal,
the promised Holy Spirit.' (v. 13: NIV)

Our 'in Christ' passage for today informs us that when we came to Christ a divine sealing took place – we were 'marked in him with a seal, the promised Holy Spirit'. Christians are divided over what this 'sealing' is and when it takes place. Some believe it occurs at a time subsequent to our salvation, in what they describe as a 'second blessing' or 'the baptism' or 'filling' with the Spirit. I certainly believe that the 'sealing' referred to in our text takes place at the time of our conversion. When we first surrender our lives to Christ, the Holy Spirit comes into us to regenerate us. 'Flesh gives birth to flesh, but the Spirit gives birth to spirit' (John 3:6). At this time an inward seal is put inside us by the Holy Spirit, indicating that we now belong to Christ. A seal is a mark of ownership and authenticity, and this sealing of the Spirit is 'a deposit guaranteeing our inheritance until the redemption of those who are God's possession' (v.14).

In Paul's time wealthy merchants would send an employee to purchase timber from a trader, and once he had selected the desired piece, he would mark it with his master's seal for collection at a later time. We are sealed at our conversion with the Holy Spirit of promise – and are waiting to be collected.

✹ O Father, I see that the presence of the Holy Spirit in my life makes me a 'guaranteed' person. I am not only assured of heaven, but with your indwelling Spirit I have heaven to go to heaven in. Thank you. Amen.

Clean of their own accord

FOR READING AND MEDITATION – EPHESIANS 1:15–23

'... ever since I heard about your faith in the Lord Jesus and your love for all the saints ...' (v. 15: NIV)

'Faith and love,' said someone, 'are the apostle Paul's Siamese twins.' They turn up together time after time in the great apostle's letters. When writing to the Thessalonians, Paul says, for example, 'Timothy has ... brought us the good news of your faith and love' (1 Thess. 3:6, RSV). In his second epistle to the Thessalonians he congratulates the converts there on the fact that 'your faith is growing abundantly, and the love of every one of you for one another is increasing' (2 Thess. 1:3, RSV). Is it just a matter of chance that faith and love are so closely connected? No, they are cause and effect – love flows out of faith.

To encourage people to love without faith is merely an exercise in futility. Genuine love must have its roots in faith in the Lord Jesus Christ. When we centre our attention on Christ, our faith grows, and we find that not only do we begin to think like Christ and act like Christ, but we begin to love like Christ. A Belgian government official said to a pastor: 'We have been pressing ... your people to clean up, but nothing happened. You come along and say something to them and they clean up of their own accord. What's the secret?' The secret was simple – one look at Jesus and they wanted to be clean 'of their own accord'.

My Father, help me to live in such a way that faith and love will be the alternative beats of my heart in everything I do and everywhere I go. I ask this in the precious Name of Jesus. Amen.

A working principle

FOR READING AND MEDITATION – EPHESIANS 1:17–23

'… That power is like the working of his mighty strength, which he exerted in Christ when he raised him from the dead …' (vv.19–20: NIV)

This passage brings us to one of the most powerful insights in Scripture. Paul affirms that the very same power that raised Jesus from the dead, also works redemptively in us, enabling us to sit with him in heavenly places – the final seat of authority. The resurrection of Christ is a dynamic that ought to affect every aspect of our lives. The same power that turned the most humiliating defeat in history into the most glorious triumph, is available to you.

To be in Christ means I am in a triumphant Christ, not a defeated Christ. I am in a Christ who wrought out the greatest victory ever seen – not as a victory for himself alone, but as a victory available to all who are in him. This is not just an interesting concept, but a working principle of the Christian life. In Christ you and I are living on the greatest power that was ever manifested – the power that raised Jesus from the dead. We plug into the power of his resurrection and go out every day to live by that power. Are you pressed down by difficult and perplexing circumstances? Then realise that resurrection power is at work in your life, not always to change the circumstances, but to bring you out from under them. If it took Christ from the sepulchre to the throne, it is well able to deliver you.

✎ O Father, forgive me that so often I think of the resurrection as something to be admired. Let it rise in me today, lifting me above all my trials. In Jesus' Name. Amen.

A look at our destiny

FOR READING AND MEDITATION – EPHESIANS 2:1–10

'For we are God's workmanship,
created in Christ Jesus to do good works …' (v. 10: NIV)

Today's passage must be looked at in the light of the two verses immediately preceding it: 'For it is by grace you have been saved, through faith – and this not from yourselves, it is the gift of God – not by works, so that no one can boast.' Verse 9 says that we have not been saved by good works, while our verse for today says we are created for good works. These two verses sum up the position regarding good works: we are not saved because of good works, but we are saved for good works. 'Salvation does not come out of good works,' said someone, 'good works are the outcome of salvation.' The good works that come out of salvation are the result of good 'workmanship'. Our Lord does not begin by changing our deeds; he begins by changing us. Good deeds come out of the good person. 'The good man,' says Scripture, 'brings good out of his good store' (Matt.12:35, MOFFATT).

'In Christ' we are destined to bring forth good works – 'good works, which God prepared beforehand' (NKJ). Just as a fish was destined to swim, so a Christian is destined for 'good works'. This is why we have such a bad time when we practise these bad works after we have become Christians. Once we are 'in Christ', we are destined and designed for good works.

Father, I see that now I am a Christian, I am destined and designed in the very structure of my being for good works. Your stamp is in my inner being, hence my good works come out of good workmanship. Thank you. Amen.

Why belong to panic?

FOR READING AND MEDITATION – EPHESIANS 3:1–13
'In him and through faith in him we may approach God
with freedom and confidence.' (v. 12: NIV)

We discover another benefit that arises from being 'in Christ' –
right of access to God and all his resources. Outside Christ there is
no access to God. No matter how strenuously someone may try,
there is simply no way by which he or she can come to know the
Almighty except through Jesus Christ. Erich Fromm, a secularist
and a humanist, wrote in one of his books, 'There is only one solution to man's problem: to face the truth, to acknowledge his fundamental aloneness in a universe indifferent to his fate, to recognise that there is no power transcending him which can solve his
problem for him. If he faces the truth without panic, he will recognise that there is no meaning to life except the meaning man gives
his life by the unfolding of his powers, by living productively.' How
different from Paul's glorious affirmation that 'in Christ' we have
access to God the Father and all of his resources.

Our Lord referred to himself in the Gospels as 'The Way'. In
Jesus the way is open out of prison into freedom, out of defeat into
victory, out of misery into mastery, out of loneliness into fellowship, out of sin into forgiveness, out of death into life. Eric Fromm
speaks of panic; Paul speaks of endless possibilities. Why belong to
panic when you can belong to possibility?

✎ *Father, I am so thankful that I belong not to panic but to possibility. 'In
Christ' I have access to everything that is good. I am rich beyond calculation
or imagination. I am so deeply, deeply grateful. Amen.*

Growing up into him

FOR READING AND MEDITATION – EPHESIANS 4:7–16

'... speaking the truth in love, we will in all things grow up
into him who is the Head, that is, Christ.' (v. 15: NIV)

This 'in Christ' passage emphasises the truth that we become what
we habitually give out – 'speaking the truth in love, we will in all
things grow up into him ... Christ'. Whilst it is true that what we
believe on the inside affects how we act on the outside, it is also
true that how we act on the outside influences and reinforces the
beliefs we hold. Whilst love must come into us before it can flow
out of us – the more love we give out, the more loving we become.

Paul connects speaking the truth to growing up in Christ. It is
as if he is saying, 'When we are in Jesus and speak the truth in love,
then we grow up in every way into him.' What if we just speak the
truth but there is no love mixed into the truth? Then – we don't
grow. Truth with love produces redemption; truth without love
produces rebellion. Bare truth can never redeem. This is why God
wrapped his truth in love and called his Name – Jesus. In Jesus love
speaks, acts and thinks in every word, every syllable, every deed.

The Amplified Bible's translation of today's verse is: '... enfolded
in love, let us grow up in every way and in all things into him ...'
Some people believe conversion to Christ stultifies the personality.
The truth is that only 'in Christ' do we find the resources that
enable us to reach our fullest potential.

❧ *Lord Jesus, I would grow up into you in all things. Let the spiritual hor-*
mones of love and truth be at work in my life, contributing to my growth
and adding inches to my spiritual stature. In Jesus' Name I ask it. Amen.

The cost of forgiveness

FOR READING AND MEDITATION – EPHESIANS 4:25–32
'Be kind and compassionate to one another, forgiving each other,
just as in Christ God forgave you.' (v. 32: NIV)

This powerful verse has been described as 'the high-water mark of morality in the universe'. We are encouraged to forgive others in the same way we were forgiven 'in Christ'. How does God forgive in Christ? Lightly? The Cross is the price he had to pay to forgive our sins. God offers forgiveness in a nail-pierced hand. Our forgiveness of others is also costly. When we forgive someone who has hurt us deeply, there is a sense in which we bear in our own souls the sins of the one who is being forgiven. We offer forgiveness in nail-pierced hearts.

I talked with a woman recently whose husband had an affair. She said, 'There was a moment when, although I knew that Christ had taken my husband's sin into his own body on the Cross, I had to take it, too. I felt the pain of my husband's sin come deep within me and I realised that unless I held it and quenched it in the love that flowed toward me from Jesus Christ, I would lash out at him day after day for the rest of our lives.' As she spoke, I said to myself, 'Would to God we could all do this.' There is no other way. If we do not forgive, we break down the bridge over which we must cross to God – the bridge of forgiveness. The forgiveness we get in Christ is the forgiveness we must give in Christ.

✒ *Loving Father – you forgive not only with a costly forgiveness, but with a generous forgiveness. Help me to forgive like that. Let me not hold any corners of unforgiveness in my heart. In Jesus' Name. Amen.*

Bound to be confident

FOR READING AND MEDITATION – PHILIPPIANS 1:1–14

'Because of my chains, most of the brothers in the Lord have been encouraged to speak the word of God more courageously and fearlessly.' (v. 14: NIV)

Today Paul is telling us that as a result of his imprisonment the Christians in Philippi were more confident in the Lord. We would have thought that they would have felt that way when he was out of prison. The early Christians thought a little differently to the usual thinking today. We expect the righteous to be exempted from suffering and pain; we think that God is working for us if we are protected from troubles and calamities. But Paul had instilled into the first century believers that when a Christian enters into a trial, he doesn't rebel against it – he uses it. The Christian takes hold of whatever comes and transforms it so that it advances him toward the goal of becoming more like Jesus Christ. The early Christians saw Paul turn his imprisonment into fruitfulness. He said, 'I am in chains for Christ.' He saw his fetters as forged in the counsels of God in eternity.

Shut up in prison, he wrote the deathless letters which have enriched the world. Some think that Paul did more from behind bars than when he was free! So the early Christians got the message, 'What does it matter if we are put into prison? We will preach to the guards and the other prisoners – and win them for Christ. When the worst happens, we can turn it into the best.'

✎ *Father, help me see that while I cannot expect to be exempted from the troubles of life, I can expect to be adequate for them. When you back me, the universe backs me. How can I be anything but confident? Amen.*

The highest joy

FOR READING AND MEDITATION – PHILIPPIANS 3:1–14

'Finally, my brothers, rejoice in the Lord!' (v. 1: NIV)

This 'in Christ' passage offers sound advice, for when you cannot squeeze a drop of rejoicing out of your circumstances, your prospects or your past, you can always rejoice in the Lord. Habakkuk found this out when he wrote, 'Though the fig tree may not blossom, nor fruit be on the vines … yet will I rejoice in the Lord, I will joy in the God of my salvation' (Hab. 3:17–18, NKJ). Habakkuk shows us in the Old Testament what Paul shows us in the New Testament, that when you cannot rejoice in what happens to you, you can rejoice in the God of your salvation.

Being 'in Christ' means that we have access to the One who said, 'These things I have spoken to you, that my joy may remain in you, and that your joy may be full' (John 15:11, NKJ). It is as if he is saying: when My joy is in you, then your own joy will reach its highest potential. His joy is not alien to our joy; they are akin. Our joy in him is supernaturally natural.

Many Christians are lacking in joy. As someone said, 'They follow their own hearse around.' Luke 10:17–22 records that the seventy-two returned with joy and said, 'Lord, even the demons are subject to us in your Name.' Jesus replied, 'Rejoice rather because your names are written in heaven' (v. 20, NKJ).

✎ Blessed Lord Jesus, let my joy be in you – then my joy will be full. Help me see that when there is nothing else to rejoice in, I can always rejoice in you. Thank you, my Saviour. Amen.

What a difference!

FOR READING AND MEDITATION – PHILIPPIANS 4:4–13
'I can do everything through him who gives me strength.' (v. 13: NIV)

Moffatt translates today's verse, 'In him who strengthens me, I am able for anything.' Once when I had preached on this verse, a person came up to me and said, 'I have come to the conclusion that there are two types of Christians – those who are power-conscious and those who are problem-conscious.' Which type are you?

Let's look at Moffatt's translation. 'In him' – not 'through him' as if he were an outside helper, 'but in him'. Since I am in him and he is in me, then I possess all his resources. '… who strengthens me', note the 'who'. He directly and immediately strengthens me. The power does not come through an intermediary, but directly from Christ himself: His life flowing into my life, his Spirit merging into my spirit. '… who *strengthens* me'. The moment we need his strength, it is there: it is always there. 'who strengthens *me*.' This means the total me: spirit, soul and body. He doesn't do everything, thus weakening my personality, but gives me enough of his strength to make a strong me. 'I am able for anything.' Strong on the inside, I can say, 'Come on, world, do your worst and see how God will match it with his best.'

✎ *O God, help me become a power-conscious and not a problem-conscious person. Show me that it is not my responsibility but my response to your ability that makes all the difference. And what a difference! Thank you, my Father. Amen.*

Pleased to dwell

FOR READING AND MEDITATION – COLOSSIANS 1:9–20

'For God was pleased to have all his fulness dwell in him.' (v. 19: NIV)

The RSV translates today's text this way: 'For in him all the fulness of God was pleased to dwell.' One commentator says of this, 'In most of us God dwells, but he dwells sufferingly. He is with us and inside us alright, but he lives there in pain – our unchristlikeness creates a stab in his heart.' In Christ, however, God is perfectly at home. The Almighty dwells in Jesus, not sufferingly, but joyously. He is the only perfect vehicle through whom God can express himself.

Some modern-day theologians contend that while he was on earth, Christ underwent a conversion experience similar to ours, in which he passed from brokenness to wholeness, from imperfection to perfection. What nonsense! On two separate occasions God spoke to him from his cloudy pulpit and confirmed the unsullied purity of his Son (Matt. 3:17 and 17:5). We have to go from brokenness, through conversion, to wholeness, but Jesus didn't. Perfect manhood and perfect Godhood flowered in him. There was nothing that could be done or can be done to make Christ more perfect in character. 'This is my beloved Son, in whom I am well pleased' (Matt. 3:17, NKJ). No wonder, for he was a perfect Son. In us lies some of the fulness of God: in Christ it is there in all its power and majesty.

♦ Father, as I see how pleased you were to dwell in your Son, my heart longs that you might find pleasure also in dwelling in me. Show me what I need to do to make you as at home in my life. For his dear Name's sake. Amen.

Effortless activity

FOR READING AND MEDITATION – COLOSSIANS 1:21–29

'... so that we may present everyone perfect in Christ. To this end I labour,
struggling with all his energy, which so powerfully works in me.' (vv. 28–29: NIV)

Here Paul shares with us his goal – bringing everyone up to their
full maturity in Christ. But wasn't that something which God could
do on his own? Isn't it the work of the Holy Spirit to bring Christians to the place of spiritual maturity? The Holy Spirit is the prime
agent in making us like Jesus Christ, but God uses others, such as
friends and counsellors, in this task. Both the divine and the human
are employed in this task.

The maturity Paul is referring to here is not just psychological,
but spiritual maturity. To the world, you are 'mature' when you can
function well in your environment. But it's a poor sort of maturity
that merely fits someone to be a cog in a social and economic
machine. Being mature 'in Christ' is being mature in love. That is
the maturity that will make a person function well in their environment without being an echo of it.

Paul's struggling was not in the energy of the flesh, but in the
power of the Spirit. Christ put into Paul the energy he expended.
Paul worked with effortless activity – pouring out what was
poured in.

*Father, help me understand even more clearly how to pour out what you
are pouring in – and to do it with effortless activity. May all the energy I
expend be all the energy you pour in. For Christ's sake I ask it. Amen.*

As – so

FOR READING AND MEDITATION – COLOSSIANS 2:6–23

'So, then, just as you received Christ Jesus as Lord,
continue to live in him.' (v. 6: NIV)

This verse tells us how we can live happily and effectively in Christ. The way we received him is the way we are to live in him. How did we receive Christ? By surrender and receptivity. We gave our lives to him and he gave his life to us. Give and take is the relationship between Christ and ourselves.

Giving on our side means giving of the one and the only thing we own – ourselves. When this is done, the way is open to receive all. God asks that we give all in order to receive all. Among the things he gives us is – ourselves. When we give ourselves to him, he cleanses the self of all its conflicts and contradictions and then gives it back to us – redeemed and ready to be used in his service. We are now at home with ourselves and with God. From birth to death we live by surrender and receptivity. The child before birth surrenders to its environment and receives everything from its mother. The little baby drawing life and nourishment from its mother's breast is a beautiful symbol of the humble, surrendered receptivity which must characterise every Christian. An unsurrendered Christian is unable to absorb the grace of God; unable to take because he has not given himself. The moment he gives himself, he can receive.

Father, I see that when I give with both hands, I can take with both hands. Let the truth of what I have been meditating upon today be driven deeply into my spirit. In Jesus' Name I ask it. Amen.

In Christ: zest to everything

FOR READING AND MEDITATION – 1 THESSALONIANS 1:1–10
'We continually remember before our God and Father your work
produced by faith, your labour prompted by love, and your
endurance inspired by hope in our Lord Jesus Christ.' (v. 3: NIV)

In today's passage Paul picks up three things he had mentioned
before – faith, hope and love – but ties them together with a new
emphasis. He talks of 'work produced by faith', 'labour prompted
by love' and 'endurance inspired by hope in our Lord Jesus Christ'.
All three flow out of being 'in Christ'. You can have work, labour
and endurance outside Christ, but then all three lack a vital ele-
ment. There is no faith in the work, no love in the labour, no hope
in the endurance. In the end it means irksome work, laborious
labour and hope-less endurance, what Bertrand Russell called 'an
unyielding despair'.

Being 'in Christ' adds zest to everything. It puts faith into our
work, for we discover ourselves doing everything for him. It puts
love into our labour, for we realise we are labouring for him whom
we love. It puts hope into our endurance, for we are assured that no
matter how hard and difficult our path may be, one day we will
receive our eternal reward. A woman walked for the first time into
a Christian church and said to the minister as she left, 'I came here
without faith, hope or love, but I have seen all three in the eyes of
these people.' Would to God it shone so clearly in all our churches.

*My Father, grant that from today forward there may be more faith in my
work, more hope in my endurance and more love in my labour. In Jesus'
Name. Amen.*

I am if you are

FOR READING AND MEDITATION – 1 THESSALONIANS 3:1–13

'For now we really live, since you are standing firm in the Lord.' (v. 8: NIV)

Today's 'in Christ' passage beautifully illustrates the identification Paul had with his converts and fellow-Christians. *The Living Bible* puts it thus: 'We can bear anything as long as we know that you remain strong in him.' In a sense, Paul is saying to the converts at Thessalonica, 'When you are happy, I am happy; when you are hurt, I am hurt.' In a certain part of Africa, whenever anyone is asked, 'How are you today?', the usual answer is, 'I am if you are.' The speaker means by this, 'I am only well if there is nothing wrong with you. If you have a problem, then it affects me, too.'

The empathy Paul shows toward his converts here is empathy at its highest level. Sympathy is feeling *like* someone; empathy is feeling *with* someone. Sympathy is wholly subjective: it goes down with the sufferer into his or her pain and then both struggle. Empathy feels the hurt the other is feeling, but retains enough objectivity to help lift him or her out of it. It must be pointed out, of course, that although Paul felt keenly the hurts and heartaches of his fellow-Christians, his own spiritual life was not anchored in them – but in Christ. He was uplifted when his converts demonstrated growth and progress, and he was saddened when they fell by the way. But he was not dependent on their growth – he was dependent on Christ.

My Father, help me to have empathy with my brothers and sisters, but let me see that it has to be limited empathy. My final and unlimited empathy is with you, for it is in you that I live. Thank you, Father. Amen.

A new perspective on death

FOR READING AND MEDITATION – 1 THESSALONIANS 4:9–18

'… and the dead in Christ will rise first.' (v. 16: NIV)

I was fascinated by the phrase 'the dead in Christ' for a long time. It appeared to be a contradiction in terms. I thought to myself: there are no dead 'in Christ'; everything in him is alive and alive for ever more. I have since realised that the phrase 'dead in Christ' refers to those who were committed followers of Jesus Christ and who died. It is interesting that prior to this statement Paul refers to death as 'sleep': 'We do not want you to be ignorant about those who fall asleep' (v. 13); 'God will bring with Jesus those who have fallen asleep in him' (v. 14); 'We who are still alive … will certainly not precede those who have fallen asleep' (v. 15). I am grateful for these references, for the word *sleep* helps to put the thought of death in its proper perspective. Those who die 'in Christ' may die physically, but they do not die spiritually. Actually, they are more alive when they are dead than when they were alive.

Some say the term *sleep* means that we remain unconscious after death. Then why did Paul say, 'I have a desire to depart and be with Christ, which is better by far' (Phil. 1:23)? Paul was enjoying the presence of Christ here on earth, but knew that after death he would enjoy it even more. Let the wonder of this take a fresh grip on your soul today.

✎ *Father, thank you for reminding me that physical death is just the tossing aside of an outworn body on the way to real life. I shall be alive after it has gone. Amen.*

All authority is from God

FOR READING AND MEDITATION – 1 THESSALONIANS 5:12–24

'… respect those who work hard among you,
who are over you in the Lord and who admonish you.' (v. 12: NIV)

The early Christian creed said, 'Jesus is Lord.' It is clear and decisive – there is one Lord. Does today's verse mean that there are underlings? I believe so. Paul had a good deal to say about the need for Christians to submit to rightful and legitimate authority. In Romans 13:1–2 he says, '… for all legitimate authority is derived from God's authority, and the existing authority is appointed under God. To oppose authority then is to oppose God, and such opposition is bound to be punished' (J.B. PHILLIPS). It would be simple if we had to obey Christ and him alone – he is so trustworthy. I said to a woman who was struggling with obeying the church authorities, 'Surrender the matter to Christ and trust him to work it out through the authorities over you.' She replied, 'It's one thing to trust Christ, it's another thing to trust his underlings.'

What's the solution? It is recognised that one of the most powerful ways of developing a strong character is learning how to submit joyfully to authority. You will never be able to lead until you know how to obey. But what if the authority over us makes a wrong decision – one which is against our interests? Then sit back and watch God quietly bring his purposes to pass. Many people struggle with this principle, but it is scriptural, nevertheless.

✎ O Father, help me to see that all legitimate authority is your authority. And help me to esteem those over me in authority with the same love that I have for you. For your own dear Name's sake. Amen.

A double glorifying

FOR READING AND MEDITATION – 2 THESSALONIANS 1:1–12

'We pray this so that the Name of our Lord Jesus may be glorified in you, and you in him ...' (v. 12: NIV)

Paul is praying that the Thessalonian converts may be made worthy of their calling 'in Christ'. He prays also that God's power may fulfil every good purpose of their lives and every act prompted by their faith. It is clear that Paul believes that through persevering and intercessory prayer it is possible to tap resources adequate for anything that needs to be done. And the result is 'that the Name of our Lord Jesus may be glorified in you, and you in him'. Paul talks here about a double glorifying. The fact that we, who are redeemed sinners, can do something to glorify the Lord Jesus Christ, is a truth that causes us to fall at his feet in awe. But to be told, in addition, that in the glorifying of Christ we ourselves are glorified!

This verse gives us a little glimpse into the great mystery of redemption. God is not only interested in glorifying the Redeemer – Christ; he is interested also in glorifying the redeemed – you and me. In the glorifying of the Redeemer the redeemed are glorified, and in the glorifying of the redeemed the Redeemer is glorified. This 'is according to the grace of our God and the Lord Jesus Christ' (v. 12). How thankful we ought to be for the grace that not only redeems us, but also seeks to glorify us.

✍ Jesus, I bow in adoration before you to thank you for the grace that not only redeems me but also glorifies me. My gratitude shall be yours throughout all eternity. Amen.

Confidence in the Lord

FOR READING AND MEDITATION – 2 THESSALONIANS 3:1–15

'We have confidence in the Lord that you are doing and
will continue to do the things we command.' (v. 4: NIV)

Today's 'in Christ' passage wonderfully links the theme of law with grace. Nowhere is Paul's deep spiritual concern for his converts seen more clearly than here. The great apostle could easily have set himself up as a lawgiver, but he is careful to focus the attention of his converts not only on his commands, but also on the power by which those commands could be carried out – God's love and grace. Had Paul simply written verse 4 of today's text, without the sentence that follows, it would have been a legalistic command similar to the commands given by Moses. Paul's next words direct the attention of his converts away from himself 'into the love of God, and into the … steadfastness of Christ' (v. 5, AMPLIFIED). Now the question of obedience was no longer between Paul and the Thessalonians, but between them and Christ. Of course, Paul was on the sidelines, urging them on to avail themselves of God's love and the hope that flowed to them through the promise of Christ's coming. This showed him not to be a dictator – but a director. Another thing emerges – he says he has confidence in the Lord about them. Paul's confidence was in the Lord. Confidence in the Lord about people: that is the secret of making people.

Father, help me see that the secret of inspiring people is to have confidence in you about them. Help me in my own relationships to stand on the sidelines and keep on believing, in spite of what they think about themselves. In Jesus' Name. Amen.

Ambitious – to serve

FOR READING AND MEDITATION – 1 TIMOTHY 3:1–13
'Those who have served well gain an excellent standing
and great assurance in their faith in Christ Jesus.' (v. 13: NIV).

A deacon in a church I once pastored said, 'There seems to be no place for an ambitious person in Christianity.' I replied, 'You are right, if by "ambitious" you mean an egocentric power-seeker, for the first thing Christianity demands is total and complete self-surrender.' The ego trying to be God must be renounced. Once that is done, there is a place for ambition. But the ambition now has a new motive and a new goal – the ambition to serve. Jesus said, 'Whoever would be great among you must be your servant, and whoever would be first among you must be your slave' (Matt. 20:26–27, RSV). So if you would be great, be a servant; if first, be a slave.

The deacon who forgets himself in selfless service discovers, as a by-product, that he gets a new standing. When he wants nothing, he gets everything – everything that is worth having. Moreover, he gains 'much confidence and freedom and boldness in the faith which is founded on and centres in Christ Jesus' (v. 13, AMPLIFIED). The more he gives himself to the faith in Christ, the more he discovers that it works; it is self-verifying. We will have great confidence in the faith when we have great confidence in the centre of our faith – Christ Jesus the Lord.

℣ Lord Jesus, help me to see that when I take your way, then it turns out to be the way – the way to everything. I sense I am on the right track. Then great confidence and peace will possess me. I am so deeply thankful. Amen.

Strong in grace ...

FOR READING AND MEDITATION – 2 TIMOTHY 2:1–13

'You then, my son, be strong in the grace that is in Christ Jesus.' (v. 1: NIV)

One of the accusations often laid against Christianity is that the doctrine of grace (i.e. the belief that progress is made in the Christian life not by strenuous effort, but by depending on God) produces weak and spineless individuals. An atheistic father writing to his son some months after the young man had become a Christian, said, 'You are so dependent on this fictitious Person called Christ that you will lose all the spirit of individualism and enterprise that I have built into you.' Well, some doctrines of grace do produce weak and spineless personalities, but not 'the grace that is in Christ Jesus'.

The Christian doctrine of grace, when properly understood and applied, produces men and women like Paul, who can stand up to everything because they have learned how to use everything. Paul was one of the strongest men who ever lived and was a great advocate of the doctrine of grace. His personal testimony was this: 'By the grace of God I am what I am' (1 Cor. 15:10, NKJ). One commentator says of our text for today, 'Jesus Christ is a strong Man creating other strong men around him.' Paul Katz says, 'The true strength of a person is not in his physical prowess, his mental ability or even in the way he manages his emotions, but in the way he mediates the grace of God.' Grace makes us strong because it makes us humble enough to receive.

✎ *O God my Father, make me also strong in the grace that is in Christ Jesus. And then help me to pass this truth on to others by sound teaching and by example. In Jesus' Name I ask it. Amen.*

Get your guidance from within

FOR READING AND MEDITATION – 2 TIMOTHY 3:10–17

'… from infancy you have known the holy Scriptures, which are able
to make you wise for salvation through faith in Christ Jesus.' (v. 15: NIV)

What part do the Scriptures play in the life of those who are committed to Jesus Christ? Once we become Christians, one of the temptations is to say, 'Now that I am in him and he is in me, I can rely upon him to guide me from within.' But if we give way to this temptation, we will soon wander off into all sorts of vagaries and speculations. Many get all their guidance from dreams, inner voices and impressions, many of which flow out of the subconscious.

Paul shows us that the Bible provides four things in particular: it teaches; it reproves; it corrects; and it disciplines. It teaches us effective Christian living; it reproves us whenever we violate any of God's principles; it corrects our wrong behaviour and shows us the steps to take in order to get back on track; it disciplines us by showing us how to avoid the mistakes we have made in the past and how to stay on the right spiritual track. Someone who tries to live without the guidance of the Scripture, is like a captain of a ship brushing aside his charts and saying he will be guided only by his intuition. No one can remain spiritual who is not scriptural.

O Father, create within me a deeper love for your Word. Take me by the hand and lead me to Christ, the eternal Word. Your Word is my inspiration and illumination. Amen.

We have what we share

FOR READING AND MEDITATION – PHILEMON 1–7

'I pray that you will be active in sharing your faith, so that you will have
a full understanding of every good thing we have in Christ.' (v. 6: NIV)

Paul writes to Philemon, the owner of a runaway slave whom Paul
had led to Christ, and urges Philemon to demonstrate his faith in
Christ by restoring Onesimus and forgiving him. Paul first focuses
on the necessity of sharing one's faith. To be 'in Christ' demands
sharing your faith, for the Christian life is such that you cannot
have your full share of Christ unless you share him with others.

Nothing is really ours until we share it. The sharing of the faith
makes it possible to share even more deeply in the faith. The reason
why many Christians get to a place of boredom in the Christian
life is because they have not learnt how to share with others
what has happened (or what is happening) to them. You can't get
any more into a full container. Paul impresses upon Philemon that
when his faith is shared, he will have 'a full understanding of every
good thing we have in Christ'. Sharing the faith means telling everyone
we can about the blessings and mercies that have come to us
through Christ. It means watching for every opportunity that
comes to share with others 'every good thing we have in Christ'.
That form of Christian witnessing is the easiest and most natural
thing in the world.

✎ Father, make me alert and responsive to those moments and opportunities
that constantly come my way to share with my friends and family the
good things that you have given me in Christ. In Jesus' Name. Amen.

Be bold – yet loving

FOR READING AND MEDITATION – PHILEMON 8–16
'… although in Christ I could be bold and order you
to do what you ought to do …' (v. 8: NIV)

To be in Christ is to be bold, for in him you have the sum total of reality behind you – cosmic backing. 'In society' you will find it difficult to be bold, for you continually look around you to see what others are thinking of you. This makes you cautious and timid – not a voice, but an echo. If you are 'in you', there is nothing behind you but you. Any boldness you develop is a self-engendered boldness – something imposed on the personality rather than exposed from within it. When you are 'in Christ', however, you are bold with a boldness that is divine. Paul knew this boldness. Instead of drawing on boldness as the basis for his remarks in today's passage, he says, 'Yet for love's sake I prefer to appeal to you' (v. 9, RSV).

How like his Master was the great apostle. Consciousness of strength was one factor of our Lord's humility: 'Jesus, knowing that the Father had given all things into his hands … rose from supper … and began to wash the disciples' feet' (John 13:3–5, NKJ). The little, the empty, the timid must keep up their precarious position, so they sit stiff. For self's sake, they refuse to bend. Paul, for love's sake, stood tall in the bending. He was bold enough to command, yet loving enough to appeal. Boldness is important, but not the last word in the Christian scheme of things – love is.

✎ *Lord Jesus, make me bold enough to face anyone in any situation, yet loving and humble enough to win them rather than browbeat them. Amen.*

Refreshed in Christ

FOR READING AND MEDITATION – PHILEMON 17–25

'I do wish, brother, that I may have some benefit from you in the Lord;
refresh my heart in Christ.' (v. 20: NIV)

Paul knew what it was to be refreshed from within – by being in Christ – but now he asks Philemon for refreshment from without: 'Yes, brother, let me have some profit from you in the Lord. Cheer and refresh my heart in Christ' (AMPLIFIED). In Christ it is possible to receive refreshment from both directions – within and without. What we must watch, however, is that we do not come to depend on the refreshment that comes from without. We can enjoy it and be built up by it – but we must not come to depend on it. I have found, in talking to many thousands of people over the years, that this is the point at which many Christians get stuck. Without realising it, so many Christians depend for their life on the refreshment that comes from without, rather than the refreshment that comes from within – from being 'in Christ'.

Relationships like the love of a husband for a wife, or wife for a husband, or the affection of a close and trusted friend, can minister and refresh the human spirit in a wonderful way – but we must not come to depend upon these for our lives. Our lives are 'hidden with Christ in God' (Col. 3:3). If we depend on Christ and on Christ alone for our primary refreshment, then whatever is added to it from 'without' is a bonus.

❧ Redeemer, refresh me so powerfully within that whether I get refreshment from without or not, I will be, secure and undisturbed. By depending on you, I joyously take anything that comes from others. Amen.

Thinking Christianly

FOR READING AND MEDITATION – ROMANS 12:1–21
'Do not conform any longer to the pattern of this world,
but be transformed by the renewing of your mind.' (v. 2: NIV)

The Christian church has always stood in danger of being brainwashed by the world, but in this present age secularism has spread its tentacles so far and wide that almost without realising we find ourselves thinking about the important issues of life with much the same mindset as the world. I am referring to those issues where there is clear and distinctive Biblical teaching. *J.B. PHILLIPS* translates today's text, 'Don't let the world around you squeeze you into its own mould, but let God remould your minds from within.'

Harry Blamires saw during the middle of this century that the church had begun to drop into the world's way of thinking, and wrote, 'The Christian mind has succumbed to the secular drift with a degree of weakness and nervelessness unmatched in Christian history. It is difficult to do justice in words to the complete loss of intellectual morale in the twentieth-century church … there is no longer a Christian mind.' He went on to say that though there is still a Christian ethic, a Christian practice and a Christian spirituality, we are in danger of losing the ability to think Christianly about the deep and perplexing issues facing us in today's world. The danger signs are there – we must do something about it.

◁ *My Father and my God, forgive us if we, your people, have allowed our thinking to be influenced by the world, so that we now think as it thinks rather than as you think. Give us a truly transformed mind. In Jesus' Name we pray. Amen.*

The divine exchange

FOR READING AND MEDITATION – 1 CORINTHIANS 2:1–16
'But we have the mind of Christ.' (v. 16: NIV)

We said yesterday that one of the great dangers of these modern times is that we who carry the Name of Christ are succumbing to the prevailing secularism of our day. In other words, we do not think about the great issues of life with a Christian mindset. A Christian mind can only think as Christ does about everything if it has deeply and thoroughly absorbed the principles and presuppositions of God's revelation written in the Bible.

Paul tells the Corinthians in the text before us today that they have the 'mind of Christ'. He meant that those who have received Christ into their lives, and in whose personality he lives, have access to his way of thinking – providing, of course, they allow his mind to engage with theirs. I remember sitting a school examination as a boy and thinking to myself, 'It's all right for the teacher out at the front. He knows the answers to all these questions. How different things would be if his mind was in me at this moment.' Alas, it could not be. The same, however, is not true of the mind of Christ. Our sovereign Lord places at the disposal of all his children his pure and perfect mind. He opens his mind to us; we must open our minds to him.

✎ O Father, I know that since I became a Christian Christ has been thinking in me, but I long that he might think in me even more. Help me be more open to him and less open to the influences of the world. Amen.

Wholesome thinking

FOR READING AND MEDITATION – 2 PETER 3:1–18

'I have written … reminders to stimulate you to wholesome thinking.' (v. 1: NIV)

We must not think that because the Scripture says 'we have the mind of Christ' we have nothing to do but sit back and let Christ think in us. *J.B. PHILLIPS* translates yesterday's text: 'But we have the mind of Christ,' in this way: 'Incredible as it may sound, we who are spiritual have the very thoughts of Christ!' Something is expected of us – a degree of spirituality. Christ is willing to think in us, not by dominating our minds with his, but by engaging his mind with ours – as we give him our consent and co-operation.

How much of Christ's thinking do we see in the minds of Christians today as they approach the different issues of life? Generally speaking, we seem to give more credence to the ideas of the world than the words of our Lord. Take the field in which I have had long experience – Christian counselling. More and more I hear and read statements such as this: 'This idea works, so let's incorporate it into our counselling approach.' Ideas are fine, but they must be scrutinised to see if they are in harmony with Christian truth. The criterion for Christians should never be 'Does it work?', but 'Is it right?' It is not so much that the ideas of the world are never good – at times they are. It is that they come out of a system where Satan reigns – they must be carefully scrutinised and compared with the Word of God before being accepted and adopted.

✎ *My Father and my God, I see that Christ will not force his thinking upon me, but gives it in relation to my co-operation and consent. You have my consent; now for my co-operation. Amen.*

What's it all about?

FOR READING AND MEDITATION – ROMANS 10:1–15

'… They are zealous for God, but their zeal is not based on knowledge.' (v. 2: NIV)

What Paul wrote about unbelieving Jews in this passage could be said of some modern-day Christians. This is because they pay more attention to things that stir their feelings than things that inform their minds. Their attitude is like that of a student I once read about. While away from his university in another country, he heard that a student protest was taking place back home. 'I wish I were there right now,' he said immediately. 'I would be right in the middle of it. What's it all about?' Enthusiasm without enlightenment – that sums up the condition of many.

Let no one think that I am in any way playing down feelings and playing up thinking. I am pleading for an equal and balanced concern for both. Some focus on the development of their intellect and come out as dry, wooden representatives of Christianity. Others focus on the development of their feelings and, like a vigorously shaken champagne bottle, are always popping their corks. Both are important, but must be held in balance. It so happens that the mind is the focus of our attention in these meditations, but that should not be taken to mean that the area of feelings is of lesser importance. It is your mind I want to get at in the weeks that lie ahead, but not in a way that ignores the other aspects of your personality. Keep that in mind!

Heavenly Father, you have made me to think and to feel, but to keep both in balance. With this challenge to my mind that I am going through at present, don't let me forget I am a feeling being also. In Jesus' Name. Amen.

The Master's yoke

FOR READING AND MEDITATION – MATTHEW 11:20–30
'Take my yoke upon you and learn from me,
for I am gentle and humble in heart ...' (v. 29: NIV)

It is time to ask ourselves: What are the marks of a Christian mind? There are at least eight of them, the first being a willingness to put one's ability to think under the tutelage of Christ. Today's text makes plain that our Lord expects all his disciples not only to be yoked to him, but to learn of him. A yoke was a wooden frame that was laid on the necks of oxen. In Scripture the term symbolises the authority of one person or system over another. Christ likens himself to a farmer and us to oxen in his service. But unlike a farmer who imposes a yoke upon the oxen whether they like it or not, Christ invites us to carry his yoke. 'Take my yoke upon you,' he says – in other words, submit voluntarily to his authority.

He begins by adopting the role of a farmer ('Take my yoke upon you') and ends in the role of a teacher ('learn from me'). The difficulty all educationalists face is getting their pupils to give their minds to them in the same way that they give their minds to their pupils. It is no less a difficulty in the school of Christ. He gives his mind to us, but are we willing to give our minds to him? One thing is sure – if Christ doesn't have our minds, then he doesn't have us. For as a man thinks, so is he.

⊴ *Lord Jesus, you give yourself to me with such willingness and openness. May I respond in like manner. Help me link my mind with your mind, my littleness with your greatness, my Saviour. For your Name's sake. Amen.*

Two different burdens

FOR READING AND MEDITATION – 1 JOHN 5:1–12

'This is love for God: to obey his commands.
And his commands are not burdensome.' (v. 3: NIV)

The message of today's verse is similar to yesterday's. New Christians are often puzzled by the fact that no sooner do they come to Christ and have lifted from them the burden of sin, than Christ places upon them another burden – the burden of service. These two different 'burdens' must be clearly understood, for those opposed to Christianity consider them to be contradictions. When seen in context, however, they appear not as contradictory, but complementary. When Christ calls those who are 'weary and burdened' to come to him, he is summoning those who are weighed down with sin and guilt. When he speaks of carrying his yoke, he is thinking of those who have had their sins forgiven and are now seeking to walk with him. The difference between the two burdens is this: the burden of sinfulness is difficult and heavy; the burden of service is easy and light.

Is it because he lays nothing of consequence upon us? No, the first commandment is love for God and it is not burdensome, because to love is what our souls were made for – when we fulfil the command to love, we fulfil ourselves. The highest characteristic in God – love – is also the highest characteristic in us. Nothing could be more demanding, yet nothing more fulfilling. This burden is only as great a burden as wings are to a bird.

◈ Father, we are grateful that you demand our total love, for in demanding a total love you are giving a total love. We receive your love. Amen.

Change your mind

FOR READING AND MEDITATION – JOHN 6:53–69

' "You do not want to leave too, do you?" Jesus asked the Twelve.' (v. 67: NIV)

The disciples willingly put their minds under the tutelage of Christ. They seemed happy to be called his 'disciples', his 'servants', even his 'slaves', and referred to him often as their 'Lord' and their 'Master'.

All this meant, of course, that their understanding of truth was shaped and moulded by the teachings of Jesus. These men, we should remember, had been brought up in the traditions of Judaism, and during the three years they were under the tutelage of Christ, they were required to change their minds about many things. Sometimes, as we can see from the passage before us today, they were shocked by our Lord's words and attitudes and appear to have been reconsidering their commitment to him.

Have you not had similar moments in your own pilgrimage with Christ? Moments when you were tempted to put your own thinking ahead of his? In the early days of my Christian life (and sometimes even now) I found myself wanting to adapt and modify the words of Jesus and bring them in line with my own ambitions and desires. How foolish and absurd! Our Lord's teachings flow from a mind that is incarnate wisdom. That is why it is pointless to argue with Christ. He is right in everything.

✎ *O Father, help me have the mind of Christ in everything. May I put his thinking ahead of mine at all times, and grow and develop in the knowledge of the Saviour. I ask this in his Name. Amen.*

God's powerful laser

FOR READING AND MEDITATION – 1 CORINTHIANS 2:1–16

'The man without the Spirit does not accept
the things that come from the Spirit of God …' (v. 14: NIV)

Who has not experienced times when their own thinking and
Christ's thinking seem to lead in opposite directions? It is due to
the effects that Adam and Eve's original sin have had upon the
human personality and mind. I have often been intrigued when
leading highly educated people to the Lord to see the struggle they
have to think correctly about the matters of the soul. They can
think correctly about other things – mathematics, physics, and so
on – but when it comes to thinking about God and their soul's salvation, you begin to perceive the deep problem that sin has produced in the mind.

Today's text reminds us that the person without the Spirit sees
the truth of God as foolishness. That is why unless the Holy Spirit
assists a person to come to Christ, he or she will never be able to
enter into his kingdom. Conversion happens when the Holy Spirit
penetrates the mind dispelling the darkness, illuminating human
reason and depositing a truth in the intellect – the truth that only
Christ saves and that no one can save himself or herself. He does it
in a way that the person concerned is able to understand. There can
be no salvation without illumination of the mind.

❧ O God, how can I sufficiently thank you for the time when the laser beam
of your Spirit first penetrated the darkness of my mind? You showed me that
without you I am nothing, but with you I am something. May that truth
never depart from me. In Jesus' Name. Amen.

Our thinking vs. God's

FOR READING AND MEDITATION – 1 CORINTHIANS 1:10–31

'For the message of the cross is foolishness to
those who are perishing …' (v. 18: NIV)

Without the correction that comes from the teaching of Christ and
the Holy Spirit we cannot hope to think properly about life's important issues. Haven't you been amazed many times when thinking through an issue to find that the Bible's approach to that same
issue is almost diametrically opposed to your own?

We tend to think that our position of leadership means other
people should serve us. Jesus said otherwise: 'The greatest among
you will be your servant' (Matt. 23:11). We tend to think that the
way to independence is by getting out from under authority. God
says differently: 'Everyone must submit himself to the go-verning
authorities' (Rom. 13:1). We tend to think the way to get ahead is
by covering up our mistakes. God says the opposite: 'He who con-
ceals his sins does not prosper, but whoever confesses and
renounces them finds mercy' (Prov. 28:13). We tend to think that if
we surrender our lives to God, we will lose them. Jesus said:
'Whoever loses his life for me will find it' (Matt. 16:25). We tend to
think that the way to overcome our enemies is to get even with
them. Jesus said: '… Love your enemies and pray for those who
persecute you' (Matt. 5:44). Isn't it obvious why we must bring our
minds under the tutelage of Christ?

*My Father, I see that my mind and your mind can so often be at cross-
purposes. I cannot rely on independent thinking – only on you. Help me
bring my thinking in line with your thinking. In Jesus' Name. Amen.*

Two stages of education

FOR READING AND MEDITATION – JOHN 14:15–31

'But the Counsellor ... will teach you all things and
will remind you of everything ...' (v. 26: NIV)

The learning of the apostles was a gradual process which began
when Christ's earthly presence was with them, and continued with
the descent of the Holy Spirit at Pentecost. Jesus himself explained
these two stages of education. Step by step the disciples matured
and developed in their thinking concerning such issues as salvation, creation, Scripture, the final glory, and so on. In so many matters they had to choose between the current Jewish beliefs and the
wisdom of Christ and the Holy Spirit. The two were often in direct
conflict. But the disciples were determined to bring their minds,
and the minds of those to whom they ministered, under the authority and continued tutelage of Christ.

Paul put it like this: 'We demolish arguments and every pre-
tension that sets itself up against the knowledge of God, and we
take captive every thought to make it obedient to Christ' (2 Cor.
10:5). The multitudinous thoughts of our minds behave sometimes like the mutinous soldiers of a rebellious army, but when
Christ's mind engages with ours, his power and presence are more
than a match for all that is against us. The more we allow Christ's
mind to engage with ours, the easier it will be to bring rebellious
thoughts into captivity.

✎ *O God, it seems too good to be true – that my sometimes rebellious
thoughts can be taken captive. But I dare to believe it. Help me give all my
mind to you so that I might take all from you. In Jesus' Name. Amen.*

Meditation and the mind

FOR READING AND MEDITATION – PSALM 143:1–12

'... I meditate on all your works and consider
what your hands have done.' (v. 5: NIV)

In today's church, 'We are more like Martha than Mary – determined to be taken up with doing things for Jesus rather than sitting at his feet, listening to his words,' as one preacher put it. Meditation on the Scriptures, something the church has taught and upheld throughout the centuries, is nowadays almost a lost art. Is it any wonder that Christians of our generation don't think Christianly when the greatest means of accomplishing this – Biblical meditation – is hardly mentioned in our churches?

Over the years I have found through talking to Christians that they fear bringing their minds under the authority of Christ is a denial of their rationality. But submitting to Christ's revelation does not mean we have to stop thinking; it means we think more effectively. A top nuclear scientist once told me, 'I think more clearly and make better decisions in my work when I have exposed my mind to the mind of Christ by prayer and meditation in the Scriptures.'

If we do not seek to know more of the mind of Christ through prayer and Biblical meditation, then how can we claim to be Christ's disciples? Every Christian is expected to be a pupil in the school of Jesus Christ. If we reject this idea, then surely our commitment to him must be in doubt.

✒ O God, help me think Christianly and understand also that to submit to your revelation is not to dismiss my rationality, but to develop it. I think my best thoughts when I think with you. Amen.

A mind imbued

FOR READING AND MEDITATION – PHILIPPIANS 2:1–11
'Your attitude should be the same as that of Christ Jesus …' (v. 5: NIV)

The second mark of a Christian mind is humility. It was the philosopher John Ruskin who said that the test of a great mind is the degree of humility it displays. The same can be said of a Christian mind. Certainly our Lord's mind was imbued with humility, as the passage before us today so clearly shows. The *Amplified* puts today's text like this: 'Let this same attitude and purpose and [humble] mind be in you which was in Christ Jesus – let him be your example in humility.' Recently I heard of a minister who during his lifetime preached close on 10 000 sermons, each of them based on this text. He claimed that Christ's humility is the essence of the gospel and the starting-point for everything. While never ceasing to be what he had always been – true God – our Lord became what he had never been before – true man.

The dictionary defines humility as 'meekness' or 'the quality of having or showing a low estimate of one's importance'. Humility is often looked down upon. It is confused with such ignoble characteristics as servility, grovelling and obsequiousness. Biblical humility is the attitude of mind that regards the interests of others as more important than one's own. This attitude is missing from much of today's thinking. Believe me, Christianity that does not begin with humility, doesn't begin.

✎ *Father, I see that the first lesson in your school is the most challenging. But I am grateful for it, as your challenges work to the development of my character. May this mindset be in me as it was in your Son. Amen.*

The basis of humility

'When I consider … the work of your fingers …
what is man that you are mindful of him …?' (vv. 3–4: NIV)

We saw yesterday that humility is a quality which is often looked down upon by the world. Aristotle, Greece's most famous philosopher, said once that he much preferred high-mindedness to humility. I feel that the people of the world do not really understand humility. As W.E. Sangster put it, 'The real understanding of humility calls for a piercing spiritual perception that is never found in coarse minds, particularly worldly ones.'

In Christian tradition, however, humility ranks high. Chrysostom, one of the church fathers, believed, 'Humility is the foundation of our philosophy.' Augustine said, 'If you ask me what is the first precept of the Christian religion, I will answer, first, second, and third, humility.'

Such appreciation of humility springs from the conviction expressed by the psalmist in today's passage that mankind is made from the dust, and is totally dependent on God for existence and survival. Indeed, the only thing of which we can be proud, is that God has visited us with salvation. To think like this, is to think Christianly.

✎ *O Father, help me to see myself in proper perspective – small, guilty, deserving of eternal death, yet loved by the world's most aggressive lover. Were it not for that love, I would be nothing. May I never forget it. In Jesus' Name. Amen.*

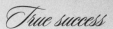

True success

FOR READING AND MEDITATION – PROVERBS 18:1–15
'Before his downfall a man's heart is proud,
but humility comes before honour.' (v. 12: NIV)

Humility is one of the chief characteristics of a Christian mind. To understand it, we must learn to distinguish it from the things with which it has become confused. Some confuse humility with an inferiority complex. True humility does not come out of a complex; it comes out of Christ. It is not the result of being mishandled in childhood, but the consequence of intimate fellowship with a loving heavenly Father, and of viewing oneself against the backdrop of his everlasting mercy and love.

Others confuse humility with lack of ambition. The truly humble are the most ambitious souls alive, but they are ambitious about the right things and for the right reasons. Though they stretch themselves in the pursuit of success, they define success not in worldly terms, but as knowing God's will for their lives – and doing it.

The hypocritical can simulated humility but those who are discerning soon see through such deception. Schemers sometimes adopt the guise of humility as an unobtrusive means of achieving their end. They take the lowest place in order to be invited to go up higher, or express low opinions of themselves hoping to be contradicted. The humble do not talk much about themselves, and if they do say something that is self-depreciating they mean what they say.

✎ *O Father, how can I set my mind in the direction of humility if I do not know what it is? Teach me to differentiate between the real and the unreal, the spurious and the spiritual. Guide me toward true humility. Amen.*

The seed-bed of humility

FOR READING AND MEDITATION – ROMANS 12:1–8

'Do not think of yourself more highly than you ought,
but rather think of yourself with sober judgment.' (v. 3: NIV)

The best definition of humility the secular mind can offer, is in the *Concise Oxford Dictionary*: 'Humble – having or showing low estimate of one's own importance.' Our Lord was the greatest example of humility the world has ever known, but who would you put as the next greatest? Personally, I would give the honour to the apostle Paul. His was a mind that thought Christianly about everything. Let us therefore draw on Paul's mind now for a definition of humility within which to think more deeply about this great Christian virtue.

Paul tells us not to have an exaggerated opinion of our own importance, but to think about ourselves with sober judgment. Humility, then, is a conscious and realistic appraisal of oneself. Where we so often go wrong is comparing ourselves with other human beings rather than with God. In another part of his writings Paul says: 'For who makes you different from anyone else? What do you have that you did not receive? And if you did receive it, why do you boast as though you did not?' (1 Cor. 4:7). Pride grows out of a wrong comparison and humility grows out of a right comparison. The more clearly we see God's greatness, the more clearly we will see our own smallness. That is the context in which humility grows.

✎ *O Father, forgive me that so often I compare myself with others rather than with you and with your Son. When I see who you are, I am better able to see myself as I am. Help me achieve this. Amen.*

Look up!

FOR READING AND MEDITATION – PSALM 121:1–8

'I lift up my eyes to the hills – where does my help come from?' (v. 1: NIV)

We ended yesterday with the thought that just as pride comes from a wrong comparison, humility comes from a right comparison. That great preacher of a past generation, Philip Brookes, put it like this: 'The true way to be humble is not to stoop until you are smaller than yourself, but to stand at your real height against some higher nature that will show you what the real smallness of your greatest greatness is.' I do not wish to detract from the great man's powerful statement by adding a comment of my own, but if I might be permitted to put it in a more condensed form, what he is saying in effect is this: stand at your very highest, look at Christ, then go away and be forever humble.

If we lose sight of Christ, then we ourselves begin to loom large. When we lose touch with God – the true God – we lose touch with ourselves and we lose touch with the source of humility. This turns the definitions of many concerning humility on their head – definitions such as this one, which I came across in my reading the other day: 'Humility never looks up, or out, but always down.' It is definitions such as this that lead people to think of humility as a cringing, obsequious attitude that, to say the least, is unappealing and unattractive. We cannot learn how to develop humility except by looking up.

❧ *O God, how can I have a right standard of comparison unless I compare myself with you? Your greatness gives me the perspective for seeing myself as I really am – God-created and God-dependent. Amen.*

Knowing who you are

FOR READING AND MEDITATION – JOHN 13:1–17

'I have set you an example that you should do as I have done for you.' (v. 15: NIV)

This passage underlines and exemplifies the fact that humility can never be understood or put into operation apart from a close relationship with God. The account says, 'Jesus knew that the Father had put all things under his power, and that he had come from God and was returning to God; so he got up from the meal … and wrapped a towel round his waist' (John 13:3–4). Here we see humility in action. But consider John's statement which precedes his description of the act of humility: 'Jesus knew …' What did he know? He knew just who he was – the Son of God and God the Son. The consciousness of his identity was the secret of his humility. Knowing who he was – the Son of God – he was able to take a towel and wash the disciples' feet.

To be humble, you first of all have to know who you are and to whom you belong. And you don't know who you are until you know whose you are. Those who see humility in terms of wilful self-disparagement or self-belittlement are in serious error. Humility begins with a sense of being rooted in God – if you like, a consciousness of greatness. The small-minded and high-minded dare not be humble; they have too much to lose. Humility as demonstrated by Jesus is a choice. He was humble because he was great, and great because he was humble.

✎ Lord Jesus Christ, once again I pray: give me your mind. For you are meek and lowly and humble in attitude. I am yours and you are mine. All glory be to your wondrous Name. Amen.

The garment of humility

FOR READING AND MEDITATION – 1 PETER 5:1–14

'All of you, clothe yourselves with humility …' (v. 5: NIV)

Time and again in Scripture we are bidden to humble ourselves. This implies that the choice is ours. But as we saw yesterday, we can never make that choice until we have a clear sense of identity, otherwise we may choose to be humble for the wrong reasons. One of the most humble men I have ever met was also one of the most educated. When I asked him how he was able to avoid the arrogance that seems to be characteristic of so many who are highly educated, he said, 'The more I know about any subject, the more I realise how much I do not know. That realisation helps me keep my place – at the feet of the Creator.'

Sir James Simpson, the surgeon who discovered the anaesthetic properties in chloroform, had a brilliant mind and was a great Christian. One day one of his students asked him what was his greatest discovery, expecting him to say, 'The use of chloroform as an anaesthetic.' He replied, 'My greatest discovery was when I realised I was a sinner and that Jesus Christ was my Saviour.' A mind characterised by humility has no arrogance, no self-consciousness, and exhibits a greater concern for others than for oneself. This is the way Christ's mind functioned. And it is the way our minds will function when his mind holds sway over ours.

✎ *O Father, I see that you have provided for me a garment of humility – and I am thankful. But I see also that it is my choice to put it on. In deep dependence upon you I make that choice now. And for Jesus' sake. Amen.*

Standing alone

FOR READING AND MEDITATION – EPHESIANS 6:10–24

'… put on the full armour of God, so that …
you may be able to stand your ground …' (v. 13: NIV)

So far we have looked at just two characteristics of a Christian mind, the first being a willingness to come under the tutelage of Jesus Christ, and the second, humility. The third characteristic is a perceptiveness that sees when to go along with the crowd and when to stand alone. God has made us as social beings, beings who relate to one another. But we must not be controlled by those relationships – we must be controlled by God.

A term often used by psychologists in the early part of this century (but little used today) is 'herd instinct'. It was used to identify the need all human beings have – the need to belong. We cannot always compare humans to animals, but it is clear that humanity has this herd instinct also. We like to be together, we try to protect one another from common enemies such as fire, floods, natural disasters, and so on. But as Christians our final allegiance is not to others; it is to God. For this reason we must be prepared to break away from the herd if we see it going in the wrong direction. Those with a truly Christian mind have never hesitated to do this. They see they are new people with a new allegiance – allegiance to Jesus.

Father, I see it is inevitable that I live my life alongside others and relate properly to them. But my springs are not to be in them; they are to be in thee. Help me never to forget this. In Jesus' Name. Amen.

Fear of others

FOR READING AND MEDITATION – MATTHEW 14:1–12

'The king was distressed, but because of his oaths and his dinner guests,
he ordered that her request be granted …' (v. 9: NIV)

The need to belong was implanted deep within us by God. The Almighty designed us as social beings and endowed us with the ability to relate. The fact that we belong to others gives us a sense of common life and a sense of security. Although we are apt to say that society seems to be breaking apart at the seams, there is still evidence of a social consciousness that manifests itself most strongly when anyone is in trouble. Without a sense of belonging we are ill at ease and frustrated.

The rogue elephant, the one that tears up trees and creates havoc, is the one that has been put out of the herd by the other male elephants. He is out of harmony with the herd, thus out of harmony with himself. We are social beings and cannot live harmoniously except in relation to others. Here, however, is the crux: we are members of society, yet we must not be dominated by it. Take the case of Herod. He made a foolish oath to give the daughter of Herodias almost anything she asked. When she asked for the head of John the Baptist, the account says: 'Because of his oaths and his dinner guests, [Herod] ordered that her request be granted.' Not the fear of God but the fear of others determined his conduct and left him a miserable murderer of the man he respected most.

O God, give me the perception of mind that knows when to merge with society and when to stand against it. Others shall feel my life, but not determine my life. In Jesus' Name. Amen.

Everybody does it

FOR READING AND MEDITATION – MATTHEW 23:1–23

'Everything they do is done for men to see …' (v. 5: NIV)

We continue with the thought that unless we are perceptive enough to see when we ought to break away from the herd, we will soon find ourselves in serious spiritual difficulties. Take the religious leaders who were around in the days when Jesus was here on earth. What tremendous possibilities opened up to them. They could have been the agents of the new order, the kingdom of God. Yet, when Christ confronted them with the real condition of their hearts, they resisted him instead of responding. In the moment of crisis their minds were filled with worry about what others might think of them. They looked around, not up, and hence, when the doors of the kingdom of God were opened to them, they turned in a different direction. They angled for the attention of men and consequently appear as some of the most pathetic figures in history.

Unless we are careful, the herd appeal can be so strong that we blindly follow it – to our peril. I talked to a young Christian couple who lived together. I waited for the appropriate moment to share with them my understanding of Scripture on this point, and when I did, their reply was this: 'But everybody does it these days – even Christians.' 'Everybody does it' is the last gurgle you will hear as men and women are submerged by the herd.

✎ O Father, give me the moral courage to be inwardly and outwardly different. Show me when to stay with the herd so that I may influence it, and when to remove myself from it, or resist it. In Jesus' Name I pray. Amen.

The signals to watch

FOR READING AND MEDITATION – MATTHEW 22:15–22
'Give to Caesar what is Caesar's, and to God what is God's.' (v. 21: NIV)

We ended yesterday with the thought that the phrase 'Everybody does it' is the last gurgle you will hear as men and women allow themselves to be submerged by the herd. Between writing those words and the start of today's meditation, I went into the town. As I started to cross the street, an old lady pulled me by the arm and warned, 'The pedestrian light is still red.' Rather weakly I replied, 'But everybody is crossing.' 'Don't follow them,' she said, 'follow the light.' Little did she know how she brought home to me the challenge of what I have been saying. Do we get our walking signals from God, or from the herd?

I always smile to myself when I read the passage that is before us today, especially the verse '… the Pharisees went out and laid plans to trap him in his words' (v. 15). Fancy trying to trap the One in whom dwelt all the fullness of divine wisdom! 'Tell us,' they asked, 'is it right to pay taxes to Caesar or not?' If he had said 'No', he would have been in trouble with the authorities. If he had said 'Yes', he would have been in trouble with the people. The answer he gave cut straight through the manoeuvring of his enemies. He sought God's favour first and last, and as a result gained more favour than any other being who has set foot on this planet. He came and knelt at our feet; now we kneel at his.

✎ *My Father and my God, I am thankful that the grip of the herd is broken when I am surrendered to you. Emancipated from the herd, I can now go back into it and influence it. Help me to do that. In Jesus' Name. Amen.*

Emancipated

FOR READING AND MEDITATION – 1 JOHN 2:7–17

'Do not love the world or anything in the world.' (v. 15: NIV)

Christians have a challenge to face in relation to the herd: if we do not belong to others, we are frustrated, and if we give ourselves to them without discrimination, we become spiritually stunted and demeaned. The way to belong to the herd is to have our minds centred on God. The tyranny of the herd is broken when we are emancipated from it by a higher loyalty. Once the power of the herd is broken, we can again be a member of it. We can be in it but not of it. We can be loyal to society as long as it is loyal to God – our supreme loyalty. When the herd is not going in God's direction, we must break with it. And it must be a clean break, not one that is infected with resentment, bitterness or self-pity.

A Christian mind is an independent mind – dependent on God, but independent of the opinions of others. It sees issues clearly and perceptively and says when necessary, 'This is not something the Lord wants me to do, even though others are doing it.' The supreme example of emancipation from the herd is, of course, Jesus. He identified with humanity so deeply that their sorrows and sufferings became his and he ultimately took them to the cross. He belonged to the human race, but he belonged also to God. With that supreme allegiance intact he went into the herd – emancipated. So must we.

✎ *O Father, since I belong supremely to you, I am emancipated from the herd. Now send my emancipated soul into the herd to influence it. The herd shall feed my social life, but it shall not determine my spiritual life. Amen.*

A difficult test

FOR READING AND MEDITATION – 1 CHRONICLES 28:11–21

'Be strong and courageous, and do the work.' (v. 20: NIV)

Some people get lost in the herd because they don't see any other way to go. A test paper given to young men who wanted to join the police force in London, said, 'You are patrolling the high street when a water-main bursts, sending a jet of water across the road. Several cars collide because of this and a number of drenched pedestrians begin to panic. While this is taking place, you spot a man whose face you saw on a "Wanted" poster in the police station that morning. A couple of motorists whose vehicles have collided, begin to shout at one another. As you walk over to them, you observe that one of them is the wife of your Chief Inspector, and as you get close you smell alcohol on her breath. A dog runs between your legs and you notice it does not have a collar [an offence in Britain], and then a man runs up to you and says his wife who is eight months pregnant has just gone into labour in a nearby shop. The shop's telephone is out of order and he asks you to call for an ambulance. How would you proceed to deal with the situation?' One applicant wrote, 'I would slip out of my uniform and get lost in the crowd!'

We might do the same in those circumstances, but a true Christian refuses to escape into anonymity. Remember – our Lord never went along with the crowd, even though it meant going to a cross.

✎ *Lord Jesus Christ, give me your mindset so that I will be saved from all running away, all evasion of responsibility, all hesitancies. Help me stand up to everything. For your own dear Name's sake. Amen.*

A tale of one small town

FOR READING AND MEDITATION – ECCLESIASTES 8:1–17

'Do not stand up for a bad cause …' (v. 3: NIV)

We're still looking at the Christian characteristic of a perceptive mind that knows when to go along with the crowd and when to stand alone. I once spent a couple of weeks on a preaching engagement in a small town in Canada, where I asked what the particular characteristic of the local people was. I was told that their distinctive characteristic was that they never committed themselves to anything. In their public meetings they looked at one another, waiting for someone to give a clue as to which way they would go, and seemed to always follow the very first suggestion that was made.

During the evangelistic crusade I conducted there, I noticed that when I invited those who wanted to become Christians to walk to the front, those present would look around and wait for someone to take the first step. Recently I met someone from the same area and made enquiries about the town. 'Things are very much the same,' I was told. 'People seem to get on only after they move away from the place.'

It reminded me that a Christian mind is a mind that sees beyond the crowd. It does not ignore the masses or seek to denigrate them, but it recognises that sometimes the crowd can be right and sometimes wrong.

✎ O Father, once again I pray – set me free from the fear of what others might think about me. And give me the spiritual backbone to be able to stand up for you at all times. In Jesus' Name. Amen.

The bowed head

FOR READING AND MEDITATION – TITUS 3:1–11

'Remind the people to be subject to rulers and authorities ...' (v. 1: NIV)

We look now at the fourth mark of a Christian mind – its acceptance of the principle of authority. Christians who have the mind of Christ have an attitude to authority that is quite different from the world's. Have you noticed how the word *authority* seems to grate on modern ears? Schoolteachers and educationalists report on the increasingly difficult task of trying to get young people to accept the principle of authority. 'For the most part,' comments a contemporary, 'we move in a world in which thinking and feeling alike are coloured with a distaste for authority which is unparalleled in history.'

The Christian mind has to come to grips with the fact that the principle of authority has been built into the universe by God, and unless we recognise this fact and understand it, we will never be able, as Paul puts it in 1 Tim. 6:13–14, to 'keep our commission free from stain' (MOFFATT). As Christ's disciples we have been commissioned to live our lives according to the revelation given to us in the Scriptures, and one aspect of that revelation is the principle of authority. Whatever the world may think about this issue, we are to think about it in terms of its divine source. God instituted it and because of that we are obliged to face it – and bow our heads, not turn our backs.

ℕ *Gracious Father, help me to catch on to this principle of authority and see it not as something extraneous to life, but something built into it – by you. Give me above all an obedient spirit. In Jesus' Name. Amen.*

Perfect freedom

FOR READING AND MEDITATION – REVELATION 12:1–12

'Now have come … the power and the kingdom of our God,
and the authority of his Christ.' (v. 10: NIV)

Our age revolts against the principle of authority. Why does 'authority' have such bad connotations in the modern world? Some think the rejection of authority is closely connected with the struggle which has gone on in this generation with regimes such as Communism and Nazism, for as these have been overthrown, the evils that underpinned them have been exposed for all the world to see. 'Never again will we allow ourselves to be dominated by the state,' has been the cry of many, particularly the young.

In Berlin some years ago I gave a talk on the need for Christians to bring themselves under the authority of Scripture and to submit to it in every way. Afterwards several young people came to speak to me and said politely, 'We have been set free from one totalitarianism; you seem to be offering us another.' I replied, 'True, but there is a profound difference. When you obey an earthly totalitarian regime, you find yourself in bondage; when you obey the laws of the Bible and the kingdom of God, you find yourself in perfect freedom.' Today's passage tells of God's kingdom bringing release, freedom and salvation. The kingdom of God, like totalitarianism, demands perfect obedience, but unlike totalitarianism it gives back perfect freedom.

✎ *My Father and my God, your reign is my realisation, your rule my release. I gladly submit to your authority, for I see it brings life – and life abundant. I am eternally grateful. Amen.*

A demand or an offer?

FOR READING AND MEDITATION – LUKE 14:25–35

'... any of you who does not give up everything
he cannot be my disciple.' (v. 25: NIV)

Some may have balked at my comparison of the kingdom of God
and totalitarianism. But look at the dictionary definition: 'a form of
government that permits no rival loyalties or parties'. It is not a complete description, of course, but it is a good start. What we Christians
have got to learn, is this: Christ expects of everyone of us total obedience in everything. This radical demand cuts deep into our desire
for independence and sometimes causes our spirits to rankle, but
the demand is there nevertheless. And we must face it.

As the stomach and poison are not made for each other, and
when brought together produce disruption and death, so life and
other-than-God's-kingdom ways are not made for each other, and
when brought together also produce disruption and death.

What is the stomach made for? Is it not food? When food and
stomach are brought together, then – other factors being equal –
health and vitality develop. The kingdom of God is the food for
which our nature craves, and when the kingdom and our nature
are brought together, we experience life, health and perfect fulfil-
ment. The kingdom of God is more than an offer; it is a demand.
But in demanding all, it offers all.

𝒩 O Father, help me see that the demands of your kingdom are not there to
cripple me, but to complete me. They cause me to bow low at your feet so that
I can stand at my tallest. This is wisdom greater than any mind can measure. Thank you, Father. Amen.

What saith Scripture?

FOR READING AND MEDITATION – 2 TIMOTHY 3:10–17

'All Scripture is God-breathed and is useful for teaching, rebuking, correcting and training in righteousness …' (v. 16: NIV)

The very nature of our Christian commitment demands an attitude to authority which modern minds find difficult to understand. God calls us to accept his revelation as given in the Bible without rationalisation or equivocation. One cannot read the Bible and look at its elementary doctrines without realising that it is either authoritative and binding, or false. There is no allowance in the divine scheme of things for humankind to approach God on their own terms. We either obey or disobey.

It is obvious to many that the anti-authority spirit of the world is creeping into the modern-day church. High-ranking spiritual leaders are calling into question the authority of the Scriptures: 'You ask too much of our reason. Let's discuss the issues further and see if we can come up with a compromise.' I say with all the conviction of my being – this attitude is fatal to the growth and development of the Christian church. It should be unthinkable for a Christian to disagree with what God has told us in his Word or argue with him about it. When we do, the credibility of our claim to be his disciples must surely be in doubt. If we cannot accept the authority of the Bible, then we can't think Christianly about anything.

✎ O God, help me see that the Bible, your one and only published work, has behind it all the authority of heaven. May I ever see it in that light, no matter what others do or say. In Jesus' Name. Amen.

I must be free

FOR READING AND MEDITATION – ROMANS 6:15–23

'You have been set free from sin and have become
slaves to righteousness.' (v. 18: NIV)

How is Christian obedience compatible with Christian freedom, is
a frequently asked question. One minister tells how he counselled a
young woman in his church who was on the point of marrying a
professed non-Christian. He pointed out to her the New Testament's
high view of marriage as a spiritual as well as a physical union, and
how the Bible commands Christians not to be unequally yoked to
an unbeliever and marry only 'in the Lord'. She felt that she must be
free to choose. 'If Christ tells me what to do, if the issue is settled
before I begin, then I am not free,' she said. 'And I must be free.' The
minister made the point that the true freedom of the Christian is
freedom to obey Christ, not to disobey him.

Many think that Christ's rule and freedom of thought are incompatible. 'How can our wills be said to be free,' they question, 'if
we are told what to do before we even think of doing it?' Or, 'If controls are placed on how we behave, then we are not free.' But the only
way the mind can be free, is to come under the authority of truth.
The mind is not free, for example, when it believes lies. On the contrary, it is in bondage to fantasy and falsehood. We are really free,
only when we submit to the authority that guides the universe – free
not to do what we want, but to do what we ought.

❧ *Gracious Father, help me understand that submission to legitimate
authority does not demean me, but develop me. Bondage to you produces
perfect freedom in my soul. Thank you, my Father. Amen.*

Meaning out of misery

FOR READING AND MEDITATION – ROMANS 13:1–14

'… for there is no authority except that which God has established.' (v. 1: NIV)

Many Christians are willing to submit to Christ's authority, but draw the line at submitting to any other kind of authority. We must be very careful – it is God who has established the principle of authority in the world. One of the greatest insights that I have gained from my years of study of the Scriptures, is the astonishing way in which God works to bring about his purposes through the authorities over us. If churches would teach this to their young people, we would see a much greater maturity among the youth.

As a pastor I worked with young people and they would often come with problems about people over them at work who 'bug' them and how they could get out from under that authority so that it would not badly affect their Christian lives. I would empathise and share that rather than getting away, it was important for them to respond to that authority in a way that will develop their characters and help them become the kind of people God wants them to be. Anyone who can't submit to authority, will never be able to wield authority. When they could see how God was using the principle of authority to polish their characters and prepare them for responsibility in his kingdom, they saw meaning in what hitherto was misery.

⋈ *Father, I am so grateful that you gave us your Word to direct us. Left to ourselves, we would continue in our costly stupidities. We see how you have established the principle of authority. Now help us obey it. Amen.*

Danger signs

FOR READING AND MEDITATION – 1 TIMOTHY 2:1–15

'I urge ... that requests ... be made for everyone –
for kings and all those in authority.' (vv. 1–2: NIV)

One mark of a Christian mind is the acceptance of the principle of authority – the authority of the Scriptures, and then authority God has built into creation – family, employment, civic authorities, the church, and so on. Christians have no choice in this matter – we obey or we disobey. Only when we are asked to do something that directly contradicts the Word of God, we may disobey authority. Even then a heart and mind that is bent on obeying more than disobeying will either appeal to the person concerned to reconsider, or come up with a creative alternative. Many clashes with authority can be avoided when an appeal is made in the spirit of Christ.

We must always ask ourselves: are we in danger of succumbing to the secularisation of the day? A survey conducted recently among a group of churches in the UK showed that the majority of people polled thought those in non-Christian religions would get into heaven as long as they were sincere and lived a good life. Yet the Bible says: 'Salvation is found in no one else, for there is no other name under heaven given to men by which we must be saved' (Acts 4:12). As Christians, we must guard that the thinking of the world does not influence our thinking.

✎ *O Father, how easily we rationalise the truths of Scripture and make them fit the mood of the day. Forgive us for trying to come up with exceptions instead of conforming to your truth. Amen.*

A disciplined mind

FOR READING AND MEDITATION – GALATIANS 5:1–18

'You … were called to be free. But do not use
your freedom to indulge the sinful nature …' (v. 13: NIV)

Dr E. Stanley Jones said, 'Whilst the pathway of discipleship is a
way of dependence, drawing strength from Another, in order to do
that we must be disciplined.' Disciplined thinking is the fifth mark
of a Christian mind. To get the balance right between dependence
and discipline is not easy. Some overemphasise dependency and
make it look as if in the Christian life God does everything and we
do nothing. Others overemphasise discipline and make it look as if
we do everything and God does nothing. Truth out of balance can
soon become error.

'Free grace' has been preached in a way that has weakened character. The acceptance of grace is a privilege, a blessed privilege,
providing it is linked to discipline. 'Dependence plus discipline,' it
has been said, 'result in dependable disciples.' Years ago I heard a
woman say that after prayer she had been healed of arthritis in her
legs. Then she prayed again, 'Lord, you have healed me of arthritis,
now what are you going to do about my overweight?' The answer
she said she received was, 'This kind goeth not out but by prayer.'
Where only dependence could heal, that was the answer. Where
only discipline could heal, that was the answer.

✎ *Lord Jesus, no one has ever been more dependent than you, and no one
more disciplined. Teach me your secret. For I see that only as my mind is disciplined, can I dance the dance of freedom. Amen.*

Love that springs

FOR READING AND MEDITATION – 1 TIMOTHY 1:1–17

'The goal of this command is love, which comes from a pure heart …' (v. 13: NIV)

I know the phrase 'a disciplined mind' does not sit well with many Christians because it suggests rigidity. MOFFATT'S translation of to-day's text says: 'The aim of Christian discipline is the love that springs from a pure heart, from a good conscience, and from a sin-cere faith'. Discipline is defined in this text as spontaneity – 'love that springs'. That is the object of discipline – to make you free. There is a false idea of freedom prevalent in our generation. Recently I watched a group of young people on television discussing this subject. When one of them said, 'I believe freedom means I am free to do what I like,' I felt like shouting, 'No it doesn't. Freedom means you are free to do what you ought.' Another boy in the group complained, 'They tell us this is a free country, but we are told to go to school, and we have to do it or take the consequences. They tell us to study. And we have to do it. Where's our freedom?' He was very serious – and in very serious trouble with himself.

I have always liked this definition: 'Freedom is not the right to do what we want, but the power to do what we ought.' Love can only 'spring' – be spontaneous – when it comes from a pure heart, a good conscience and a sincere faith. Any supposed freedom that leaves us with an impure heart, a bad conscience and an insincere faith ends not in springing and singing, but in sighing and dying.

✎ O Father, teach me the way of discipline, for I want to be free – free to sing and not to sigh. Your will is freedom; my will is bondage. When I take my way, I end in a mess; when I take your way, I end in ministry. Amen.

Freed by fire!

FOR READING AND MEDITATION – 2 TIMOTHY 1:1–7
'For God did not give us a spirit of timidity,
but a spirit of power, of love and of self-discipline.' (v. 7: NIV)

Discipline is our aim. The result of discipline is courage – 'a spirit of power'. Christians who have discipline in their lives, have a sense of courage; they are not afraid to face anything that comes, because they know that God is behind them. They have a 'love' that both springs and sings. The idea of the disciplined person as disagreeable is false. The disciplined person is full of rhythm and song, for he or she is attuned to life. It is true that Jesus said: 'Everyone has to be consecrated by the fire of discipline' (Mark 9:49, MOFFATT), but this 'fire of discipline' only burns away the things that bind. When the three Hebrew lads were thrown into the burning fiery furnace – (Daniel 3) the fire served only to loose them from their bonds. They were freed by the fire.

It has been said that 'beauty is the purgation of superfluities'. Discipline strips away superfluities, shuts us up to the essentials, and makes life beautiful. You can't have an undisciplined life and be beautiful. A very attractive woman once said, 'You can't hate and be beautiful.' Those who can't have outward beauty, can always have inner beauty that comes from inner discipline. The disciplined mind is a beautiful mind.

Father, I see that I must surrender myself to the discipline of something – either to the discipline of the pressures around me, or to the discipline of your will and purposes. Help me make your discipline my discipline. Amen.

A mind set on God

FOR READING AND MEDITATION – PSALM 27:1–14

'Wait for the Lord; be strong and take heart and wait for the Lord.' (v. 14: NIV)

Many Christians accept the gift of God's free grace,' said a quaint Welsh preacher, 'but then a lot of it leaks out because of a lack of discipline.' I often wonder to myself if that is the reason why many who cry out to be filled with the Spirit don't have their prayers answered – they leak. God isn't going to pour his power into a vessel that leaks because of undisciplined living.

This brings us to the question: What is the first requirement of a disciplined mind? It is to spend time with God in prayer. There is a good deal of misunderstanding concerning prayer in the Christian church. Some people think of it as the means by which we get God to do things for us. That is not the primary purpose of prayer. It is to bring the whole of life into the presence of God for cleansing and decision-making.

It is only the arrogant who think they can run their lives on the knowledge they gained during their years of education. I have known many in my time, brilliant thinkers and highly educated, who have made the most foolish decisions in their professions and their marriages because they did not take the time to submit their minds to God in a daily tête-à-tête with the Almighty. If our minds are not set on God, then we cannot have a Christian mindset.

❧ Father, how tender and wise you are. You always put first things first. Thank you for reminding me that time with you must come first. May I listen to this and learn. In Jesus' Name I ask it. Amen.

Opening up the Word

FOR READING AND MEDITATION – PSALM 119:129–136

'The unfolding of your words gives light;
it gives understanding to the simple.' (v. 130: NIV)

A Christian mindset recognises the importance of accepting the discipline of prayer. It will go to prayer whether the soul feels like it or not. The Christian mind is not controlled by feelings. It knows the necessity of entering into communion with the Almighty, and does so though the feelings may not be in agreement. A Christian mind will not be content only with giving itself to prayer, but giving itself also to the daily discipline of reading God's Word. Some people get cross with me for encouraging the daily reading of the Scriptures, believing that this tends to bring people into bondage. A better word, they say, is 'regularly'. I see their point, because some people do get into bondage over this. They think that if they miss reading a daily passage of Scripture, God will punish them, for instance by pushing them under a bus!

So let me put it this way: make it a daily goal to read the Scriptures, but don't be overly concerned if you happen to miss a day now and then. Our thoughts need to be constantly corrected by God's thoughts, as they are clearly laid out for us in the Bible. The more we consult it, the clearer our own minds will be.

O God, the entrance of your Word gives light, and the neglect of your Word gives darkness. Help me to take your light as my light, then I shall walk with a sure and steady tread. In Christ's Name I pray. Amen.

The good store

FOR READING AND MEDITATION – MATTHEW 12:22–37

'The good man brings good things out of the good stored up in him ...' (v. 35: NIV)

A truly Christian mind will always want to bring discipline to bear upon areas of life that are out of control – failures such as these: a sex habit that saps the life-blood from the central purposes of existence; the evasion of responsibility; taking the line of least resistance instead of standing for one's principles; being critical, negative and always raising objections to positive plans; picking flaws in others; living always in a state of self-reference, and so on. These tendencies and others that are incompatible with the Christian life must be disciplined.

Talking about discipline as it relates to bad habits, we must also look at the positive side of replacing the old with the new. You can build up good habits so that they become part of your life. Our text for today talks about 'the good stored up'. Every good act we perform drops into the unconscious mind and becomes an action that easily repeats itself. Good comes out of a good store. The good which is brought forth is the sum total of accumulated good and godly habits which have passed into attitude and character. No good action is lost. Even if it may not seem to have an effect upon others, it becomes part of your good store and ready to be used again and again.

✎ O Father, what a thought – good acts and good habits become a part of my store, a part of me. Teach me to discipline myself and to watch day by day the little things that make me. I want to be good through and through. From the inside out. Amen.

What is

FOR READING AND MEDITATION – DEUTERONOMY 4:32–40

'From heaven he made you hear his voice to discipline you.' (v. 36: NIV)

We have seen a truly Christian mind is disciplined to spend time with God in prayer, to dip daily (or regularly!) into the Bible, to eliminate all bad habits, and to build up good and godly ones. Now think about the discipline of carrying things through. A great many good but ineffective people are disciplined at the beginning of an undertaking, but fail to carry it through. Their lives are strewn with the wreckage of good beginnings but poor endings. Sometimes this is because they take up things they shouldn't. Pray about everything that comes along and ask God if he wants you to get involved in it. Learn to say 'No' to things which you are not sure God wants you to get involved in. Save yourself not simply for the good, but for the best. Discipline yourself also to accept 'what is'. There are many who dream of what they would do and be if they were not where they are. We always have to live where God has put us at the moment. The children of Israel lived on manna in the wilderness – they survived on God's provision for their everyday lives. So must we.

And then discipline your disciplines. Don't allow discipline to make you rigid and stilted. Remember, you are being disciplined into Christlikeness. And no one has ever been more spontaneous than Christ.

Lord Jesus, you lived in dependence and gloriously on the Spirit in the silent years in Nazareth. Help me to live in close relationship with you, and be as disciplined and as spontaneous as you. For your own dear Name's sake. Amen.

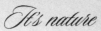
It's nature

FOR READING AND MEDITATION – 1 JOHN 1:1–10

'If we claim to be without sin, we deceive
ourselves and the truth is not in us.' (v. 8: NIV)

The sixth mark of a Christian mind is a clear awareness that the
world is a battleground between good and evil. Most would say,
'Isn't that stating the obvious?' All Christians may understand it,
but not all are aware of the more sombre implications which I want
to consider with you over the next few days. Have you noticed that
one of the differences between this generation and the ones of the
past is that men and women no longer try to make themselves look
better than they are? Indeed, in some quarters they advertise their
lower propensities with positive blatancy. Topics that were once
considered improper in decent conversation, are now freely dis-
cussed. The typical biographer of today dwells at length on the
secret sins of his or her subject. The things that biographers of past
generations would have drawn a curtain across, are now exposed
to public gaze.

There are no idols today, we are told. All have feet of clay. Some
Christians say that this indicates a sense of sin. What it indicates,
is a sense of realism that urges us to take and accept human nature
and sin as we find it. Don't allow the modern passion for realism to
brainwash us into taking human nature as we find it. If we say that
we have no sin, says the Scripture, we deceive ourselves.

*O Father, I want realism, but only the kind that is set against the back-
drop of the Scriptures. May your infallible Word be the guide to all my thinking. In Jesus' Name. Amen.*

Look out for euphemisms

FOR READING AND MEDITATION – ROMANS 12:1–21

'Who can say, "I have kept my heart pure; I am clean and without sin?" ' (v. 9: NIV)

There is an acceptance of evil by even the leaders of present-day society that is quite frightening. A high-ranking politician in the UK referred to a colleague's long-term adultery as 'a silly indiscretion'. I am deeply concerned. Will we as Christians become infected with the spirit of this age that reduces the sublime and eternal distinction between right and wrong to the level of 'a silly indiscretion'? The tendency of this age is to minimise sin. The true Christian mind will never accept this – not because it delights to sit in judgment on people (God forbids it!), but because the Bible says plainly, 'The wages of sin is death' (Rom. 6:23).

The Scripture's way of dealing with sin is to enable us to recognise it as wrongdoing, repent of it, claim forgiveness from God, and then go on to hate evil for the loathsome thing it is. Watch out for the euphemisms creeping into our language nowadays that describe sin by some other name. A lie is called a 'fib'. Adultery is called 'love'. Avoiding payment for something is described as 'being smart'. Fornication (sex before marriage) is called 'a premarital sexual relationship'. The world is glossing over the descriptions of sin that the Bible gives by using less offensive names. It is one of the ways in which the path to sin is greased.

✎ O Father, help me never to blur the distinctions between good and evil by falling for the way of the world and calling a serious thing by a light name. May I always see sin in the way you see it, and stand against it as you stand against it. Amen.

No excuse

FOR READING AND MEDITATION – PROVERBS 19:1–16

'A man's own folly ruins his life, yet his heart rages against the Lord.' (v. 3: NIV)

The way of the world is to blame wrongdoing on difficult circumstances. Christians must watch that we don't allow that same attitude to take root in our own minds. Often in counselling a person
says they got involved in a wrong relationship through loneliness.
But others have been lonely and have not succumbed to temptation. Loneliness may have been a factor; the lack of firm moral
principle was the real cause. And the failure to claim and use the
help of God.

Consider the sin of gossip. When asked why people passed on
gossip, they often reply that they thought there was no harm in
telling someone else. The truth was, of course, that they felt good
about being the conveyor of something that was not generally
known. The same applies to slander. Do not only pass on what you
were told. People often tell untruths. Scrutinise the things people
tell you. And even if a report is correct, ask if it is right to pass it
on. Isn't it true that we are eager to gossip because we don't like the
person about whom we gossip?

There is nothing so conducive to spiritual growth than to drop
all evasions and admit a fault. Circumstances are no excuse.

*My Father, may I have done with all rationalisations, all excuses, and
accept the fact that sin can never be justified by circumstances. I sin because
I fail to claim and use your help. Help me never to forget that. Amen.*

That's so Victorian!

FOR READING AND MEDITATION – ROMANS 7:1–13

'… so that through the commandment sin might become utterly sinful.' (v. 13: NIV)

We looked yesterday at the modern tendency to excuse sin by blaming it on circumstances. Look with me now at yet another argument of secular society in relation to what we are discussing – the idea that morality varies from one generation to another.

One of the many stupid dismissive remarks which people use to excuse their moral flaws, is to say of the severer ethical code, 'Oh, that's so Victorian!' But we are not dealing with the Victorian when we deal with sin; we are dealing with the eternal God. When God gave the Ten Commandments to the children of Israel those long years ago, he meant them to be the basis of morality not just for a few Semitic tribes, but the whole of humanity. As a poet has put it, 'Engraved as in eternal brass, the Ten Commandments shine, nor can the powers of darkness raze, those everlasting lines.'

Time makes no difference to the moral counsels of God. They are for kings and commoners, for people of all colours, for every era. Customs and fashions may change, but God's Word – never.

✣ O Father, help the world to see that the Ten Commandments are commandments and not merely suggestions. And help us, your people, see this more clearly, too. In Christ's Name. Amen.

A sin little talked about

FOR READING AND MEDITATION – PROVERBS 16:1–20
'Pride goes before destruction, a haughty spirit before a fall' (v. 2: NIV)

Another great problem of our day is the tendency to limit evil to certain well-known categories. If you were to poll a non-Christian section of the population about what constitutes evil, the answers would probably read like this: murder, robbery, massive fraud, rape, child molestation, and so on. Few, if any, would list alongside them vices such as pride, self-centredness or expediency. Yet, these are just as evil as the other things listed. We must recognise that the secular mind – or as some might describe it, the establishment – sees sin and evil in quite different terms from the Christian mind. It was the establishment, we should remember – the ruling class of the day – that crucified our Lord.

The true Christian mind will go further than the secular mind and will identify as one of the chief evils something that is little talked about in the world – pride. In the Christian moral system this is the sin of all sins, because it perverts the will and asserts self as the centre of the universe. And when we put self in the centre, we displace God. It was pride that made a devil out of an angel and overturned the purposes of the Almighty in the Garden of Eden. Indeed, one might measure the blunting of Christian sensibilities by how little we talk about pride.

❧ *Father, I see more clearly still how easy it is for us as Christians to have our minds blunted by the environment in which we live. May I be as clear as you about everything – especially what constitutes evil and sin. Amen.*

Self-examination

FOR READING AND MEDITATION – 1 CONRINTHIANS 11:17–34

'A man ought to examine himself before
he eats of the bread and drinks of the cup.' (v. 28: NIV)

The secular mind tends to see the law-abiding citizen as good, and the law-breaker as bad. But the discerning Christian knows that a man or woman can so live that though they do not violate the code and laws of society, they may be violating the laws of God. People can pass as respectable citizens and yet their hearts may be filled with a diabolical vanity in which they strive at every moment to minister to the desires of their own inflated ego. Indeed, some rise to a position in society where they are called upon to judge others for their sins and may, because of the pride and self-centredness that fill their hearts, be more eaten up by evil than some of the people they judge.

The Christian mind must not overlook this possibility. Do not gloat over such a realisation, but allow it to guide us as we relate to people – especially as we pray for them. Mature Christians will also want to use this realisation to examine their own lives themselves, and check that pride and self-centredness has not taken hold of them to such a degree that they themselves are just as evil (if not more so) than the man or woman who stands trembling in the dock, or is being pilloried in the press. If we do not judge ourselves, then we mustn't complain if we are judged by the Lord.

O God, help me in my evaluation of life and of others to be sensitive to my own condition. May all the knowledge and insight I gain be directed to the right end – to become more and more like your Son day by day. Amen.

A soft code?

'Why do you look at the speck of sawdust in your brother's eye and
pay no attention to the plank in your own eye?' (v. 3: NIV)

The Christian mind must be sharp enough to discriminate between
right and wrong and cut through the befuddled moral jungle which
constitutes the ethics of our day. Because the world does not understand the full gamut of evil, its judgments are sometimes topsy-
turvy. A man is given a sentence of years for robbing a bank, while a
man who almost beats a child to death is given months. The world
seems to distort the well-known statement of Jesus concerning
those who hurt his 'little ones' (Matt. 18:6) and changes it to 'Who-
soever injures a child shall be moderately punished, but he who robs
a bank, it were better that a millstone were hanged about his neck.'

But society is fiercely materialistic, and we can expect that to
be reflected in its moral judgments. It does not mean that we can
look around us in a superior way and say, 'What a terrible world we
are living in.' Let's take the plank out of our own eye before attempting to take the speck of sawdust out of someone else's eye. We
thank God that there is a code of ethics in society, but must realise
that in some ways it is a soft code, modified to buttress the securi-
ties of a materialistic society. The Christian code, on the other
hand, is rock-hard. When we can distinguish the difference, we
think Christianly.

*O Father, search me and see if there be any pride within me or anything
which I do not want to or see. Bring it to the light so that my judgments and
discernments shall be free of all that befuddles. Amen.*

Inner division

FOR READING AND MEDITATION – LUKE 11:14–28
'Any Kingdom divided against itself will be ruined,
and a house divided against itself will fall.' (v. 17: NIV)

The seventh mark of a Christian mind is singleness of purpose. Jesus reminds us in our text for today that a house divided against itself cannot stand. Both Christianity and psychology agree on that. It is a universal law. Inner division soon produces outer disruption. Once I saw two posters side by side. One said, 'Health and fitness come first.' The other said, 'Smoke brand X of cigarettes.' In the Bible there are many characters who came to grief because of a mind that did not have singleness of purpose. Take Amaziah for example. 'He did what was right in the eyes of the Lord, but not whole-heartedly' (2 Chron. 25:2). One translator puts it this way: 'He did what was right in the sight of the Lord, but not with an undivided mind.' This inner division was his undoing. The account goes on to say that he brought back the gods of the people of Seir and set them up as his own, bowing in homage before them. Not long after, there was a conspiracy against him and he was killed.

Outwardly a divided mind gives the impression of correctness, but the inner division soon reveals itself in disloyalty. This, in turn, leads to personal downfall. A divided mind, unless corrected, soon results in the downfall of the personality.

O God, give me that singleness of purpose that commits itself to the right things with dedication and commitment. May I be so united within that I will be able to stand up to anything that comes from without. Amen.

Civil war within

FOR READING AND MEDITATION – ISAIAH 30:1–14

'… this sin will become for you like a high wall, cracked and bulging …' (v. 13: NIV)

Is not having an undivided mind sin? It can be if it is not quickly corrected. Today's text is rendered by one translator thus: 'This guilt of yours shall split you.' Failure to give ourselves whole-heartedly to God and follow him with singleness of purpose means that we are not sure about him, which amounts to lack of trust. And lack of trust, unless dealt with, can become sin.

One of the major reasons why people seek Christian counselling, is because of inner division. They don't know whom to serve – God or themselves. One woman said to me some years ago, 'I may look calm on the surface, but beneath I am a veritable battlefield.' There is nothing worse than to live with a civil war within. United within, we can stand anything without, but divided within, the smallest circumstance can blow us over. A Christian counsellor told me recently how he had dealt with a young Bible College student who was teetering on the verge of a nervous breakdown. He thought at first that her problem was too much studying, but after exploring the issues with her found that she had taken up part-time employment in a betting shop to make extra money to put herself through college. She was trying to serve Christ with one part of her mind and contributing to an unbiblical system with another. The pay-off was that she became two persons at war with each other.

O God, I want to be one person, not two. Outwardly correct and inwardly correct. You made me, dear Father, and you can remake me. I am a candidate to be remade from top to bottom. Help me. In Jesus' Name. Amen.

Which is me?

FOR READING AND MEDITATION – MATTHEW 22:34–46
'Love the Lord your God with all your heart and
with all your soul and with all your mind.' (v. 37: NIV)

We continue reflecting on the fact that a Christian mind is a mind that is shot through with singleness of purpose. Edwin Sanford Martin has brought clearly into focus the plight of the inwardly divided in these powerful words:

Within my earthly temple there's a crowd,
there's one that's humble, one that's proud.
There's one that's broken-hearted for his sins,
and one, who, unrepentant, sits and grins.
There's one who loves his neighbour as himself,
and one who cares for naught but fame and self.
From such corroding care I would be free
if once I could determine which is me.

The way to determine who you are is to give yourself to Christ whole-heartedly. There must be no idea that you can serve Christ with one part of your mind and serve yourself with the other. There must be no Dr Jekyll and Mr Hyde business in the Christian life. We must be all out for God with all we have.

✎ *Lord Jesus Christ, it is clear that you lived your life here on earth with a single eye and a single purpose. Help me to do the same. For your own dear Name's sake. Amen.*

On the right side

FOR READING AND MEDITATION – ROMANS 7:14–25
'Who will rescue me from this body of death?
Thanks be to God …' (vv. 24–25: NIV)

A divided mind is one of the greatest contributors to ineffective-ness as a Christian. A minister in Yorkshire once had to withdraw from his pulpit for a while due to ill health. His doctor (who was a member of his congregation) said to him, 'There's nothing wrong with you physically, but I think I know what might be the reason for your problem. You are preaching the gospel as a postscript.' The minister appeared nonplussed, so the doctor went on, 'Your ser-mons are filled with pessimistic reports of the world and then, in the last few minutes, the gospel is dragged in. It appears you are not sure of the power of the gospel, but that you have an obligation as a minister to say something about it. Try believing in the gospel, stop playing up pessimism and see what happens.' He took the doctor's advice, got alone with God, regained his confidence in the gospel and quickly recovered.

You have to be inwardly committed. No one can afford to hold any conflict within. Resolve it as quickly as possible. The attempt to hold both sides of a dilemma in order to feel secure, results in a central insecurity in the person concerned. Always throw yourself whole-heartedly on the right side of an issue.

✎ O God, I see I can't live in the 'I'm not sure what I want to do' frame of mind without being inwardly disrupted. And the more important the issue, the greater the disruption. Help me resolve any conflict I may be facing along this line today. Amen.

No rest in places

FOR READING AND MEDITATION – PHILIPPIANS 4:1–9

'And the peace of God … will guard your
hearts and your minds in Christ Jesus.' (v. 7: NIV)

A mind that continually goes in two different directions is not a Christian mind. We all have times, of course, when we can't make up our minds, but on Christian issues we can't afford to prevaricate. We must make up our minds that what God says is what we are determined to do. We are made for inner integrity, and inner division breaks us down. It is like a woman that is not married to the man she lives with, although everyone she knows believes this to be so. She is full of guilt. Until the matter is brought out into the open, the church members informed, repentance made, forgiveness given, and the couple properly married before God.

I still remember the days when anyone who seemed to be verging on a breakdown was encouraged to go on a sea voyage. But when people did this, they found that they carried their conflicts with them – sometimes all the way around the world. Jesus said in Luke 11:24 that 'when an evil spirit comes out of a man, it goes through arid places seeking rest and does not find it'. I use the illustration only to make the point that the unclean spirit tried to find rest in 'arid places'. It can't be done. One can never find rest for the soul in 'places'. It is to be found only in a Person – Christ.

✒ Lord Jesus Christ, you are the only way out of all my conflicts and divisions. Help me to bring all my inner conflicts and array them before your kindly eye. Then together deal with them. Amen.

Like a child

FOR READING AND MEDITATION – MATTHEW 6:19–34
'But seek first his kingdom and his righteousness.' (v. 2: NIV)

I read about a couple who had built for themselves a large house with 14 rooms. But after a while they couldn't get along with each other any more, so each had seven rooms and lived entirely apart. It was a home divided against itself, and although on the outside it appeared to be a magnificent mansion, on the inside it was a magnificent misery.

Thomas Edison's wife, when talking about him to a friend, said, 'He works hard and long, then lies on the couch and goes immediately to sleep. Never does he show any disunity of mind. He has no obsessions and no impeded flow of energy. He is like a child in God's hands. Nature's man. Perhaps this is one reason God can pour all those wonderful ideas through his mind.' Note the phrase, 'Never ... any disunity of mind.' Because of that, his mind has literally lighted up the succeeding generations.

As one person puts it, 'There may be a score of active motives within us, but only one must dominate, the rest must co-operate, not mutiny. We are made for obedience, one of the first laws of life. We must choose what we will allow our minds to be dominated by.' Seek first the kingdom of God; then everything falls into its proper place, co-ordinated, happy and free.

✎ O Father, if it is so that I can choose what will dominate my mind, then I choose you. I want my motives not to be a crowd but a company, all marching in step and in one direction. Grant that it shall be so. Amen.

Inner division suppressed

FOR READING AND MEDITATION – ZECHARIAH 5:1–11

'He said, "This is wickedness," and he pushed her back into the basket ...' (v. 8: NIV)

What a strange passage of Scripture presents itself for our attention today. Zechariah is given a vision of a basket, the cover of which is made of lead. An angel takes the cover off the basket and reveals a woman sitting inside. The woman, says the angel, represents 'wickedness'. Then, having announced this fact, he promptly proceeds to put the lid on her again. We do something similar. We push our conflicts down inside us, put a leaden lid on them, and think they have gone away. But they are still there, and work away as a hidden complex. We must face and deal with whatever is stopping us being single-minded, and not just hope that if we put the lid on, it will go away.

On one occasion Jesus said two apparently contradictory things: 'Fear him' and 'Don't be afraid' (Luke 12:5, 7). But the meaning is this: once we fear God, then we have no reason to fear anything else. To fear God means to revere him, and when we do this supremely, then all other issues become secondary. Low at his feet we stand straight before anything else. Loving God supremely, we then love all other things marginally. Mixed loyalties give way to a master loyalty. Jesus put it another way: 'When thine eye is single, thy whole body also is full of light' (Luke 11:34, AMPLIFIED).

☨ *O Father, may my life from this day forward take on a new power as I surrender all my conflicts to you and invite you to take control. Help me develop a mind that is free from all division. One that is single-minded and always under your control. Amen.*

Eternity in time

FOR READING AND MEDITATION – 2 CORINTHIANS 5:1–10

'For we must all appear before the judgment seat of Christ …' (v. 10: NIV)

We have reflected over the past weeks on the first seven marks of a Christian mind. The eighth mark of a Christian mind is this: a mind that looks out on eternity. It looks beyond this life to another one, and allows the future to intrude on everyone of life's major decisions. Harry Blamires, a Christian writer to whom I often refer, and whose thoughts have triggered many of my own on this subject, puts it like this: 'The mind of a Christian is supernaturally oriented and brings to bear upon all earthly considerations the fact of heaven and the fact of hell.'

I wonder how many of us who name ourselves after the Name of Christ see our earthly affairs in the light of eternity. Our tendency is to see eternity as something we will enter into when we die. Most non-religionists go through life with the assumption that all is over when they die; that after 60 or 70 years they sign off for good; that eating, drinking, sleeping, working, breeding and the rest constitute the totality of things; that in worldly acquisitions and experiences lies the source of all meaning and value. Christians know, however, that we must all appear before the judgment seat of Christ that each of us might receive what is due to us. Surely, then, we ought to live so that eternity has the casting vote in every decision we make here on earth.

✎ *Father, forgive me that sometimes I am so taken up with the affairs of this world that I give no thought to the world to come. Grant that in future eternity shall figure in my thoughts as much as the present time. Amen.*

Proprietors or stewards?

FOR READING AND MEDITATION – LUKE 12:13–21
'This is how it will be with anyone who stores up things …
but is not rich toward God.' (v. 21: NIV)

Issues take on a different aspect when we bring to bear upon them a mind which reckons not just with time, but with eternity; not just with a human life span, but with a destiny beyond the grave. Take the subject of money. Are we as Christians the proprietors of our money, or merely stewards? The true Christian mind will not struggle on that point. It will acknowledge that a Christian is only a trustee, holding the money on behalf of Another.

I love the story of the bishop who preached a sermon on the theme 'God is the Owner – we are debtors.' A wealthy man who heard the sermon invited him to his home and took the bishop for a drive. They reached the crest of a hill and he pointed to the hundreds of acres ahead of him and said, 'Bishop, if this doesn't belong to me, to whom does it belong?' The bishop quietly replied, 'Ask me that question a hundred years from now.' My father once wrote in the flyleaf of a new Bible I had purchased, 'We take nothing into eternity except our characters, and what we deposit in other people's characters.' I have never forgotten that. We cannot serve God and mammon, but we can serve God with mammon. Focus on how what we have in our hands is contributing to eternity. This, too, is thinking Christianly.

✎ O Father, I need to learn the lesson that I am a steward and not a proprietor. My safe will not get into eternity, but my soul will. Help me use whatever financial resources I have to advance the cause of your kingdom. Amen.

No greater word

FOR READING AND MEDITATION – ROMANS 8:28–39

'And we know that in all things God works
for the good of those who love him …' (v. 28: NIV)

The popular term you hear everywhere nowadays is 'world-view'. As well as a world-view, Christians should develop an other-world view. We saw how the eternal perspective affects our view of money; now we examine how it affects us in relation to the dampening disappointments that come to us all along our way.

Have you been deeply disappointed? Then look again at today's text. My favourite text is Romans 8:28, because I have found it to be one of the most sustaining texts. It shows that nothing can work successfully against us. Disappointments, when seen in the light of eternity, become his-appointments. God takes the obstacles and turns them into opportunities; he marches in through the door of every disappointment to bring something good out of it.

So, if the 'time-side' of life is a bit rough at the moment, then let the 'eternity-side' hold you steady. Something good comes out of disappointment. You'll see!

◁ *Gracious God, teach me how to rest not in the immediate but in the ultimate – in you. Remind me that nothing can happen in time that can't be taken care of by eternity. You have the last word in everything. Thank you, my Father. Amen.*

The pain God guides

FOR READING AND MEDITATION – 2 CORINTHIANS 7:1–16
'Godly sorrow brings repentance that leads to salvation …
but worldly sorrow brings death.' (v. 18: NIV)

Disease and suffering take on a completely different perspective to the eternally-oriented Christian mind. To the non-Christian it is something entirely negative that cannot be reconciled with justice or meaning. The MOFFATT translation of today's text begins 'The pain God is allowed to guide …' Paul saw that some pains lead to death and some lead to life. When we keep our pains in our own hands and deal with them on an entirely human level, they make us bitter, cynical and full of self-pity. They lead to the death of hope, meaning and purpose. When we bring God into our pains and allow him to guide them, he turns them from what seems senseless suffering into spiritual character. The pain itself may have come from an evil source, but the question is, where is it going? It depends on whether we have a spiritual perspective and see the pain as fitting into an eternal plan.

One of the greatest Christians I have known, was struck down with poliomyelitis. Instead of lying back lamenting the fact, he reflected on how his condition would be different when he got to heaven. He became so enthused that he began to talk to others about it too. From an invalid carriage he won more souls to Christ than any layman I have known. It was a pain God was allowed to guide.

✎ O Father, thank you that your Son turned the pain of the Cross into redemption that will go on eternally. May my pains contribute to eternal things, too. Amen.

An other-world view

FOR READING AND MEDITATION – 2 CORINTHIANS 4:1–18

'So we fix our eyes not on what is seen, but on what is unseen.' (v. 18: NIV)

An eternal perspective totally alters the character of such matters as possessions, disappointment, suffering, pain. But the eternal perspective also transforms things such as success, prosperity and achievement. For the Christian mind earthly wellbeing and happiness is not the greatest good, just as pain and suffering is not the greatest evil. Earthly wellbeing may be the goal of those whose minds are bound by the terrestrial, but the Christian mind sees them as transitory and limited only to time. We can see how the Christian mind clashes with the secular mind, for the non-Christian views happiness in this life as the greatest goal, whereas the Christian is willing to forfeit happiness in this world knowing that there is the guarantee of everlasting joy in the world to come.

We don't hear much about nuclear war any more, but there was a time when people saw the destruction of life on this planet as the final evil. Beyond, so they believed, there is nothing. The Christian mind, while never ceasing to pursue ways to avoid such a catastrophe, never surrendered to the gloom that characterised non-Christians, for ultimately they knew that to be swept out of this world is to be swept into heaven. Sudden death – sudden glory. There is nothing that can happen in human life that will not look different to the Christian mind than to the secular mind.

Father, how different the things of earth look in the light of eternity. Help me to have an eternal perspective on all things. In Jesus' Name. Amen.

Spring in the heart

FOR READING AND MEDITATION – 2 TIMOTHY 1:8–18

'... our Saviour ... has destroyed death and has brought life and
immortality to light through the gospel.' (v. 10: NIV)

Nothing highlights the difference between the Christian and the non-Christian mind more dramatically than the subject of death. The Christian faith is the only faith that lights up that mysterious and dark area – not with a word, but with the Word made flesh. Jesus went through death and the word of resurrection became flesh in him. Anyone who lives in him is deathless. It was said of Emerson, the American philosopher, that he did not argue, but simply let in the light. The same can be said of Jesus. He did not argue the fact of immortality; he simply showed himself alive after men had put him to death.

Victor Hugo said, 'Winter is on my head, but eternal spring is in my heart. The nearer I approach the end, the plainer I hear around me the immortal symphonies of the world to come. When I have gone down to the grave, I shall have ended my day's work, but another day will begin the next morning. Life closes with the twilight, but opens with the dawn.' That is the language of faith. Compare it with the words of the sceptic Robert Ingersoll, who said at his brother's grave, 'Life is a narrow vale between the cold and barren peaks of two eternities. We cry aloud and the only answer is the echo of our wailing cry.' Jesus demonstrated immortality so that we can believe in it, too.

Father, I see that I shall need eternity to grow up in. You have brought life and immortality to light through the gospel. I am eternally grateful. Amen.

Look through the window

FOR READING AND MEDITATION – 1 JOHN 3:1–10

'Everyone who has this hope in him purifies himself, just as he is pure.' (v. 3: NIV)

It is important to understand that 'living in time and eternity simultaneously' does not mean that earthly struggles and problems will have no effect upon us. Some do believe that, but it is not a belief I share. Although our minds may be oriented toward eternity, this will not stop us from feeling acutely the pain that comes from the struggles and disappointments of life. What is the benefit, then, of being a Christian? This – though we struggle, sometimes severely, and fear, anger and discouragement rise within our souls, there steals over us, from eternity, the sense that God is in control and that he is working out his purposes, no matter how things may look to the contrary. Then, much to your amazement, you find yourself growing a little more patient, you check irritability when it arises, you discover yourself to have a strange confidence even in the midst of panic. Your soul rests on the guarantee that badness will never overcome goodness, and that when the last chapter of this life is written, the eternal one begins. There all wrongs will be made right, all reunions will bring unparalleled joy, and all relationships will be exempt from selfishness.

Learn to look through the window of eternity. It will fire you with perseverance. Be careful, though, that you don't think too much about eternity and lose sight of your responsibilities now.

✒ *O God my Father, I realise that if I do not have within me that which is beyond me, I will soon give way to that which is around me. Help me keep an eternal perspective in all things. In Jesus' Name. Amen.*

The end of the beginning

FOR READING AND MEDITATION – PHILIPPIANS 2:1–11

'Your attitude should be the same as that of Christ Jesus …' (v. 5: NIV)

We end this edition on the Christian mind by reminding ourselves of the eight distinguishing marks at which we have looked in detail. A Christian mind, we said, is a mind that puts itself under the tutelage of Christ, is imbued with humility, is keenly perceptive, is accepting of authority, is disciplined in its thinking, is aware of the reality of good and evil, is undivided and has an eternal perspective. Perhaps at no other time in history has there been such a need for minds that think Christianly than there is at this hour. How do we deal with such questions as these: Should a woman with an unwanted pregnancy seek a legalised abortion? Ought a young couple who plan to get married experiment to see if they will be sexually compatible? Is it right for a wife whose husband is sterile to be inseminated by a donor? What is a Christian lifestyle in a world of hunger? The list could be lengthened almost indefinitely. For guidance, should we look to society or to the Scriptures? Are we in the end just worldly Christians who follow the crowd? Or do we make a conscious attempt by soaking ourselves in the Word, and through prayer and discussion with other Christians seek to discover the mind of Christ in all things? Having the mind of Christ does not mean giving up our own. God wants us to think, but to think with him, not apart from or against him.

꙳ *O God, may I go on from here to have a mind that is trained by your Spirit, informed by your Word and equipped to handle all decisions that come my way with the mindset of my Master. Amen.*